ROYAL
SHAKESPEARE
COMPANY

The **RSC** Shakespeare
Toolkit for Teachers

methuen | drama

First published 2010
Revised edition published 2013 by
Methuen Drama
An imprint of Bloomsbury Publishing Plc
50 Bedford Square, London, WC1B 3DP

www.bloomsbury.com

ISBN 978-1-4725-1548-3

Photograph credits:

Front cover, clockwise from left: In-school spoken word project 2010, Photographer Nick Spratling; Performance from a Learning and Performance Network primary school as part of the Regional Schools Celebration 2012, Photographer Stewart Hemley; International Youth Ensemble performing at Worlds Together Conference 2012, Photographer Kwame Lestrade; Students taking part in a Teaching Shakespeare workshop in Stratford-upon-Avon 2011, Photographer Nick Spratling.

Back cover: Students taking part in a workshop led by an RSC practitioner in preparation for their performance in their Regional Schools Festival for the Learning and Performance Network 2011, Photographer Nick Spratling.

P7, clockwise from top left: Romeo and Juliet in-school project 2004; In-school workshop, RSC Learning and Performance Network 2008; In-school workshop, RSC Learning and Performance Network 2008; RSC Regional Schools Celebration 2008, Photographer Ellie Kurttz; In-school workshop, RSC Learning and Performance Network 2008; Stand up for Shakespeare assembly 2009, Photographer Stewart Hemley; RSC workshop 2008, Photographer Ellie Kurttz; In-school workshop, RSC Learning and Performance Network 2008; RSC workshop 2008, Photographer Ellie Kurttz.

P11, clockwise from top left: RSC Regional Schools Celebration 2009, Photographer Ellie Kurttz; In-school workshop, RSC Regional Tour 2009; Romeo and Juliet in-school project 2004; RSC Regional Schools Celebration 2009, Photographer Ellie Kurttz; RSC Regional Schools Celebration 2009, Photographer Ellie Kurttz; In-school workshop, RSC Regional Tour 2009; RSC Regional Schools Celebration 2009, Photographer Ellie Kurttz; Stand up for Shakespeare assembly 2009, Photographer Stewart Hemley; In-school workshop, RSC Regional Tour 2009; Romeo and Juliet in-school project 2004; (centre) RSC workshop 2009, Photographer Nick Spratling.

P289: Romeo and Juliet in-school project 2008, Photographer Ellie Kurttz.

P304: RSC workshop 2009, Photographer Nick Spratling.

CONTENTS

CONTENTS

"Shakespeare wrote plays and young children are geniuses at playing. Ask them to comment on a great work of literature and they will shrink away. Give a child the part of Bottom, Tybalt or Lady Macbeth and watch them unlock their imagination, self esteem, and a treasure trove of insight into what it's like to be alive that will feed them for a lifetime. Shakespeare remains one of the world's favourite artists because his living dilemmas of love, mortality, power and citizenship remain unresolved, vivid and urgent today".

From Michael Boyd's introduction to *Stand Up For Shakespeare*, the RSC's manifesto for Shakespeare in schools.

"My dad said Shakespeare was boring, but he's got it wrong! I'm gonna tell him about Hamlet. It's got murders and ghosts and castles and stuff and that's not boring. What are we doing next?"

Ben, age 8, Devon after doing a unit of work with his teacher on *Hamlet*

Most of us encounter Shakespeare for the first time at school. I certainly did. It was at primary school in Preston, I think, that I first heard a recording of Mendelssohn's incidental music for *A Midsummer Night's Dream*, with extracts from the play performed by actors. When Puck declared that he would "put a girdle round about the earth, in forty minutes", I was amazed. My dad had told me that Sputnik, the first space satellite sent up by the Soviet Union, took over an hour and a half to orbit the globe. Puck was twice as fast as Sputnik!

The Russian satellite might have launched the space age, but Puck launched Shakespeare for me. I was hooked. But many find their first encounter with Shakespeare harder. The plays are too wordy perhaps, or the language old-fashioned, or the stories just plain irrelevant. This book has been written to support the thousands of teachers in the UK and across the world who aim to bring Shakespeare's work vividly to life for their students.

Shakespeare is probably the most prescribed author in education systems internationally. Responses to a survey conducted by the RSC and the British Council indicate that approximately 50% of schoolchildren across the world are encountering Shakespeare at school; it is hard to imagine another artist coming close to this. Our priority is in ensuring that these early encounters with Shakespeare's work secure the richest rewards for students of all ages.

The RSC's education practice is centred on our manifesto for Shakespeare in schools, *Stand up for Shakespeare*, with its call for children and young people to: Do Shakespeare on their Feet; See it Live; and Start it Earlier. Over many years of working with young people we have found that engaging students directly and physically with the sound, shapes and rhythms of the text allows them deeper access to it and invites personal responses from them about it. We know that it is the personal connections that young people make with any artist's work that has the potential to open up a lifelong relationship for them with that artist or artistic practice. When we encourage young people to see themselves as active, capable agents in the artistic process, real learning and real ownership happen.

The lesson plans we've devised are inspired by the way we work in the rehearsal room, which is really just another kind of classroom. During a rehearsal period we develop a play together and at the end of the process we all share a common understanding of the play as well as its relevance to the world we live in and to our own lives. We've shared this approach in the toolkit.

Cicely Berry, Voice Director at the RSC, first started our work in schools and her influence is evident throughout the book. We owe her a huge debt of gratitude, not least for her unwavering belief that working actively with Shakespeare's language unlocks it in a way that simply reading words cannot. Cic's most often quoted phrase is from Thomas Kyd's play *The Spanish Tragedy*: *"Where words prevail not, violence prevails."*

I hope that you get great enjoyment and pleasure from trying out the work with your students and from finding your own connections between the classroom and the rehearsal room.

Gregory Doran
Artistic Director
Royal Shakespeare Company

INTRODUCTION

"Instead of just delivering the knowledge, I've learnt alongside my students, and learnt from them. They've seen things in the play I'd never noticed, come up with interpretations I never would have considered. The essence of this is what makes Shakespeare come alive."

Lucy, secondary school teacher, Cornwall

"Our ever growing trust enables us to experiment, improvise and rework. This ensemble is a secure environment without ever being a comfort zone. All of us are continually challenging ourselves and being inspired by those around us"

Geoffrey Streatfeild, RSC Ensemble actor

At the heart of this book is a belief that Shakespeare's work can inspire and engage students of all abilities. It is a complete resource for an active approach to teaching Shakespeare in the classroom, inspired by the work that happens in RSC rehearsal rooms. Employing the techniques in the toolkit will help you to:

■ Teach Shakespeare actively.

■ Set the pace and challenge of learning across the ability and age range.

■ Manage student behaviour and relationships.

■ Use advanced teaching skills in questioning, developing personal, learning and thinking skills in your class.

■ Encourage students to make their own informed interpretive choices.

We have successfully trialled all the activities in classroom settings with students of different ages, abilities and backgrounds. This book is based on years of direct teaching and learning experience and represents our current understanding of best practice.

At the RSC we see direct parallels between teaching and learning in the classroom and the way our theatre company works. The process of rehearsing a play is collaborative. It is a focused artistic inquiry in which the actors and director make discoveries by working playfully together. As a group they make choices about the interpretation of plot, characters, themes and language of the play. This process is similar to an inquiry in the classroom where teacher and students explore a play text together.

As a theatre company, we also operate as an ensemble; a group who learn from each other, and a group that gets stronger as we get to know and trust one another. You cannot perform a play without relying on each other, and it is often the quality of the relationships between companies of actors that distinguishes an average performance from an excellent one.

> "I really look forward to doing Shakespeare ... Instead of just writing what happens in the play, like conversations between characters, we actually live it and we try to feel how the characters must feel. I think that that is a good way of learning."
>
> Rowanne, 11 years old, South Yorkshire

> "The students grew as a co-operative and collaborative team, with their curiosity shaping the direction the lessons progressed in. Instead of the traditional teacher-student power structure, the group became more empowered themselves as they began to recognise that their active exploration was the route to as many answers as asking a member of staff. "
>
> Jo, secondary school teacher, Cheshire

> "I heard one pupil say, 'Why haven't we watched the film like everyone else?' and another pupil replied 'Why would we need to?' "
>
> Celia, secondary school teacher, Cumbria

Similarly, as teachers, we all know the importance of relationships in the classroom, and have the pleasure of working with groups of learners who are already a healthy ensemble. But we also know those groups where the personal, social and thinking skills of the learners could be developed. We believe that the more active and collaborative our work is in the classroom and the rehearsal room, the more effective it will be for all learners. The more the teacher or director works as an enabler and fellow explorer, the better the outcomes.

We firmly believe that Shakespeare belongs to everyone and that his work is an important part of our cultural inheritance: an inheritance that all students should have access to and feel ownership of. We also believe the learning exchanges we offer in our classrooms should be inclusive, accommodating the multiple intelligences and learning styles of every individual child. This book celebrates in particular those pupils who learn by doing; those kinaesthetic learners who sometimes present challenging behaviour when asked to sit still and analyse objectively. In these lessons, we encourage pupils to experience the play on their feet, to read the words actively and then confidently articulate their discoveries, sometimes by speaking and listening to each other and sometimes by writing about them. Many of the activities require an intuitive, spontaneous response, which is then consolidated through reflective enquiry and questioning. We also know that this way of working can produce sophisticated analytical responses, both verbal and written, challenging the most able learners as well as motivating the most reluctant.

The activities outlined here can generate a range of evidence demonstrating pupil understanding of:

■ Character and motivation.

■ Themes and ideas.

■ Language.

■ The plays in performance.

You will not need any specialist training in the fields of Shakespeare or drama to teach these lessons. Some of them may seem more adventurous than others, so our advice is to start where you are comfortable and work from there. One of the most significant lessons we have learnt from the rehearsal room is that we have the right to try things out: sometimes the same idea will work brilliantly in one set of circumstances, less well in another. The right to fail is built into the rehearsal process, and it is the right of every reflective classroom practitioner.

Marc and Shane, two boys in a Year 8 low ability group, were both struggling in English for different reasons. Marc was one of the weakest members of the group, working at a Level 3, but he was self-confident and keen to make progress. Shane was academically one of the strongest in the group, working at a Level 4, but was de-motivated and had recently been moved down from a higher set. Their teacher, Tara, found that both boys were excited by the opportunity to explore meaning and they got into a heated discussion with each other about the best way to deliver just one line in a scene from *Macbeth*. Both boys offered interesting and reasoned arguments for their own interpretation. For Marc, the achievement here was in articulating a complex response and for Shane, the achievement was in his complete engagement and need to put his views across. Tara commented:

"The process of being able to experiment with ways of reading and then consider the movement of presentation and characters had provided them with a sense of ownership."

Tara wanted to assess how active approaches to Shakespeare would impact on the reading attainments of her class. Prior to the Shakespeare unit, she had specifically targeted Reading AF3 (the ability to infer, deduce and interpret) through more traditional methods but no one in her class had attained a Level 5.

Following the Shakespeare unit, Tara found that more than a third of her pupils could now attain Level 5 because the active approaches had allowed them to speculate about, as one student put it, *"what was going on in the heads"* of characters. Reading the plays was no longer a passive activity, and, as one girl explained:

"It's easier to understand when you use drama as you can see it and you can remember it better."

If you are new to these approaches, you could work with another member of staff to teach some of the lessons as a team. A paired approach can be less daunting and can also give you the encouragement and support you need to try new things out. Experience has shown us that the best learning takes place when we are slightly out of our comfort zones and that if you model the necessary courage your pupils will quickly follow. If you are a reflective practitioner seeking to inspire your students through active learning techniques, we think this toolkit will help you.

RSC Education team

HOW TO USE THIS BOOK

Each chapter in the toolkit offers a different approach to working actively with Shakespeare's plays. It is important to note that all of the activities can be applied to any of Shakespeare's texts, as well as many other stories, poems and plays.

In the chapter on *Macbeth* we take a step by step journey through the narrative, each lesson designed to animate key moments of the action.

The *Romeo and Juliet* chapter offers you a 'pick and mix' of active lessons, as we anticipate you already have a number of tried and tested strategies that our lessons can support and add value to.

With the activities on *A Midsummer Night's Dream* we emphasise a visual, auditory and kinaesthetic approach to the very different worlds and environments that the play inhabits.

All of the lessons have been structured for Key Stage 2 and Key Stage 3 pupils and the objectives for learning are drawn from the Framework for secondary English[1] and the Primary Framework for Literacy[2] so they will be compatible with the approaches to teaching in your school. The activities have been created for classrooms where tables and chairs have been pushed back to create the open space needed for active learning.

Each lesson plan contains a starter, main and plenary activity and some include additional suggestions for homework; they also contain a list of the resources you will need for each lesson. In the lessons, we refer to **resource sheets** and **worksheets**. Resource sheets are for teachers to work from whilst worksheets are for pupils.

We have not given timings for the lessons as these will differ according to the context you are teaching in, but the plans are predicated on a lively approach with time allowed for all-important reflective activities. You will make choices about which exercises you want to take out and which you want to spend more time over according to the needs and abilities of the group you are working with. We estimate that each chapter contains between 15 – 20 hours of teaching material. You don't have to use the lesson plans as we've suggested, but it's important that the lessons are complete, rounded experiences in themselves.

---

[1] Correct at time of going to print, January 2010

[2] Correct at time of going to print, January 2010

To enable quick and easy navigation of the lesson plans, we have used icons as follows:

Teacher Note
This icon highlights the pedagogical foundation of the lesson and anything practical you will need to know. Teacher notes also include information about the social and historical context of the play which you can choose to weave into your lesson narrative as and when appropriate.

Differentiation
This icon highlights where we have provided text resources differentiated for younger / less able pupils or older / more able pupils. Shakespeare's language can be a daunting prospect for actors and pupils alike. So, to build confidence, we suggest introducing the words gradually and cumulatively. We often edit the text, scaffolding activities with single words, phrases or lines drawn from the play. Sometimes we edit a speech or a scene so that it is manageable for active learning before tackling the full text. Equally, we know that pupils enjoy the challenge of handling complex texts. Even the most difficult passages of text are accessible if we approach them playfully, and one of the aims of this toolkit is that every pupil is immersed in Shakespeare's language.

Common Bank of Activities and Terms
This icon directs you to fuller explanations of frequently used activities or terms. This section can be found at the back of the book from p.289 onwards. We strongly recommend that you refer to it since it contains the core set of strategies used throughout the book. These are also transferable to other play texts and other kinds of literature.

Pair Work

Small Group Work

Whole Group Work

These three icons give you an 'at a glance' overview of how the pupils are working together in the lesson.

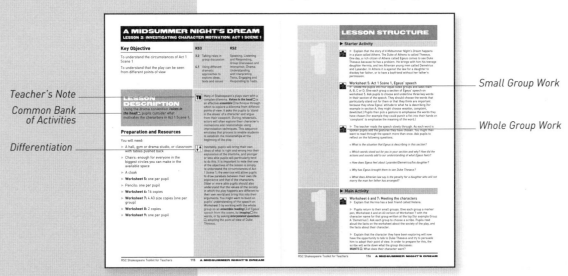

Teacher's Note

Common Bank of Activities

Differentiation

Small Group Work

Whole Group Work

▶ The CD-ROM

The enclosed CD-ROM provides all the teacher notes, resource sheets and worksheets as printable PDFs, as well as extra image and text resources for some lessons. For further information, including system requirements, please see the inside front cover.

MACBETH

The following sequence of work on *Macbeth* is designed to take pupils on a journey of discovery through the play. Following this sequence will mean that they encounter the ***world of the play*** ⊏⊐, its story, the characters, and their language, in the order that Shakespeare presents them. They will be able to discover for themselves the effect of the witches' prophecy on Macbeth and his kingship, and to question whether or not the prophecy is self-fulfilling: ultimately, is it only because Macbeth believes what the witches tell him that the tragedy unfolds? The lesson sequence also provides an opportunity for teachers and pupils to discuss and reflect on modern-day Macbeths, who may have been corrupted by ambition and power or fallen prey to paranoia and suspicion.

Display suggestions

The work in this unit could be mapped with a classroom display using four headings: Language; Character and Motivation; Themes and Issues; Text in Performance.

Title photograph: RSC Production of *Macbeth* (2004)
Photographer **Manuel Harlan**

CONTENTS

MACBETH
LESSON 1: MACBETH IN BATTLE, ACT 1 SCENE 2

Key Objective

To understand the battle described at the opening of *Macbeth* and the relationships between Macbeth and his peers.

KS3

1.1 Developing active listening strategies and skills

4.1 Using different dramatic approaches to explore ideas, texts and issues

KS2

Listening and Responding, Drama, Understanding and Interpreting Texts, Engaging and Responding to Text

LESSON DESCRIPTION

Pupils enact the battle at the opening of *Macbeth* and explore the relationships between Macbeth and his peers in Act 1 Scene 2.

Preparation and Resources

You will need:

▶ A hall or drama studio, or classroom with tables pushed back

▶ A drum that you can carry easily

▶ **Resource Sheet 1** – read this in advance and ideally prepare to tell the story without the sheet

▶ **Worksheet 1** displayed on a whiteboard, flipchart or sugar paper on the wall

▶ **Worksheet 2** cut into six separate lines

▶ An image of a heath or moor

▶ Post-It notes

 Macbeth was written in 1606, early in the reign of King James I, who was also James VI of Scotland. King James was a patron of Shakespeare's acting company and *Macbeth* clearly reflects the playwright's relationship with his sovereign. Shakespeare deliberately sets up the 'good' reign of King Duncan in opposition to the corrupt and 'bad' reign of Macbeth. This would have resonated at the royal court, where James was busy reinforcing his position as the lawful Christian King, not least through commissioning the authorised version of the Bible (1611) which is still used today.

In this first introductory lesson, pupils approach the opening of the play physically. Encouraging pupils to inhabit the action, as actors do, accommodates the multiple intelligences (particularly the kinaesthetic and visual) that are present in any group of learners. By being in the action, pupils are *experiencing* the play: the feelings and the multi-sensory environment. This is a unique process to each new group of people who explore the play, whether in a RSC rehearsal room or your classroom.

LESSON STRUCTURE

▶ Starter Activity

Pupils spread out in the room so that they are equally spaced, facing you. Work through the following, allowing a couple of minutes for each exercise.

▶ Pupils move around the room at a steady walking pace. Explain that you will play a game to see how fast and how slowly they can move. Their usual walking pace is pace 2. Now ask them to slow down so that they are moving as slowly as they can. Slow motion walking is pace 1. Now ask pupils to walk as fast as they can without running. High speed walking is pace 3. Explain that you will call out 1, 2 or 3 and pupils must adjust their pace accordingly.

▶ When pupils are comfortable changing pace, ask them to become aware of the other pupils moving in the room, and to feel when they get too close for comfort to another member of the group. Explain that when they feel they are getting too close, they should make a deliberate turn away from the other pupil.

▶ Stop pupils to demonstrate this exercise. Find a space on the floor where no one else is, jump into it and call 'Mine!' in a loud and clear voice. Explain that pupils will move round the room, looking for spaces and claiming them with the word 'Mine!' Once they have claimed a space, they move on and find another.

▶ Pupils find a partner. Explain that you will give them a title for a *freeze frame* ⬕ (see titles below), which they will only have five seconds to make. Each time, call the title of the statue and then count down slowly from five: *5, 4, 3, 2, 1 and Freeze!*:

■ *A king and his subject*

■ *Best friends celebrating*

■ *Friends sharing a secret*

■ *Friends who don't trust each other anymore*

▶ As each freeze is formed, choose a pair for the rest of the group to look at and ask the other pupils questions about what they see *(How do these two characters feel about each other? How do you know? What might this character be about to say? What might this character be thinking?)* Each time, draw the pupils' attention to details in facial expression and body language in order to provoke a discussion about what we expect from our friends, what it feels like to share a secret, and what it feels like when trust is betrayed.

▶ Main Activity

▶ Introduce a drum, and explain that you will beat the drum and call out *high*, *middle* or *low*. Pupils move around the room, listening for the drum and the word. When they hear it, they spontaneously make a frozen shape responding to the word that they hear, i.e. a shape that is high, middle or low. Encourage inventive physical shapes by asking pupils to make a different shape each time.

▶ Pupils find a partner and name themselves A and B. Ask B to lead first. On the beat of the drum, they will make a shape that is either high, middle or low, and their partner must instinctively respond with a shape in a different dynamic, i.e. if B makes a high shape, A must make a middle or low shape in response.

▶ On the beat of the drum, A leads the next shape, B replying spontaneously with a shape in a different dynamic. Pupils continue to alternate A and B leading on each beat.

▶ Ask pupils to plan a sequence of five paired moves, which they can remember and repeat. Give pupils five minutes working with their partner to prepare a sequence.

▶ Pupils sit on the floor with their partner. Now introduce the context: *We are going to tell a story today which starts with a great battle between Scotland and Norway. A is a soldier for Scotland and B is a soldier for Norway: they are sworn enemies.* Ask: *What is the soldiers' attitude towards each other?* (Pupil responses may include: 'they hate each other'; 'they are scared of one another'; 'they are eager to get into battle to prove they're better soldiers'.)

▶ Explain that pupils will use the five moves they have prepared to perform the battle. They should show how the soldiers feel about each other by making direct eye contact with their partner. They should imagine that they have a weapon in their hands but they should not make physical contact. Pupils could include sounds to go with each move: battle cries.

▶ Give pupils five minutes to prepare their battle moves with their partner.

▶ Now explain that, in their pairs, the whole group will now perform their battle moves simultaneously, cued by five beats on the drum. Beat the drum slowly as the pupils perform, so that every pair has time to complete their moves.

▶ Sit pupils down for a moment. Ask:

■ *The battle takes place on a heath, or moor. Has anyone ever been to a moor? What was it like?* (Introduce a photograph of a heath or moor if pupils are unfamiliar with the setting). Ask pupils to imagine the heath as they perform.

▶ Explain that you will tell the story of the battle, and that in the middle of the story the drum will beat and the pupils will perform their battle. When the battle has finished, pupils should continue being soldiers, listening and responding to the story. Ask pupils to stand and face their partner, ready to begin.

Resource Sheet 1: The story of the battle

▶ Tell the story, incorporating any ideas that the pupils have had about the heath to heighten the atmosphere. Cue the battle moves with the drum. After you have finished telling the story, ask pupils to sit down on the floor, close their eyes and imagine the scene on the heath after the battle. Ask them to listen to these questions and answer them silently in their heads:

■ *What could the soldiers see?*

■ *What could they hear?*

■ *What could they smell?*

■ *What did they feel?*

▶ Pupils open their eyes. Ask the questions again, this time encouraging individuals to answer them verbally. (Alternatively, pupils could share their thoughts with a partner first.) Note the responses on a flipchart or whiteboard.

Worksheet 1: Act 1 Scene 2

▶ Explain that Scotland wins the battle, and that there are two friends who have fought fiercely for Scotland: two lords called Macbeth and Banquo. Display the description of Macbeth's part in the battle and read it aloud. Ask:

■ *What event is being described?*

■ *What picture of Macbeth do you have in your head? What does he look like? What is he doing?*

■ *Are there any unfamiliar words? What do you think they mean?*

▶ Ask for two volunteers. Explain that Macbeth and his friend Banquo find each other at the end of the battle and leave the battlefield together to celebrate their victory. Explain that the volunteers are going to make a ***freeze frame*** ◘ of Macbeth and Banquo at this moment and everyone else is going to help them. Negotiate a physical position for the two characters. Ask:

■ *What would Macbeth and Banquo be doing?*

■ *How close are they to each other? What are they doing with their arms?*

■ *What expression is on their faces?*

■ *What would King Duncan of Scotland feel about these two characters?*

▶ Ask another volunteer to join the freeze frame as King Duncan, showing how he feels about Macbeth and Banquo. Again, use the rest of the group's ideas to find a specific physical position for the King.

Worksheet 2: Descriptions of Macbeth
▶ Distribute lines describing Macbeth to six other pupils and ask them to read their line to themselves. Then ask those pupils to join the freeze frame as other Scottish lords, showing clearly how their lord feels about Macbeth. They speak their lines aloud to Macbeth, in order.

▶ Ask the rest of the group:

■ *How do the rest of the Scottish lords feel about Macbeth at the beginning of the story?*

■ *What do you think 'Thane' means? (lord). Explain that Macbeth is Thane of Glamis, and that Glamis is an area of Scotland.*

■ *What single word would you use to describe Macbeth? Record these on Post-It notes as the students voice them and save them for use in the plenary session.*

Thought Track ◆ Pupils speak aloud what Macbeth or Banquo might be thinking at this moment.

▶ Plenary

▶ Ask:

■ *Did the statue of Macbeth and Banquo remind anybody of the statues that we made at the beginning of the lesson? Which one and why?*

▶ **Role on the wall ◆** Create an outline drawing of Macbeth. Add the Post-it note descriptors of Macbeth to the drawing. You could use the drawing in future lessons to help track the progress of Macbeth's character through the play.

▶ Homework

Ask pupils to research Elizabethan beliefs about witches and witchcraft in preparation for the next lesson.

■ *Why did the Elizabethans believe in witches and witchcraft?*

■ *What kinds of people were thought to be witches?*

■ *What happened to people who were thought to be witches?*

■ *Can you find any images of witches from the Elizabethan period?*

■ *Can you find any images of witches today?*

The story

The great armies of Scotland and Norway were ready on the barren heath. (*Add to this any details about the heath that the pupils have discussed.*)

The wind whistled across the empty space between them. It was bitterly cold. Their fingers were frozen, gripping their weapons, waiting. Their breath made clouds as it condensed in the air. They listened. A moment of dreadful silence fell as they held their breath, every muscle tensed, ready. Waiting for the battle cry. Then, King Duncan of Scotland let out a great roar and...

(*At this point, beat the drum slowly five times while the pupils perform their battle moves and sounds (if used). As soon as the last move has finished, continue telling the story.*)

As the smoke of battle cleared, the exhausted soldiers slowly started to be aware of what was happening around them. Across the battlefield, they saw the injured and dying, friends and enemies alike, bleeding onto the cold earth. They felt the icy wind blow through them, as they took in the scene. They could see, hear, smell and feel the aftermath of battle.

MACBETH
WORKSHEET 1

Act 1 Scene 2

For brave Macbeth – well he deserves that name –
Disdaining Fortune, with his brandished steel
Which smoked with bloody execution,
Like valour's minion carved out his passage
Till he faced the slave,
Till he unseamed him from the nave to th'chops
And fixed his head upon our battlements.

▶ **Notes**

'Disdaining Fortune': ignoring fate
'brandished steel': sword ready to use
'slave': villain
'valour's minion': bravery's favourite
'unseamed': ripped in two
'nave to th'chops': navel to the jaw

MACBETH
WORKSHEET 1

Act 1 Scene 2

For brave Macbeth – well he deserves that name –
Disdaining Fortune, with his brandished steel
Which smoked with bloody execution,
Like valour's minion carved out his passage
Till he faced the slave,
Till he unseamed him from the nave to th'chops
And fixed his head upon our battlements.

▶ **Notes**

'Disdaining Fortune': ignoring fate
'brandished steel': sword ready to use
'slave': villain
'valour's minion': bravery's favourite
'unseamed': ripped in two
'nave to th'chops': navel to the jaw

MACBETH
WORKSHEET 1

Act 1 Scene 2

For brave Macbeth – well he deserves that name –
Disdaining Fortune, with his brandished steel
Which smoked with bloody execution,
Like valour's minion carved out his passage
Till he faced the slave,
Till he unseamed him from the nave to th'chops
And fixed his head upon our battlements.

▶ **Notes**

'Disdaining Fortune': ignoring fate
'brandished steel': sword ready to use
'slave': villain
'valour's minion': bravery's favourite
'unseamed': ripped in two
'nave to th'chops': navel to the jaw

1. **Worthy gentleman**

2. **Valiant cousin**

3. **Worthy Thane**

4. **Peerless kinsman**

5. **Great Glamis**

6. **Brave Macbeth**

MACBETH
LESSON 2: MEETING THE WITCHES, ACT 1 SCENE 3

Key Objective

To explore the meeting between Macbeth, Banquo and the Witches in Act 1 Scene 3, and to make interpretive choices about the staging of the scene informed by the text.

KS3

4.2 Developing, adapting and responding to dramatic techniques, conventions and styles

5.2 Understanding and responding to ideas, viewpoints, themes and purposes in texts

KS2

Speaking, Listening and Responding, Group Discussion and Interaction, Drama, Understanding and Interpreting Texts, Engaging and Responding to Text

LESSON DESCRIPTION

Pupils explore the meeting between Macbeth, Banquo and the witches in Act 1 Scene 3.

Preparation and Resources

You will need:

▶ A hall or drama studio, or classroom with tables pushed back

▶ **Worksheet 3:** displayed on a whiteboard, flipchart or sugar paper on the wall

▶ **Worksheet 4:** one copy per pupil

 The first of two lessons exploring Act 1 Scene 3: the meeting of Macbeth and Banquo with the three 'weird sisters'. The themes of superstition and witchcraft, which are central to the story of *Macbeth*, would have appealed to the contemporary audience, many of whom believed in witches, and also to King James who had written his own book on *Daemonologie*. The book refers to necromancy – prophecy by the dead – which it describes as a '*black and unlawful science*'. Witches were thought to have demon followers and a variety of powers such as the ability to create storms and to shape shift (transform themselves into animals). It was also believed that witches and soothsayers could predict the future. In the stories and sermons of the day, witches were associated with evil, disorder in nature and the disruption of the divine right of the King. Therefore, women who were suspected of witchcraft were shunned, and many were killed. In 1606, social outsiders were commonly described as witches.

In both this lesson and the next, pupils discuss the events of Act 1 Scene 3 and consider how the meeting with the witches, and the prophecies they make, affect the relationship between Macbeth and Banquo. In this lesson, pupils focus on their ideas about the witches, informed by the social and historical context we have provided. In doing so, they are making the kinds of interpretive choices that any actors approaching the play must make. Enabling pupils to make their own choices about a scene is a critical feature of an active approach. In making these choices, pupils are developing the personal, social and thinking skills at the root of personalised learning.

LESSON STRUCTURE

▶ Starter Activity

▶ **Re-call** Pupils make a *freeze frame* ◘ of Macbeth and Banquo leaving the battlefield. Ask the pupils to make two freeze frames from Lesson 1:

■ Friends sharing a secret

■ Friends who don't trust each other anymore

▶ Sit pupils down on the floor in a circle and explain that in this lesson they will be finding out about the secret the two men share. Invite pupils to report back on the homework task from Lesson 1. Establish that the group has a clear understanding of the power of the witches (so that they can recognise the impact they have on the two men) by asking:

■ *Why did the Elizabethans believe in witches and witchcraft?*

■ *What kinds of people were thought to be witches?*

■ *What happened to people who were thought to be witches?*

■ *How might a meeting with witches affect Macbeth and Banquo?*

▶ Explain that as Macbeth and Banquo are leaving the heath after the battle they meet three witches. Invite pupils to share any images of witches they found through the homework task. Ask:

■ *What do witches look like? Think of three words that describe what a witch might look like. Share these with a partner.*

▶ Collect some of the words. (Your class may come up with lots of different ideas or their ideas may be similar.) Explain that *Macbeth* has been performed thousands of times since it was written and that in every production the witches are different.

Worksheet 3: Banquo sees the witches
▶ Display and read aloud what Banquo says about the witches. Ask:

■ *What can we tell about the witches from what Banquo says?*

▶ Main Activity

Worksheet 4: Act 1 Scene 3 (edit)
▶ Distribute the worksheet and explain that it is an edited version of Act 1 Scene 3. The words in italics are stage directions, and you will read those. Ask confident readers to take parts as Macbeth, Banquo, first, second and third witch. Read aloud, then ask:

■ *Who can remember what Thane means?*

■ *What do the witches prophesy for Macbeth? Ask pupils to put the prophecy into their own words.*

'In the eyes of England, Scotland was seen as a wild place that was really beyond everyday experience and I think Shakespeare is playing on that to create an atmosphere of danger, otherness, difference and strangeness in the popular imagination.' Dominic Cooke, RSC Associate Director and Director of *Macbeth*, 2004

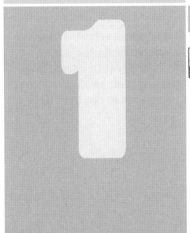

■ *What do the witches prophesy for Banquo? Ask pupils to put the prophecy into their own words.*

▶ Divide pupils into groups of three and ask them to cast themselves as first, second and third witch. Any additional pupils in each group will direct the scene, so will have the final say in deciding how it should be staged and acted.

▶ Ask pupils to discuss where the witches have come from? *Why have they come to see Macbeth and Banquo? Why are they speaking the spell?*

▶ Next, ask them to decide what the witches are like physically. *How do they move? Together or separately? Is one of them the leader? How do they speak?*

▶ Using **Section One** of the worksheet, ask each group to work out how the witches meet together on stage, how they speak and how they move, both individually and as a trio. Ask them to decide on clear start and end positions for this section, and remind them that they will share their work with the rest of the group so they must present Section One in a way that means everyone else in the room will be able to see.

Perform
▶ Explain that every group will perform their work for the class. As soon as the first group has finished, the next one will start. Number the groups so that they know which order they are performing in. Ask each group to pay particular attention to the group that follows theirs, to see what differences or similarities they can spot. They should watch carefully to see how the scene they have created is different from the others. (You could share the discussion questions in the plenary section with all pupils to support their ability to reflect on what they've seen.)

▶ Plenary

▶ Discuss the key interpretive choices that have been made. Ask:

■ *What words would you use to describe the witches in this group?*

■ *How did the way these witches spoke help us to understand what they were like?*

■ *How did the way these witches moved differ from the way other witches moved?*

▶ Explain that there is no right way of doing this scene, and that professional actors and directors go through exactly the same process: making choices based on clues in the text to decide how to interpret the scene. Applaud the pupils for their work so far and explain that they will continue working on the scene in the next lesson.

Act 1 Scene 3: *Banquo sees the witches*

BANQUO: What are these,
So withered and so wild in their attire,
That look not like th'inhabitants o'th'earth
And yet are on't?— Live you, or are you aught
That man may question?

Act 1 Scene 3:

Section One

Thunder. Enter the three Witches.

FIRST WITCH: Where hast thou been, sister?

SECOND WITCH: Sister, where thou?

THIRD WITCH: A drum, A drum,
Macbeth doth come.

ALL: Thrice to thine, and thrice to mine
And thrice again, to make up nine.
Peace, the charm's wound up.

Section Two

Enter Macbeth and Banquo.

MACBETH: So foul and fair a day I have not seen.

BANQUO: What are these,
That look not like the inhabitants o'the earth,
And yet are on't?

MACBETH: Speak if you can: what are you?

Section Three

FIRST WITCH: All hail, Macbeth: hail to thee, Thane of Glamis!

SECOND WITCH: All hail, Macbeth: hail to thee, Thane of Cawdor!

THIRD WITCH: All hail, Macbeth, that shalt be king hereafter!

Section Four

BANQUO: Speak then to me, who neither beg nor fear
Your favours nor your hate.

FIRST WITCH: Lesser than Macbeth, and greater.

SECOND WITCH: Not so happy, yet much happier.

THIRD WITCH: Thou shalt get kings, though thou be none.

ALL: Banquo and Macbeth, all hail!

Section Five

The Witches vanish.

MACBETH: Your children shall be kings.

BANQUO: You shall be king.

MACBETH

Key Objective

To explore the meeting between Macbeth, Banquo and the Witches in Act 1 Scene 3, and to make interpretive choices about the staging of the scene informed by the text.

KS3

4.2 Developing, adapting and responding to dramatic techniques, conventions and styles

5.2 Understanding and responding to ideas, viewpoints, themes and purposes in texts

KS2

Speaking, Listening and Responding, Group Discussion and Interaction, Drama, Understanding and Interpreting Texts, Engaging and Responding to Text

LESSON DESCRIPTION

Pupils continue to explore the first meeting of Macbeth and Banquo with the witches in Act 1 Scene 3.

Preparation and Resources

You will need:

▶ A hall or drama studio, or classroom with tables pushed back

▶ **Worksheet 5:** one copy per pupil

▶ **Worksheet 6:** one copy

▶ **Worksheet 7:** one copy

▶ **Worksheet 8:** one copy

▶ **Worksheet 9:** one copy

▶ Four simple percussion instruments

▶ **Resource Sheet 2:** Read this in advance and ideally learn it so that you can deliver the message without the sheet. (Alternatively you could ask a pupil to learn it in advance)

 This lesson offers pupils an opportunity to deepen their understanding of Act 1 Scene 3. They are asked to place themselves in the position of Macbeth and Banquo and to speculate about how the witches' prophecy affects their state of mind, their feelings and their friendship.

For the majority of this lesson, pupils will work in small groups, and each group will need a director. You could leave this as a free choice for each group to make, but we have suggested that you choose a director for each group. As teacher you can give this responsibility to someone you know will be able to work well as a facilitator in the group. This will usually be someone with a strong personality, who can command the respect of his or her peers, but may not always be the obvious choice. As you develop an active approach in your classroom, you may find that pupils who find written tasks challenging would relish the opportunity to direct. One of the most satisfying aspects of working actively is that you are developing a new group dynamic, where all pupils can achieve, regardless of pre-conceptions about ability.

▶ Starter Activity

Worksheet 5: Act 1 Scene 3 (edit)
▶ Distribute the worksheet and explain that during this lesson the pupils will continue exploring Act 1 Scene 3. Once again, ask confident readers to take parts as Macbeth, Banquo, first, second and third witch. Read aloud, then ask:

■ *Who can remind us what the prophecy made to Macbeth means?*

■ *Who can remind us what the prophecy made to Banquo means?*

■ *What did we find out about the witches in the scene during the last lesson?*

■ *Does anybody else in the play know what the witches say to Macbeth and Banquo?*

▶ Remind the pupils that the prophecy is a secret that Macbeth and Banquo share and during this lesson they are going to act out the rest of the scene. Explain that the Thane of Cawdor and King Duncan are alive and well. Not only that, the King has two sons called Malcolm and Donalbain, who are his heirs.

▶ Main Activity

Worksheet 5
Divide pupils into four equally sized groups. Explain that their task is to investigate a short section of the scene. Each group has a number of decisions to make as they bring their section to life.

▶ Choose a director in each group. Explain that everyone will work together on the scene, and that the director must listen to everybody's ideas, and try out the ideas that are suggested. The director will have the final say about how to bring the scene to life.

▶ Ask pupils to choose a Macbeth, a Banquo and three witches to be in their scene.

▶ Any remaining pupils will help the audience to understand what Macbeth and Banquo are experiencing, using sound effects. Distribute a percussion instrument to each group. Explain that they can use this instrument, as well as sounds they can make using whatever is available in the classroom, and also vocal sounds. Their job is to make sure that the audience understand which moments are important for Macbeth or Banquo, and what they are feeling. The director will have the final say about how the sound effects will be used.

Worksheets 6,7,8,9: Questions about the scene
▶ Distribute Worksheet 6 to the director in the first group, Worksheet 7 to the next director, Worksheet 8 to the next director and Worksheet 9 to the next director.

▶ Explain that there are some questions on the worksheets which each group will explore the answers to. Reassure pupils that there are no definitive answers to the questions. They are allowed to make their own decisions, based on what they know from reading the scene and what they think or feel about the characters. Explain that this is what professional actors and directors do when they are interpreting a scene. Ask the director to read to their group the questions they must answer together in order to bring the scene to life.

▶ Give the pupils a ten-minute time limit in which to bring their scene to life, preparing a performance of their section for the rest of the class.

▶ After five minutes, remind pupils to add in sound effects if they haven't already.

▶ After a further five minutes, ask the pupils to have one last run through, making sure that the audience can see and hear everything.

Perform

Explain that every group will perform their work for the class. As soon as the first group has finished, the next one will start.

▶ Discuss the key interpretive choices that have been made, using the questions on Worksheets 6, 7, 8 and 9.

■ Ask each group to decide on a *freeze frame* for their Macbeth and Banquo which shows how they feel about what the witches have prophesied and how they feel about each other at the end of the scene.

■ All pupils except the Macbeths and Banquos form an audience at one end of the room. The Macbeths and Banquos form their freeze frame over a count of five, and hold it. Count them down: *5, 4, 3, 2, 1, Freeze!* Ask the audience if these freeze frames remind them of the 'Friends sharing a secret' or 'Friends who don't trust each other anymore' images.

Thought Track ▣ *Ask four or five individual pupils in the audience to suggest what Macbeth or Banquo might be thinking or saying.*

Resource Sheet 2: Act 1 Scene 3, Messenger

▶ Finally, choose one of the Macbeth or Banquo pairs and explain that, just after the witches have made their prophecy, a messenger comes from King Duncan. Ask Macbeth and Banquo to re-make their freeze frame, and explain that they will come to life when the messenger comes in and react to the news that he brings. You will take on the role of the messenger. Kneel down in front of Macbeth and deliver the news on the sheet. As soon as you have finished, freeze Macbeth and Banquo again. Ask:

■ *What might each of the characters be thinking now?*

■ *Do they trust each other now? Why / Why not?*

▶ Plenary

▷ Ask:

■ *What impact will meeting the witches have on the friendship between Macbeth and Banquo? Will it change as a result of the meeting?*

■ *Has Macbeth always wanted to be King, or does the meeting with the witches make him think about it for the first time?*

■ *Why might Macbeth be influenced by what the witches have said?*

■ *Refer to the **Role on the Wall** ☒ from Lesson 1 and the things that were said about Macbeth. Ask pupils to write down any new words that might describe Macbeth's character.*

Adapted from speeches delivered to Macbeth in Act 1 Scene 3 by two Scottish lords: Ross and Angus.

MESSENGER: The King hath happily received, Macbeth, the news of thy success, and gives thee greater honour. The Thane of Cawdor is a traitor, who has confessed to treason against Scotland. The King gives his titles and his lands to you, Macbeth. Hail! Thane of Glamis and Thane of Cawdor!

Act 1 Scene 3 (edited):

Section One

Thunder. Enter the three Witches.

FIRST WITCH: Where hast thou been, sister?

SECOND WITCH: Sister, where thou?

THIRD WITCH: A drum, A drum,
Macbeth doth come.

ALL: Thrice to thine and thrice to mine
And thrice again, to make up nine.
Peace, the charm's wound up.

Section Two

Enter Macbeth and Banquo.

MACBETH: So foul and fair a day I have not seen.

BANQUO: What are these,
That look not like the inhabitants o'the earth,
And yet are on't?

MACBETH: Speak if you can: what are you?

Section Three

FIRST WITCH: All hail, Macbeth: hail to thee, Thane of Glamis!

SECOND WITCH: All hail, Macbeth: hail to thee, Thane of Cawdor!

THIRD WITCH: All hail, Macbeth, that shalt be king hereafter!

Section Four

BANQUO: Speak then to me, who neither beg nor fear
Your favours nor your hate.

FIRST WITCH: Lesser than Macbeth, and greater.

SECOND WITCH: Not so happy, yet much happier.

THIRD WITCH: Thou shalt get kings, though thou be none.

ALL: Banquo and Macbeth, all hail!

Section Five

The Witches vanish.

MACBETH: Your children shall be kings.

BANQUO: You shall be king.

In your group, discuss answers to the following questions:

- How might Macbeth and Banquo have become friends? How long might they have known each other for? For example, did they meet in King Duncan's court? Or have they known each other since they were children? Or have they only become friends recently by fighting side by side? Or...

- How might they be feeling as they walk away from the battle? For example, are they injured, proud, exhausted, excited? Or...? How does this affect the way they enter the scene?

- What might the witches do to get their attention? For example, do they whisper from a distance, or surround them so they cannot escape? Or...?

- Why do you think Macbeth asks the witches to speak?

In your group, discuss answers to the following questions:

- What do you think the witches are trying to achieve in giving Macbeth his titles? Are they:

  - mocking him?
  - honouring him?
  - tempting him?
  - or... ?

- How does this affect where they stand and move in relation to Macbeth when they speak to him?

- How does Macbeth react to each part of the prophecy? What does he do?

- How does Banquo react to what he hears and sees?

In your group, discuss answers to the following questions:

- Why does Banquo ask the witches to speak to him? How do you think he feels about them? For example, is he frightened of them or not?

- How do the witches give their prophecy to Banquo? Do they treat him differently to Macbeth?

- How does Banquo react? What does he do?

- How does Macbeth react? Does he do anything?

In your group, discuss answers to the following questions:

■ How do the witches vanish?

■ What is Macbeth thinking when he says to Banquo, *'Your children shall be kings.'*?

■ What is Banquo thinking when he says to Macbeth, *'You shall be king.'*?

Key Objective

To understand the persuasive tactics that Lady Macbeth uses to influence Macbeth.

KS3

2.2 Using and adapting the conventions and forms of spoken texts

6.2 Analysing how writers' use of linguistic and literary features shapes and influences meaning

KS2

Listening and Responding, Drama, Understanding and Interpreting Texts, Engaging and Responding to Text

LESSON DESCRIPTION

Pupils enact moments from Act 1 Scene 5 and Act 1 Scene 7 and explore the relationship between Lady Macbeth and Macbeth.

Preparation and Resources

You will need:

▶ A hall or drama studio, or classroom with tables pushed back

▶ **Worksheet 10:** one per pupil

▶ **Worksheet 11:** one per pupil

▶ **Worksheet 12:** one per pupil

▶ Cloak and crown: to represent King Duncan

▶ Chairs

▶ **Worksheet 13:** for older or more able pupils

▶ A whiteboard or flipchart

 In this lesson pupils begin to speculate about the relationship between Lady Macbeth and Macbeth using the clues in the text. Actors in rehearsal work in the ways outlined here, they negotiate meaning collaboratively by speaking the lines and playing the scene in a variety of different ways. The lesson first of all explores Lady Macbeth's reaction to the witches' prophecy and then explores the decision to kill King Duncan. Something to note with your pupils as you go through the lesson activities is that Shakespeare's audience would have been appalled by the idea that the Macbeths kill King Duncan. Not only is he a divinely appointed ruler, he is also their guest of honour. Being a good host, with the responsibility to keep your guests safe and happy, was the socially-accepted code of the time, and to break this code was unthinkable.

 Older or more able pupils could use an edited version of the scene (**Worksheet 13**) in pairs and use the *Scene Studies* ◖◗ outlined in the Common Bank of Activities. This would replace the main activity in this lesson.

▶ Starter Activity

Worksheet 10: Character facts about Macbeth and Lady Macbeth

▶ **Freeze Frames** ☐ Pupils read the facts about the characters and make a freeze frame which shows the relationship between Lady Macbeth and Macbeth. They then bring their freeze frame to life and speak aloud Macbeth's and Lady Macbeth's lines. Pupils can choose who speaks first, how the lines are spoken, and whether the lines are spoken by the characters to each other or to the audience.

▶ **Spotlighting** ☐ Pairs make their freeze frame again. Explain that you have an imaginary spotlight in your hand and you will move around the room. When the spotlight shines on a pair, they will show their work. Move round the room spotlighting each pair. (At this point you could share some of the reflective questions in the next discussion section with pupils to inform their observation of the work).

▶ Ask:

■ *What did you see in other pairs' work that was different from in your own?*

■ *What did the physical position of the characters show about the relationship?*

■ *How did the order of the lines change what we understood about the relationship?*

■ *What did you notice about how the lines were said?*

▶ Now explore with the group what they have learned about the Macbeths' relationship. Ask

■ *What have you learnt about the relationship between Macbeth and Lady Macbeth?*

■ *Do you think that Macbeth will tell his wife what the witches have prophesied? Why / why not?*

▶ Tell pupils that Macbeth writes a letter to Lady Macbeth informing her about the prophecy. While she is reading that letter a messenger comes to tell her that her husband is on his way home with King Duncan. The King is coming to stay at their house to celebrate Scotland's victory in the battle and honour Macbeth as a hero.

▶ Main Activity

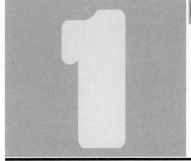

Worksheet 11: Act 1 Scene 5, Lady Macbeth

▶ Distribute Worksheet 11. Explain that the worksheet contains some of the things that Lady Macbeth says after she has read the letter from her husband. Use **Ensemble reading** ☐ to familiarise the class with the speech.

▶ Divide the class into groups of **three**. Give each group one of the short sections of Lady Macbeth's speech numbered one to seven (more than one group can have the same section). One pupil in each group sits on the chair and is Macbeth. The other two pupils share saying Lady Macbeth's lines. They should find a way of speaking the lines, and moving in relation to Macbeth, that clearly shows how Lady Macbeth feels about her husband.

▶ Then tell pupils that Lady Macbeth comes up with a plan. Ask:

■ *What do you think the plan might be?*

■ *What makes you think that?*

▶ Explain that when Macbeth and King Duncan arrive at the castle, Lady Macbeth has arranged a great feast in the King's honour. The Macbeth's decide that they are going to kill King Duncan that night. However, during the feast, Macbeth realises that he cannot go through with it and he leaves and goes into another room on his own. Lady Macbeth follows him. Macbeth tells her that he does not want to kill King Duncan.

Worksheet 12: Act 1 Scene 7, Lady Macbeth
▶ Explain that the worksheet contains some of the things that Lady Macbeth says to Macbeth to persuade him to go through with the murder, in the order that she says them.

▶ Allocate one of the short sections to each group of three. Ask them to discuss responses to the following questions, allowing a couple of minutes for each.

■ *What is Lady Macbeth saying?*

■ *Why is she saying it? What effect does she think her words will have on Macbeth?*

■ *If Lady Macbeth was speaking in modern English, what would she be saying?*

■ *What is she trying to make him feel?*

■ *Why would her words have an impact on Macbeth?*

■ *What actions might go with the words?*

■ *What are the most important words?*

▶ Ask one pupil to sit on the chair and be Macbeth. Ask the other two to label themselves as A and B. They are both Lady Macbeth, but A will speak Shakespeare's words and B will speak in modern English. Their aim is to convince Macbeth to kill the King. They can both use actions to persuade him to do what they want but they are not allowed to touch him. Macbeth is not allowed to say anything except '*I dare do all that may become a man*', but he can say this whenever he wants to and in whatever way he wants. If the pupil playing Macbeth feels persuaded by his/her Lady Macbeth's, he should stand up to indicate his readiness to murder the King. Otherwise, he should stay seated on the chair. His response will be influenced by Lady Macbeth's attitude; he may feel angry, nervous, sulky or frightened in response to her. Any of these is reasonable and pupils need to make the choice that feels right for them. Give the group five minutes to experiment, then ask:

■ *Did any of the Macbeths stand up?*

■ *Why / Why not?*

▶ Plenary

 ▶ Write 'For' and 'Against' on the whiteboard or flipchart. Ask pupils for the reasons why Macbeth should kill King Duncan. For example, the witches have already prophesied it, it will please his wife, he might make a good, brave king. List them in the 'For' column. Then ask why he should not kill King Duncan and list them in the 'Against' column. For example, King Duncan has recently honoured him, the King is a guest under his roof, he might get caught.

 ▶ **Conscience Threes** ▣ Working in their groups of three, ask pupils to form a line across the centre of the room with their Macbeth standing in the middle, between pupil A and pupil B. Place a cloak and a crown on a chair at one end of the room to represent King Duncan.

▶ Explain that A will try to convince Macbeth to kill King Duncan. They can use the 'For' arguments to help them. B will try to convince Macbeth not to kill King Duncan. They can use the 'Against' arguments. If Macbeth is convinced by the 'For' arguments, he will take a step towards the cloak and crown representing King Duncan; if he is convinced by the 'Against' arguments, he will take a step away. The groups work simultaneously. Give them two or three minutes to do this.

▶ Ask the pupils to stop and stay where they are. Ask the Macbeth in the group that is nearest to King Duncan to say why they got so close and which were the most persuasive arguments that they heard. Ask the Macbeth in the group that is furthest away which was the most persuasive argument they heard. Finally, ask:

■ *Is Macbeth determined to kill King Duncan by this point in the play?*

Why / Why not?

▶ Invite pupils to return to the **Role on the Wall** ▣. Ask:

■ *How has Macbeth changed from our first encounter with him?*

Provide Post-it notes and ask pupils to write one comment in response to this question supported by evidence from the text.

MACBETH

- He is a Scottish lord and a brave fighter in King Duncan's army.

- He has just helped win a war for Scotland against Norway.

- He has no children.

He says: *'I dare do all that may become a man.'*

LADY MACBETH

- She is married to Macbeth, a Scottish lord.

- She would like to be more powerful than she is.

- She wants Macbeth to be more powerful than he is.

- She is now childless.

She says: *'Art thou afeard?'*

Act 1 Scene 5 (edited)

LADY MACBETH:

1 Glamis thou art, and Cawdor, and shalt be
What thou art promised:

2 Yet do I fear thy nature:
It is too full o'th'milk of human kindness
To catch the nearest way.

3 Thou wouldst be great,
Art not without ambition.

4 What thou wouldst highly,
That wouldst thou holily: wouldst not play false,
And yet wouldst wrongly win.

5 Hie thee hither,
That I may pour my spirits in thine ear
And chastise with the valour of my tongue
All that impedes thee from the golden round.

6 The raven himself is hoarse
That croaks the fatal entrance of Duncan
Under my battlements.

7 Come, you spirits
And fill me from the crown to the toe top-full
Of direst cruelty.

▶ Notes

'milk of human kindness':	compassion / natural kindness
'wouldst':	want to
'highly':	ambitiously
'holily':	innocently
'play false':	betray
'hie':	hurry
'chastise':	tell off
'impedes':	holds you back
'golden round':	the king's crown

Act 1 Scene 7 (edited)

LADY MACBETH:

1
                     Was the hope drunk
Wherein you dressed yourself? Hath it slept since?
And wakes it now, to look so green and pale
At what it did so freely? From this time
Such I account thy love.

2 Art thou afeard
To be the same in thine own act and valour
As thou art in desire?

3 When you durst do it, then you were a man:
And to be more than what you were, you would
Be so much more the man.

4 I have given suck, and know
How tender 'tis to love the babe that milks me:
I would, while it was smiling in my face,
Have plucked my nipple from his boneless gums,
And dashed the brains out, had I so sworn as you
Have done to this.

Act 1 Scene 7 (edited)

LADY MACBETH: He has almost supped. Why have you left the chamber?

MACBETH: Hath he asked for me?

LADY MACBETH: Know you not he has?

MACBETH: We will proceed no further in this business:
He hath honoured me of late, and I have bought
Golden opinions from all sorts of people,
Which would be worn now in their newest gloss,
Not cast aside so soon.

LADY MACBETH: Was the hope drunk
Wherein you dressed yourself? Hath it slept since?
And wakes it now, to look so green and pale
At what it did so freely? From this time
Such I account thy love. Art thou afeard
To be the same in thine own act and valour
As thou art in desire?

MACBETH: Prithee, peace.
I dare do all that may become a man:
Who dares do more is none.

LADY MACBETH: What beast was't, then,
That made you break this enterprise to me?
When you durst do it, then you were a man:
And to be more than what you were, you would
Be so much more the man.
I have given suck, and know
How tender 'tis to love the babe that milks me:
I would, while it was smiling in my face,
Have plucked my nipple from his boneless gums,
And dashed the brains out, had I so sworn as you
Have done to this.

MACBETH: If we should fail?

LADY MACBETH: We fail?
But screw your courage to the sticking-place
And we'll not fail.

MACBETH

Key Objective

To understand how Macbeth makes the decision to kill Duncan.

KS3	KS2
4.1 Using different dramatic approaches to explore ideas, texts and issues	Speaking, Listening and Responding, Group Discussion and Interaction, Drama, Understanding and Interpreting Texts, Engaging and Responding to Texts
5.2 Understanding and responding to ideas, viewpoints, themes and purposes in texts	

LESSON DESCRIPTION

Pupils map Macbeth's decision-making process in the speech *'Is this a dagger which I see before me'* and act out their choices in an exercise based on 'Grandmother's Footsteps'.

Preparation and Resources

You will need:

▶ A hall or drama studio, or classroom with tables pushed back

▶ A whiteboard or flipchart

▶ A supply of coloured pens or markers

▶ A crown and a dagger

▶ **Worksheet 14/14a:** one per pupil

 Unlike Lady Macbeth, who appears to trade honour for power in the blink of an eye, Macbeth agonises over his decision to kill Duncan. One of his most prominent qualities is his ability to see many sides to a question and to want to investigate these in detail, an aspect of his character which Lady Macbeth finds intensely frustrating. Taking his reflection for cowardice, she warns him not to let "'I dare not' wait upon 'I would'." Interestingly, Lady Macbeth herself pays the price for the suppression of her own feelings: in the Act 5 sleepwalking scene we see how her guilt has at last overwhelmed her and driven her mad. Macbeth's dynamic is a different one and his self-examination is very evident in the *'Is this a dagger'* soliloquy, during which he examines the possible consequences of murdering Duncan.

Children's games can provide useful frameworks for exploring a scene and often feature in rehearsal room practice. Here, 'Grandmother's Footsteps', one of the most frequently played games in RSC rehearsal rooms, is used as a starting point for investigating Macbeth's emotional journey. As pupils act out their choices in this exercise, it will be helpful to remind them that Macbeth has been played in many different ways and that there are passages within the speech where a range of different choices can be made and justified.

 Worksheet 14a provides an edited version of Macbeth's speech for younger or less able pupils.

▶ Starter Activity

Worksheet 14/14a: Act 2 Scene 1

▶ Pupils will be picking up the story from the point where Macbeth is deciding whether to kill Duncan or not. Read them the words that Macbeth speaks to the audience in his soliloquy, just after Lady Macbeth has left him. As you read the speech aloud, ask pupils to close their eyes and echo all the words which create pictures in their imaginations. Ask:

■ *What are your first impressions of the speech?*

■ *Which words strike you as especially important?*

▶ Now ask pupils to speak the speech. Any of the following methods can be used:

■ all reading together

■ **ensemble reading** ▣

■ pupils sharing the speech round the circle, each taking one verse line

■ the group divides in half with one half speaking the first line while the second half speaks the second line, and so on.

'Grandmother's Footsteps'

▶ Choose a pupil to be crowned King. This pupil stands at one end of the space, his back to the others. The rest of the group line up as far away as possible from the King with the single-minded ambition of claiming his crown for themselves. As long as the current King cannot see them, they can move toward him in order to snatch the crown from his head. When he turns around, any player he sees moving is sent back to the starting line. Repeat the game with the winner of the crown playing the King.

▶ Discuss their strategies and their feelings during the exercise.

■ *What different ways of moving did you use?*

■ *What did you feel as you tried to claim the crown?*

■ *What if there were severe penalties for being caught rather than just being sent back to the start line – how would you feel about the risk-taking then?*

■ *How did the current King feel about people creeping up on him, wanting to take his crown?*

► Main Activity

Worksheet 14/14a: Act 2 Scene 1

► Pupils use coloured pens to map Macbeth's dagger soliloquy. They must make joint decisions about how Macbeth is feeling at the prospect of murdering King Duncan, exploring three possible choices:

■ Macbeth is intent on the murder.

■ Macbeth is horrified by the prospect of murder.

■ Macbeth is undecided.

Use three different colours to represent each of the different choices: green = he is intent on murder; red = he is horrified and wants to stop; amber = he is undecided. Ask pupils to decide which lines could relate to each particular choice and use the appropriate colour to mark the worksheet accordingly. Advise them that you will be asking them to 'walk' the speech in a way which reflects their choices: when they want to commit the murder they will move towards a dagger which you will hold; when they feel horrified they will move away; and when they can't decide what to do they will stand still. A further challenge is to ask pupils to decide *how* they move at any point. For example, when they move toward or away from the dagger do they edge sideways or crawl or rush?

► Now you stand at the far end of the space, holding the speech in one hand and the dagger in the other. Pupils, in their pairs and with their marked worksheets, form a line facing the dagger. As soon as you begin reading the speech, they begin walking their choices.

► Plenary

► Tell pupils what you observed about their choices and ask them to explain why they moved as they did. Some pairs will reach the dagger very early; others just at the last moment. Characteristically, Shakespeare is offering the actor a wide range of interpretative possibilities, and performance history tells us they have all been played in various productions.

► Homework

► Ask pupils to write detailed reasons on their worksheets, justifying their choices for moving at each point. Younger or less able pupils could pick three reasons. For older pupils this may form the basis for a piece of coursework entitled 'Why Macbeth decides to kill Duncan' which might incorporate their thinking from the *Conscience Threes* ▣ exercise in Lesson 3 (p.44) as well as their knowledge of other scenes from the play.

Act 2 Scene 1: Making the decision

MACBETH: Is this a dagger which I see before me,
The handle toward my hand? Come, let me clutch thee:
I have thee not, and yet I see thee still.
Art thou not, fatal vision, sensible
To feeling as to sight? Or art thou but
A dagger of the mind, a false creation,
Proceeding from the heat-oppressèd brain?
I see thee yet, in form as palpable
As this which now I draw.
Thou marshall'st me the way that I was going,
And such an instrument I was to use.
Mine eyes are made the fools o'th'other senses,
Or else worth all the rest. I see thee still,
And on thy blade and dudgeon gouts of blood,
Which was not so before. There's no such thing:
It is the bloody business which informs
Thus to mine eyes. Now o'er the one halfworld
Nature seems dead, and wicked dreams abuse
The curtained sleep: witchcraft celebrates
Pale Hecate's off'rings: and withered murder,
Alarumed by his sentinel the wolf,
Whose howl's his watch, thus with his stealthy pace,
With Tarquin's ravishing strides, towards his design
Moves like a ghost. – Thou sure and firm-set earth,
Hear not my steps which way they walk, for fear
Thy very stones prate of my whereabout
And take the present horror from the time
Which now suits with it. – Whiles I threat, he lives:
Words to the heat of deeds too cold breath gives.
I go, and it is done: the bell invites me.
Hear it not, Duncan, for it is a knell
That summons thee to heaven or to hell.

▶ Notes

'have thee not': cannot feel you in my hand
'sensible to feeling as to sight': able to be felt as well as seen
'heat-oppressed brain': the mind under pressure from fear or worry
'palpable': real
'marshall'st': guide
'worth all the rest': more reliable than the other senses

'dudgeon': handle of the dagger
'gouts of blood': drops of blood
'the one halfworld': one half of the world
'alarumed': called into action
'sentinel': guard
'watch': signal
'sure': solid
'prate': gossip about
'threat': make threats

Act 2 Scene 1:
Making the decision (edited)

MACBETH: Is this a dagger which I see before me,
The handle toward my hand? Come, let me clutch thee:
I have thee not, and yet I see thee still.
Art thou not, fatal vision, sensible
To feeling as to sight? Or art thou but
A dagger of the mind, a false creation,
Proceeding from the heat-oppressèd brain?
I see thee still,
And on thy blade and dudgeon gouts of blood,
Which was not so before.
Thou sure and firm-set earth,
Hear not my steps which way they walk, for fear
Thy very stones prate of my whereabout.
Whiles I threat, he lives.
I go, and it is done: the bell invites me.
Hear it not, Duncan, for it is a knell
That summons thee to heaven or to hell.

▶ Notes

'**have thee not**': cannot feel you in my hand

'**sensible to feeling as to sight**': able to be felt as well as seen

'**heat-oppressed brain**': the mind under pressure from fear or worry

'**dudgeon**': handle of the dagger

'**gouts of blood**': drops of blood

'**prate**': gossip about

'**threat**': make threats

MACBETH
LESSON 6: THE MURDER OF KING DUNCAN

Key Objective

To understand the 'offstage action' implied at the opening of Act 2 Scene 2, and to analyse how Shakespeare organises and structures the opening of the scene to influence meaning.

KS3

4.1 Using different dramatic approaches to explore ideas, texts and issues

6.2 Analysing how writers' use of linguistic and literary features shapes and influences meaning

KS2

Speaking, Listening and Responding, Group Discussion and Interaction, Drama, Understanding and Interpreting Texts, Engaging and Responding to Text

LESSON DESCRIPTION

Pupils enact the murder of King Duncan, create a soundscape using clues in the text and analyse the opening of Act 2 Scene 2.

Preparation and Resources

You will need:

▶ A hall or drama studio, or classroom with tables pushed back

▶ **Resource Sheet 3:** displayed on whiteboard, flipchart or sugar paper

▶ **Resource Sheet 4:** displayed on a whiteboard, flip chart or sugar paper

▶ **Worksheet 15:** one per pupil

▶ **Resource Sheet 5:** displayed on a whiteboard, flipchart or sugar paper

▶ A selection of about ten simple percussion instruments

TN In every play, there are events that we know must have happened, but which are not included in the action: 'offstage scenes'. Shakespeare chooses not to show his audience the scene in which the Macbeths murder King Duncan and his guards, (you might want to discuss with your pupils why they think he made this choice, for example, an imagined horror is more powerful than one you can see). However, the actors must ask themselves how this event took place, how the characters feel about it and what the mechanics of the event have been, in order to make sense of the rest of the play. In rehearsal, this can be achieved by improvising the 'offstage' action and this exercise reflects that process. The theatre is a live, multi-sensory medium: the director and designer want to engage all of the audience's senses so that we can feel and understand the atmosphere and setting of the play. Lighting, music, sound effects and special effects are all deployed to transport the audience in their imaginations to another time and place. This exercise draws on the multi-sensory aspects of the setting to deepen the pupils' understanding of atmosphere and to deepen empathy with the characters.

At the time the play was written, the theme of bad versus good kingship, embodied by Macbeth and Duncan respectively, would have resonated at the royal court where King James was busy establishing his divine right to be King. Macbeth kills the rightful, divinely anointed King Duncan. Shakespeare's audience would have seen this regicide as the most horrible crime imaginable – the equivalent of killing God on Earth.

LESSON STRUCTURE

1

▶ Starter Activity

▶ Remind pupils of the work they did in Lesson 4. In that lesson they discovered that King Duncan is staying overnight at the Macbeths' castle and Lady Macbeth and Macbeth are giving a dinner party in his honour. Ask:

- *When the dinner party is over, what time of night will it be?*
- *Where would the King sleep if he were their guest of honour?*
- *Who would be outside the King's door?*
- *Would Macbeth automatically become king if Duncan dies? Who are the heirs to the throne?* (Malcolm and Donalbain, King Duncan's sons)
- *How can Lady Macbeth and Macbeth murder the King and get away with it? They must not leave any evidence that would incriminate them.*

▶ Explain that we do not know exactly what happens on the night of the murder, but we do know that King Duncan's guards also die, and that no one appears to blame Macbeth and Lady Macbeth for the crime.

1

▶ Main Activity

▶ Pupils work in groups of five. Explain that you want them to ***improvise***/act out what happens on the night of the murder. One pupil will be the sleeping King Duncan, two pupils will be the King's guards and two will be Macbeth and Lady Macbeth. There is one rule:

- Each character may speak just once: the rest of the action must be clear from what the characters do. King Duncan should also speak, for example he could say good night to the guards or he could wake at the point Macbeth kills him and say something to him.

▶ Give pupils five minutes to prepare their scene. Explain that they must have a very clear beginning and end position.

2

▶ Arrange the groups around the room so that they will be able to see each other's work. Nominate an order in which the groups will perform. Explain that everyone will start in their opening position, and that as soon as the first group has finished, the next group will start and so on.

Resource Sheet 3: Reflective questions

▶ Ask each group to watch carefully and specifically the group that is performing directly after them. The last group should watch the first group. Explain that you will ask for feedback from them about the group they have been watching. Share the reflective questions on Resource Sheet 3 with the group before starting the performances by displaying them on a whiteboad, flipchart or sugar paper.

▶ After the performances, sit pupils down on the floor. Ask:

■ *What did you enjoy about the group that you were watching?*

■ *What did you notice that was different from your own work?*

■ *What did you notice about the relationship between Macbeth and Lady Macbeth? Who was in charge?*

■ *How did they deal with the guards? Why did the guards not suspect what was about to happen?*

■ *How did Macbeth feel when King Duncan spoke to him? How did the words the group had chosen affect how we feel about Macbeth?*

■ *From what you saw, do you think Macbeth and Lady Macbeth would get away with the murder? Who would people blame?*

Resource Sheet 4: Act 2 Scene 3, Lennox

▶ Ask pupils to close their eyes and listen. Slowly read aloud the description of the night of the murder from Act 2 Scene 3. Then ask pupils to keep their eyes shut, but this time to whisper any words that stand out to them as soon as they hear them. Read the description again, as pupils whisper, echoing the key words. Ask:

■ *What was the weather like on the night of the murder?*

■ *What was the atmosphere like?*

■ *What sounds could Macbeth hear on that night?*

▶ As pupils make suggestions, ask:

■ *What would that sound like?*

■ *What sounds could be heard outside the castle?* (The whistling wind, an owl screeching, rain drumming against the roof)

■ *What sounds could be heard inside?* (Doors creaking, windows rattling, footsteps, muffed voices down below, a clock striking midnight)

■ *How did Macbeth feel on the night of the murder? What sounds could he hear inside his own mind and body?* (A heartbeat, shallow breathing, words that his wife or King Duncan have said to him)

▶ Select one group to perform their murder scene in the middle of the room. Ask this group to remove any words, so that everything the audience needs to know is shown in the action.

▶ Give each remaining group a **soundscape** ⬡ to create. They must create a sequence of sounds with a beginning, middle and end. Give the groups one or two simple percussion instruments to help them, and explain that they can use their voices. The soundscapes are:

■ the weather

■ sounds in the distance, including animals

■ sounds inside the castle

■ sounds inside Macbeth's own mind and body

Worksheet 15: Act 2 Scene 2

▶ Whilst the soundscapes are being created, give the group selected to perform the murder scene an edited version of what Macbeth and Lady Macbeth say to each other after the murder. The two pupils playing these characters read the script aloud. The other three help them rehearse this short exchange, answering the questions on the worksheet. After they are happy all the questions have been answered, they add this scene onto the end of their murder scene.

Resource Sheet 5: "Sleep no more, Macbeth does murder sleep."

▶ Ask the soundscaping groups to pause for a moment. Display the line from Act 2 Scene 2. Ask each group to incorporate this line into their soundscape. Whilst pupils are working, circulate and find out what they have created. When you are satisfied that everyone is ready, ask pupils to stop work and sit on the floor.

▶ Time for the performance. Explain that you will be the conductor. Pupils must watch carefully. When you point to a group, they start their soundscape. Your hands are the volume control: if they are closer to the floor, the volume is turned down; if they are closer to the ceiling, the volume is turned up. When everyone is watching, allow each soundscape group to perform their work, experimenting with volume.

▶ Now ask the murder scene group to get ready to perform. Ask members of the group:

■ *At what point in the action do you think the weather sounds should start?*

■ *At what point in the action should the sounds inside Macbeth's own mind and body start?*

■ *When do you think the volume should increase?*

■ *Are there any sounds that should happen at exactly the moment that King Duncan is killed?*

■ *What should happen when Lady Macbeth and Macbeth start speaking?*

The pupils should watch carefully for their 'cue' and the volume control. Start the murder scene, pointing clearly to each group when you want them to join in, indicating volume with your hands. Use the pupils' ideas to conduct the whole scene and ask them to give each other a round of applause.

▶ Plenary

▶ Pupils sit in a circle. Explain that, when actors are rehearsing a play, they have to decide where they have just come from when they enter a scene. For example, the actors playing Lady Macbeth and Macbeth would need to decide what the murder scene in King Duncan's room looked like in order to inform how they enter the stage in Act 2 Scene 2. Ask:

■ *Did acting out the murder scene help you to imagine what happened?*

■ *Did the pupils who were playing Macbeth and Lady Macbeth do the scene differently because of the sounds they could hear? In what ways?*

■ *What do you think the line on Resource Sheet 2 means, and why do you think Shakespeare included it in the play?*

Worksheet 15: Act 2 Scene 2
▶ Ask all pupils to read along silently, whilst the pupils who played Macbeth and Lady Macbeth read it aloud. Explain that everyone will be exploring this scene in more detail next lesson. Explore responses to the questions on the worksheet with the group. Explain that these are some of the questions that directors and actors will discover the answers to as they rehearse the play. Ask pupils what they think might happen next in the story.

▶ Homework

▶ Ask pupils to imagine that they are a servant who has secretly witnessed the events of the murder. They are to write an eyewitness account of the events of the murder, using first person narrative. This could either be an informal piece of writing to another servant, or a formal piece of writing to an investigating officer. They should include:

■ A description of the atmosphere.

■ Full details of where, when, how and why the murder took place.

■ Their impressions of Macbeth and Lady Macbeth.

■ An indication of what they think might happen next.

Questions to think about when you are watching other groups perform:

- What did you enjoy about the group that you were watching?

- What did you notice that was different from your own work?

- What did you notice about the relationship between Macbeth and Lady Macbeth? Who was in charge?

- How did Macbeth and Lady Macbeth deal with the guards? Why did the guards not suspect what was about to happen?

- How did Macbeth feel when King Duncan spoke to him? How did the words the group had chosen affect how we feel about Macbeth?

- From what you saw, do you think Macbeth and Lady Macbeth would get away with the murder? Who would people blame?

Act 2 Scene 3

LENNOX: The night has been unruly. Where we lay,

Our chimneys were blown down, and, as they say,

Lamentings heard i'th'air, strange screams of death,

And prophesying with accents terrible

Of dire combustion and confused events

New hatched to th'woeful time: the obscure bird

Clamoured the livelong night. Some say the earth

Was feverous and did shake.

▶ **Notes:**

'**Lamentings**': cries of grief
'**accents terrible**': terrifying words
'**dire combustion**': dreadful confusion
'**New hatched**': newly born
'**the obscure bird**': an owl

Act 2 Scene 2: (edited)

MACBETH: I have done the deed. Didst thou not hear a noise?

LADY MACBETH: I heard the owl scream and the crickets cry.
Did not you speak?

MACBETH: When?

LADY MACBETH: Now.

MACBETH: As I descended?

LADY MACBETH: Ay.

MACBETH: Hark!
This is a sorry sight.

LADY MACBETH: A foolish thought, to say 'a sorry sight'.

▶ **Questions to resolve:**

Where might Lady Macbeth and Macbeth be when they have this conversation?
Where is the murder weapon/s? (We know that Macbeth brings the dagger/s with him from the murder scene but Lady Macbeth doesn't notice them at first.)
Is there blood anywhere?
How do you think Macbeth feels?
How do you think Lady Macbeth feels?
Who do you think is in charge?
Do Lady Macbeth and Macbeth look at each other?
Do they look back in the direction of the murdered king?
How will you show the audience that it is the end of the scene?

Sleep no more, Macbeth does murder sleep.

MACBETH

Key Objective

To understand the Macbeths' reactions to their murder of Duncan and to discover how Shakespeare's verse technique supports and reveals their feelings.

KS3	KS2
4.1 Using different dramatic approaches to explore ideas, texts and issues	Speaking, Listening and Responding, Group Discussion and Interaction, Drama, Understanding and Interpreting Texts, Engaging and Responding to Texts
4.2 Developing, adapting and responding to dramatic techniques, conventions and styles	
6.3 Analysing writers' use of organisation, structure, layout and presentation	

LESSON DESCRIPTION

Pupils use practical strategies to investigate the pace, rhythms and atmosphere of the post-murder scene between the Macbeths and speculate about the future of their relationship.

Preparation and Resources

You will need:

▶ A hall or drama studio, or classroom with tables pushed back

▶ A whiteboard or flipchart

▶ **Worksheet 16**: one per pupil

TN The sequence of events leading up to the murder of King Duncan happens very quickly. Shakespeare could have written a play that culminated in the act of regicide but instead he's written one that focuses on the consequences of that act. This lesson explores in detail the short exchange between Macbeth and Lady Macbeth immediately after the murder of Duncan. Shakespeare captures the characters' feelings and the atmosphere of a scene in the sounds of words and especially their rhythms. For example, a sequence of long and lazy vowels conjures up one atmosphere, while a collection of punchy consonants may conjure up another. Prose can shift to poetry and back again and the verse rhythms can be disturbed or changed entirely to suit character, situation and mood. Pupils can appreciate Shakespeare's immensely skilful technique by 'walking' the words and feeling in their bodies the way rhythm and sound affect actors and audience alike. In this exchange, the rhythm of the words spoken between Macbeth and Lady Macbeth is particularly interesting, containing as it does a mixture of urgent *shared lines* ◘ and pauses.

▶ Starter Activity

▶ Pupils stand in a circle and pass a clap around. Begin by turning to the pupil on your left and clapping in his/her direction. They clap at the pupil on their left and so the clap goes round the circle until it arrives back with you. Now pass a clap to the right. The third time pass the clap faster, reminding pupils to keep the speed consistent. How fast can they pass a clap? Can claps be passed in both directions at the same time and arrive safely back at the start?

Worksheet 16: Act 2 Scene 2

▶ Explain to the pupils that you will be exploring the scene between Macbeth and Lady Macbeth, which they heard last lesson, in more detail. Ask pupils to pass the words of the scene, one word at a time, around the circle. Pass them around again in the other direction, going faster, then a third time, faster still. Ask pupils if they think this scene should be played slowly or quickly. Why?

▶ Main Activity

Worksheet 16

▶ Working in pairs, ask pupils to read the scene through together twice, one playing Macbeth and the other Lady Macbeth. The first time they should pause for a slow count of two at every full stop (count this aloud for them so they understand how slow it needs to be). The second time they should not pause at all but read swiftly through the scene. Ask:

■ *Which version worked better? Why?*

▶ Ask pupils if they notice anything unusual about how the scene looks on the page. Explain what **shared lines** ◳ are. Ask pupils why they think Shakespeare would be using a number of shared lines in this scene – how do these reflect the emotional state of the characters and what is going on in the scene?

▶ Introduce **iambic pentameter** ◳ Explain that a line of poetry or verse in Shakespeare is made up of five poetic 'feet.' There are various kinds of poetic 'feet' that writers use and the kind Shakespeare mostly uses is called an 'iamb.' This foot is made up of one unstressed syllable followed by a stressed syllable: de, DUM. So a line of iambic pentameter would be: de, DUM, de, DUM, de, DUM, de, DUM, de, DUM. Does that rhythm remind pupils of anything (a heartbeat)? Use a pupil's name as an example:

■ *Do we say, Sar AH or SAR ah? Which syllable is stressed?* (The first.) *So is Sarah's name an iambic foot?* (No.) *Does anyone have a name, either first or last, with an iambic foot in it?*

▶ Beat out the first names and surnames of a number of pupils so that they understand that their names have a rhythm. Then find the rhythm for an ordinary sentence which uses an iambic beat: Your TEA is GOing COLD please EAT it NOW. Beat this through on knees or on the floor several times and then ask pupils how many iambic feet it has. Write it on the whiteboard or flipchart and mark the stressed syllables.

▶ Now use a line of Shakespeare's. Write up: *'If MUsic BE the FOOD of LOVE play ON'* and ask how many feet the line has. (This opening line to *Twelfth Night* is a classic example of iambic pentameter). You can also explore Macbeth's first line in the play (Act 1 scene 3) *'So foul and fair a day I have not seen'*: another line of iambic pentameter. Finally, ask pupils if Lady Macbeth's line *'I heard the owl scream and the crickets cry'* (Act 2 Scene 2) is a line of iambic pentameter? (Yes.) Now try Macbeth's first line *'I have done the deed. Didst thou not hear a noise?'* (No, because the first syllable is stressed and there are six feet in the line.)

▶ Explain that when Shakespeare is writing in iambic pentameter and he breaks that rhythm, this is a clue. It gives us information about how the character is feeling and/or what is going on in the scene. Ask:

■ *Why does Shakespeare choose to stress the first syllable of Macbeth's first line?* (Because Macbeth is saying, *'I have done this'*.)

■ *Can you find another example of a perfect iambic line?* (Lady Macbeth's last line)

▶ If you are dealing with a very able group, include the following exercise. Explain that when a line is shorter than five feet, when it is missing one or more syllables, Shakespeare is signalling that a pause could be taken to fill the missing beats. There are three moments in the scene where syllables are missing and so pauses could be taken. Ask pupils:

■ *Where in the scene are there missing syllables?* (Nine syllables are missing before or after Lady Macbeth's 'Ay' and another nine before or after Macbeth's 'Hark.' Four syllables are missing before or after 'This is a sorry sight.') Tell pupils that it is the actor's choice whether to take the pauses before or after these words or phrases. So, Macbeth could pause before he says, *'This is a sorry sight'* or Lady Macbeth could pause before she says, *'A foolish thought to say a sorry sight.'*

■ *Where do you think the pauses work best?*

▶ Pairs review their choices about where the pauses come in the scene. They must find reasons for the characters to pause and fill those pauses with action. Ask for volunteers to show their work.

Worksheet 16
▶ Model the **Follow Chase** ◲ with a pupil. In this scene Lady Macbeth should set off through the space at a very rapid pace, Macbeth following her. Tell pupils that at some point in the scene Macbeth will feel the need to stop rather than follow Lady Macbeth. They should decide when that is and stop accordingly. When she realises Macbeth is no longer following her, Lady Macbeth must decide what she will do next. Will she carry on walking, return to where Macbeth is now standing or go somewhere else? Pupils should try to incorporate pauses into this exercise, whether or not these have been chosen by applying an understanding of missing syllables.

▶ Plenary

▶ Ask:

■ *How has Shakespeare constructed the scene to help the audience understand how Macbeth and Lady Macbeth are feeling?* (Short sentences, questions, the rhythm of the scene)

■ *Who asks more questions in the scene, Macbeth or Lady Macbeth? Who makes the most statements? What might this suggest to us about how the characters are feeling at this point?*

■ *What do you think will happen to the Macbeths now?*

■ *How does this exchange compare with the pre-murder scene ('Was the hope drunk...?') which we explored in Lesson 4?*

▶ Homework

▶ Ask pupils to annotate their worksheets. They should write detailed stage directions for their production of this scene, indicating where the characters move, when they pause and what happens during the pauses. Older or more able pupils could accompany the annotation with three or four paragraphs explaining their choices.

Act 2 Scene 2

MACBETH: I have done the deed. Didst thou not hear a noise?

LADY MACBETH: I heard the owl scream and the crickets cry.
Did not you speak?

MACBETH:　　　　　When?

LADY MACBETH:　　　　　Now.

MACBETH:　　　　　　　　As I descended?

LADY MACBETH: Ay.

MACBETH: Hark!
Who lies i'the second chamber?

LADY MACBETH:　　　　　　　Donalbain.

MACBETH: This is a sorry sight.

LADY MACBETH: A foolish thought, to say 'a sorry sight'.

MACBETH
LESSON 8: FEARS AND IMAGININGS

Key Objective

To understand the motivations of Macbeth and Banquo in the aftermath of the murder of King Duncan.

KS3

2.2 Using and adapting the conventions and forms of spoken text

4.1 Using different dramatic approaches to explore ideas, texts and issues

5.1 Developing and adapting active reading skills and strategies

KS2

Speaking, Listening and Responding, Group Discussion and Interaction, Drama, Understanding and Interpreting Texts, Engaging and Responding to Text

LESSON DESCRIPTION

Pupils make a presentation showing what is going on in the minds of Macbeth and Banquo, in order to better understand their motivations.

Preparation and Resources

You will need:

▶ A hall or drama studio, or classroom with tables pushed back

▶ **Worksheet 17:** one per pupil

▶ A dagger

TN This lesson picks up the narrative after the discovery of the murder of King Duncan and returns to the relationship between Macbeth and Banquo. We review their relationship at this point in the action, and look closely at the language each character is using to speculate about what they are thinking and feeling. The decision to arrange the murder of his friend Banquo and Banquo's son Fleance is made by Macbeth in isolation. He does not consult his wife, who has been so instrumental in his decision to murder the King. Macbeth is at a crossroads as he decides what to do. This sort of decision, where there are no easy answers and where Shakespeare is exploring the complex psychology of a character with conflicting loyalties, desires and responsibilities, is rich in terms of teaching and learning. By 'standing in the shoes' of the characters at these moments, we are practising what it must be like to make these complex decisions, with all the ethical, moral and spiritual considerations that such a decision implies.

Shakespeare frequently chooses to explore the lives of the powerful: rulers and kings. So in the tragedies we may feel moved by circumstances greater and nobler than our own everyday existences. But we are also encouraged to identify with the personal details of these people's lives and share their humanity.

▶ Starter Activity

▶ Explain that, when the murder of King Duncan is discovered, everyone in the castle is horrified. The guards' bodies are covered in blood, and the daggers used to murder the King are found in their hands. When morning comes, the King's sons and heirs to the throne, Malcolm and Donalbain, have fled Scotland. Ask:

■ *Who might people suspect committed the murder and why?*

■ *Why might Malcolm and Donalbain have fled?*

▶ Explain that people turn to the hero of the battle, Macbeth and he is crowned King of Scotland. Ask:

■ *What did the witches prophesy for Macbeth?*

■ *Who was there when the witches made that prophecy?* (Only Macbeth and Banquo – they share the secret.)

▶ Explain that Banquo has been unable to sleep since the night of the murder, and he does not go to the coronation of Macbeth. Ask:

■ *What did the witches prophesy for Banquo?*

▶ Explain that Banquo has a young son called Fleance.

▶ Invite two pupils to represent Banquo and his son Fleance in a **freeze frame** ⬡. Ask the rest of the pupils:

■ *Why do you think Banquo can't sleep? How can we show that in our freeze frame?*

■ *How does he feel about his son, Fleance? How can we show that in our freeze frame?*

▶ Invite another pupil to represent Macbeth in the freeze frame. Ask:

■ *At the beginning of the play, what was the relationship between Macbeth and Banquo?*

■ *Do you think they are still friends? Why / Why not?*

■ *How could Macbeth make sure that Banquo's prophecy does not come true?*

■ *Where should Macbeth be in the freeze frame and why?*

▶ Main Activity

Worksheet 17: Act 3 Scene 1

▶ Using *ensemble reading* ⟡ pupils read through what Banquo says about Macbeth. Ask:

■ *What words tell us how Banquo is feeling?*

■ *What is he worried about?*

■ *What does he suspect Macbeth has done? Why has he not told anyone what he suspects?*

■ *Banquo is remembering the moment when the witches made their prophecy. What does he think might happen in the future?*

■ *Why does he say 'hush, no more' at the end of the speech?*

▶ Pupils read through what Macbeth says about Banquo. Again, the speech is read round the circle, punctuation mark to punctuation mark. Ask:

■ *What words tell us how Macbeth is feeling?*

■ *What is he worried about?*

■ *Macbeth is remembering the moment when the witches made their prophecy. Why did the witches speak to Banquo?*

■ *What does Macbeth think might happen in the future?*

▶ Divide the class into four equal-sized groups. Give Group One the first section of Banquo's speech and Group Two the second section of his speech. Give Group Three the first section of Macbeth's speech and Group Four the second section.

▶ Explain that each group will create a presentation. Choose two people in each group to speak the lines. The rest of the group must show the images that are running through the characters' minds. They will represent the people and things that Macbeth or Banquo are thinking about. The witches, Lady Macbeth, Macbeth, Banquo and Fleance might be represented as the text is spoken. Give pupils five minutes to prepare their presentation.

▶ Ask pupils to pick out the three most important words in their section of text. As a group they must find a way of emphasising these words together, and add this to their presentation. Allow them two more minutes to do this.

▶ Arrange the groups around the room so that they will be able to see each other's work, and nominate an order in which the groups will perform. Explain that everyone will start in their opening position and that as soon as the first group has finished, the next will start, and so on.

▶ Ask each group to carefully watch the group that is performing directly after them. (The last group should watch the first group.) In particular, they should watch out for which words stand out, and why. Share the reflective questions in the next bullet point with the group and ask them to consider these as they watch the performances.

▶ Sit pupils down on the floor. Ask:

■ *What did you enjoy about the group that you were watching?*

■ *Which words stood out and why?*

■ *What is the most important picture in Banquo's / Macbeth's mind?*

▶ Plenary

▶ Ask:

■ *Can Macbeth trust Banquo?*

■ *Who would Macbeth have to get rid of to keep his secret safe?*

■ *How could he get rid of Banquo and Fleance?*

Place a dagger or something that represents a dagger on a chair in the middle of the room. Explain to pupils that you are going to do **chair thermometer** ⬗. They should ask themselves:

■ *Will Macbeth kill Banquo and Fleance?*

■ *Will it be an easy decision for him?*

▶ Pupils then stand in the room in relation to the dagger. They should stand closest to the dagger if they think Macbeth is ready to kill Banquo and Fleance and it is an easy decision, and furthest away if they think Macbeth could not possibly murder them. They can choose to stand anywhere in between. They must be able to tell the rest of the group why they have chosen their position. Once they are in position, ask five or six pupils to explain why they have chosen to stand where they have, including the pupil closest to the dagger and the one furthest away.

Finally, explain that Macbeth does now arrange the murder of Banquo and Fleance, and that is what happens next in the play.

▶ Having made their decisions, ask pupils to consider how far away Macbeth is from the man we met at the start of the play. What words would they now use to describe him? Update the **Role on the Wall** ⬗ accordingly.

Act 3 Scene 1 (edited)

BANQUO (*talking about Macbeth*):
Thou hast it now: King, Cawdor, Glamis, all
As the weyard women promised, and I fear
Thou played'st most foully for't. Yet it was said
It should not stand in thy posterity,
But that myself should be the root and father
Of many kings.

                If there come truth from them —
As upon thee, Macbeth, their speeches shine —
Why, by the verities on thee made good,
May they not be my oracles as well,
And set me up in hope? But hush, no more.

MACBETH (*talking about BANQUO*):
Our fears in Banquo stick deep,
And in his royalty of nature reigns that
Which would be feared. There is none but he
Whose being I do fear. He chid the sisters
When first they put the name of king upon me,
And bade them speak to him:

                      then prophet-like
They hailed him father to a line of kings:
Upon my head they placed a fruitless crown,
And put a barren sceptre in my grip,
No son of mine succeeding.

MACBETH
LESSON 9: STAGING THE BANQUET SCENE, ACT 3 SCENE 4

Key Objective

To explore staging choices for Act 3 Scene 4 and their implications for an audience's relationship with Macbeth.

KS3

4.1 Using different dramatic approaches to explore ideas, texts and issues

4.2 Developing, adapting and responding to dramatic techniques, conventions and styles

KS2

Speaking, Listening and Responding, Group Discussion and Interaction, Drama, Understanding and Interpreting Texts, Engaging and Responding to texts

LESSON DESCRIPTION

Pupils experiment with different ways of staging Act 3 Scene 4 of Macbeth.

Preparation and Resources

You will need:

► A hall or drama studio, or classroom with tables pushed back

► **Worksheet 18:** one for each group

► **Worksheet 19/19a:** one per pupil

► A whiteboard or flipchart

► Chairs, enough for one between three pupils

 In Act 3 Scene 4 Macbeth and Lady Macbeth welcome their guests to a banquet to celebrate Macbeth becoming King. As they are about to start, the First Murderer enters with the news that Banquo is dead and his son Fleance has escaped. The bloody Ghost of Banquo, which only Macbeth can see, then appears at the dinner table. Later, Macbeth tells his wife he's going to find out why Macduff (another lord who has fought alongside Macbeth in battle) did not attend their banquet; he hints that there may be more bloodshed, but first decides he will speak to the witches again.

Whilst the appearance of Banquo's Ghost can be a spectacularly thrilling moment in the play, it it is one of the most difficult scenes to stage. The actor playing Banquo returns to the action and the audience has to believe that only Macbeth can see him. Sometimes, the choice is made not to have an actor playing the ghost on stage so the audience is in the same position as Lady Macbeth and the other guests at the feast in not being able to see the cause of Macbeth's distress. This is not something that can be worked out by sitting down and reading the scene; it is essential to be on your feet trying out different staging approaches.

In this lesson, pupils will isolate some of the key moments in Act 3 Scene 4 in order to make *staging* ◘ decisions about the scene.

 Worksheet 19a provides an edited version of Act 3 scene 4 for younger or less able pupils.

LESSON STRUCTURE

▶ Starter Activity

▶ Ask pupils to stand up and be ready to create an instant reaction to the following cues when you read them out. Explain that all the reactions you'll be asking for are in some way connected to events in Act 3 Scene 4. Responses should be larger than life. Pupils should hold their reaction for three or four seconds until you give them the next cue:

■ *You see a huge table laid with the most beautiful food.*

■ *You are warmly welcoming people to your home.*

■ *You see a murderer covered in blood.*

■ *You discover that your enemy has escaped unharmed.*

■ *You see a bloody ghost sitting at your dinner table.*

■ *You are embarrassed by your husband/brother/friend's behaviour.*

■ *You see your friend in trouble and try to cover for them.*

■ *You take charge of the situation and tell people not to worry.*

▶ Main Activity

▶ Put pupils into groups of three to play **High**, **Medium**, **Low**. Each group has a chair. Explain that when you say *change* pupils will take a position that is either high, medium or low. Sitting or lying on the floor is 'low', sitting on the chair is 'medium' and standing up is 'high'. Only one pupil can adopt a high position, a medium position or a low position at any one time. The idea is for the group to move to a new position quickly and without discussion, so that each time you say *change* there is a new person in each position. Begin slowly, giving a count of eight to change position, then four, then two, and finally a single hand clap or the call *change*. Once pupils have mastered the moves, encourage them to add the following rules, one at a time:

■ *Exaggerate the positions as much as possible.*

■ *Be in physical contact with each other.*

■ *Show how you feel about and relate to each other.*

▶ Now ask pupils to build pictures using the same set of rules in the same way, showing moments in the banquet scene from *Macbeth* which you will call out:

■ *Lady Macbeth welcomes people, and at the same time Macbeth sees a Murderer at the door.*

■ *Macbeth and the Murderer talk to each other, while Lady Macbeth looks on.*

■ *Macbeth turns to see Banquo's Ghost sat in his chair, while Lady*

Macbeth looks on.

■ *Macbeth is transfixed, Ross ushers people to leave, and Lady Macbeth tells them to sit down.*

■ *Macbeth is calm, Lady Macbeth is calm, and Ross is relieved.*

■ *The Ghost reappears, Macbeth is horrified, and Ross looks on concerned.*

Worksheet 18: Act 3 Scene 4

▶ Pupils work in groups of six and cast themselves as the characters in the scene (Macbeth, Lady Macbeth, Ross, Lennox, Banquo's Ghost, a lord. Any additional pupils can play other lords or guests at the dinner). Ask them to remember what they have learnt about the scene so far – its physical and emotional dynamics and the characters' internal and external reactions.

▶ They will now create a silent movie version of the entire scene which will be structured around six key moments of action, inspired by six lines of text from the scene. For younger or less able pupils we've supplied the lines of text on Worksheet 18. Older or more able pupils may prefer to dispense with the worksheet and identify their own lines of text. Groups should use their lines to introduce each section of action, for example by displaying them on flipchart paper.

▶ Encourage groups to perform each section of the scene in an exaggerated way. Their challenge is to ensure that the audience know exactly what is happening.

Worksheet 19/19a: Act 3 Scene 4, the banquet scene

▶ Ask pupils to read through the edited version of the scene using **ensemble reading** ⚡, then to prepare a staged version of it. They have a few minutes to rehearse and prepare their work. Groups then **showback** ⚡ their scenes to the rest of the class. (Share some or all of the plenary questions with the group before their performances.)

▶ Plenary

▶ Ask:

■ *If you were directing this scene onstage, how would you tackle it?*

■ *How do you want the audience to feel during the scene, and how will you ensure you provoke that feeling?*

■ *How would you present the ghost? Would you have an actor playing him?*

■ *In some productions Banquo doesn't appear on stage during the scene. Instead, the audience sees what the lords and Lady Macbeth see – an empty chair. What difference would this make to how involved we are with Macbeth as a character?*

■ *How would you indicate that he is a ghost and that only Macbeth can see him? For example, would you light him differently from the other characters?*

▶ **Homework**

▶ Ask pupils to imagine they are one of the lords (for example, Lennox or Ross) and have just left the banquet. They write an informal letter to a friend telling them what happened at the banquet, about Macbeth's strange behaviour and what they thought of it. Ask them to include at least one or two direct quotes from the play.

Act 3, Scene 4 (edited)

The banquet is prepared. MACBETH, LADY MACBETH, ROSS, LENNOX, LORDS, and Attendants. All are on their feet, waiting for a toast from Macbeth

1 MACBETH
Good digestion and health!

2 LENNOX
May't please your highness sit.

3 MACBETH
The table's full.

4 ROSS
Gentlemen, rise: his highness is not well.

5 LADY MACBETH
My worthy lord,
Your noble friends do lack you.

6 MACBETH
Avaunt, and quit my sight! Let the earth hide thee!

Act 3, Scene 4 (edited)

The banquet is prepared. MACBETH, LADY MACBETH, ROSS, LENNOX, LORDS and attendants are all on stage. They are on their feet, waiting for a toast from Macbeth

LADY MACBETH: My royal lord,
You do not give the cheer.

Enter the Ghost of Banquo, and sits in MACBETH's place

MACBETH: Sweet remembrancer.
Now, good digestion wait on appetite,
And health on both!

LENNOX: May't please your highness sit.

MACBETH: Here had we now our country's honour roofed,
Were the graced person of our Banquo present.

ROSS: His absence, sir,
Lays blame upon his promise.

MACBETH: The table's full.

LENNOX: Here is a place reserved, sir.

MACBETH: Where?

LENNOX: Here, my good lord. What is't that moves your highness?

MACBETH: Which of you have done this?

LORDS: What, my good lord?

MACBETH: Thou canst not say I did it: never shake
Thy gory locks at me.

ROSS: Gentlemen, rise: his highness is not well.

LADY MACBETH: Sit, worthy friends: my lord is often thus,
And hath been from his youth. Pray you keep seat.
(*To Macbeth*) Are you a man?

MACBETH: Ay, and a bold one, that dare look on that
Which might appal the devil.

LADY MACBETH: O, proper stuff!
This is the very painting of your fear:
This is the air-drawn dagger which you said
Led you to Duncan.
Why do you make such faces? When all's done,
You look but on a stool.

MACBETH: Prithee see there! Behold, look, lo!

Exit Ghost of Banquo

MACBETH: If I stand here, I saw him.

LADY MACBETH: Fie, for shame!
My worthy lord,
Your noble friends do lack you.

MACBETH: I do forget. –
Do not muse at me, my most worthy friends,
I have a strange infirmity which is nothing
To those that know me. Come, love and health to all,

Enter Ghost of Banquo

LORDS: Our duties and the pledge.

MACBETH: Avaunt, and quit my sight! Let the earth hide thee!

LADY MACBETH: Think of this, good peers,
But as a thing of custom: 'tis no other,
Only it spoils the pleasure of the time.

MACBETH: Hence, horrible shadow!
Unreal mock'ry, hence!

Exit Ghost of Banquo

Why, so: being gone,
I am a man again. Pray you sit still.

LADY MACBETH: You have displaced the mirth, broke the good meeting
With most admired disorder.

Act 3, Scene 4 (edited)

The banquet is prepared. MACBETH, LADY MACBETH, ROSS, LENNOX, LORDS, and attendants are all on stage. They are on their feet, waiting for a toast from Macbeth

LADY MACBETH: My royal lord,
You do not give the cheer.

Enter the Ghost of Banquo, and sits in MACBETH's place

MACBETH: Sweet remembrancer.
Now, good digestion wait on appetite,
And health on both!

LENNOX: May't please your highness sit.

MACBETH: The table's full.

LENNOX: Here is a place reserved, sir.

MACBETH: Where?

LENNOX: Here, my good lord. What is't that moves your highness?

MACBETH: Which of you have done this?

LORDS: What, my good lord?

MACBETH: Thou canst not say I did it: never shake
Thy gory locks at me.

ROSS: Gentlemen, rise: his highness is not well.

LADY MACBETH: Sit, worthy friends: my lord is often thus,

MACBETH: Prithee see there! Behold, look, lo!

LADY MACBETH: My worthy lord,
Your noble friends do lack you.

MACBETH: Avaunt, and quit my sight! Let the earth hide thee!

Exit Ghost of Banquo

Key Objective

To appreciate Shakespeare's skill as a poet and playwright and to understand how the rhythms, sounds and patterns of words, as well as their meanings, create the character.

KS3	KS2
6.2 Analysing how writers' use of linguistic and literary features shapes and influences meaning	Listening and Responding, Drama, Understanding and Interpreting Texts, Engaging and Responding to Texts
6.3 Analysing writers' use of organisation, structure, layout and presentation	

LESSON DESCRIPTION

Pupils explore contrasting examples of Macbeth's language from two different points in the play, in order to understand how much he is changed by the events of the play.

Preparation and Resources

You will need:

▶ A hall or drama studio, or classroom with tables pushed back

▶ A whiteboard or flipchart

▶ **Resource Sheet 6**

▶ **Worksheet 20:** one per pupil

TN There is an enormous amount of information contained in the words a character speaks: what the character is thinking and feeling; what he/she wants; what he/she is doing and planning to do. Some of this information can be discovered in the character's vocabulary, the words this specific person chooses to speak. Equally important, however, are the clues in other aspects of the character's speech: the sounds of the words, their rhythms and their patterns. When a character goes on a significant emotional journey, their experiences alter the way they speak. Tracking those changes helps us to understand what is happening to the character.

The following sequence illustrates the changes that happen to Macbeth from the moment he first hears the witches' prophecy in Act 1 Scene 3 to the point when he is trapped in the castle surrounded by his enemies in Act 5. It invites pupils to speculate about the causes of such a character change. The same exercises could be used to explore any character's emotional transformation, as well as differences between characters. For an example of the latter, see Lesson 8 in the chapter on *A Midsummer Night's Dream*: 'Discovering characters through the language.'

LESSON STRUCTURE

▶ Starter Activity

Worksheet 20 / Resource Sheet 6: Act 1 Scene 3

▶ Use the *interpolated questions* ☐ on the Resource Sheet to prompt pupils to speak Macbeth's speech in Act 1 Scene 3. Ask pupils to put themselves in Macbeth's shoes at this point in the play and remind them of the work they did on this scene in Lessons 2 and 3. Divide the group into two: as you say the speech again, one half repeat all the words which suggest Macbeth is excited and hopeful about what he has heard, and the other half echo all the words which suggest he is doubtful or doesn't believe what he has just seen and heard.

Worksheet 20: Act 1 Scene 3

▶ Pupils work in groups of three or four. Model the exercise first with two volunteer pupils. One sits in a chair with their eyes closed while another whispers in their ear the first speech ('*Stay, you imperfect speakers...*'); at the same time, the third and possibly the fourth pupil (or you in the modelling exercise) echo all the words which are significant, repeating them more than once. Ask all the groups to do the exercise and make sure that each pupil plays all the roles – whisperer, echoer and listener.

▶ Ask pupils for their response to listening to the speech. *How does it feel to be Macbeth at this point in the play? Does he seem hopeful or doubtful or perhaps both at the same time?*

▶ Main Activity

Worksheet 20: Act 1 Scene 3 and Act 5 Scene 3

▶ Create an open space and ask pupils to spread out so they are equidistant from one another. Use *Punctuation Shift* ☐ with the first speech on the worksheet. Remind pupils that they will be changing direction every time they encounter a punctuation mark and that this is done as an individual exercise – they will not all be speaking in unison.

▶ When all pupils have completed the exercise, ask for individual words which describe the way this person is feeling. All words are welcome, including ones that describe a physical state. Possibilities include: dizzy, confused, excited, worried, eager, happy, hopeful and doubtful.

▶ Do the same with the second speech ('*I'll fight till from my bones...*') and again ask for words to describe this person.

■ *How does he compare now to the person who spoke the first speech?*

■ *What might explain this change in mood – good events or bad?*

(Note that the second speech on Worksheet 19 is made up of a sequence of short speeches by Macbeth in Act 5 Scene 3.)

2

Worksheet 20
▶ Pupils form two lines facing one another, about six feet apart. Label one line 'Team A' and the other 'Team B'. Tell them that often in Shakespeare the first and last words of verse lines are especially important and carry extra information. They will be performing an experiment to see whether Macbeth's vocabulary changes from one speech to the other. They will start by examining the last words of the first speech. Team A will begin and say '*more*' to Team B; Team B then says '*Glamis*' to Team A, and so on.

▶ Now ask pupils to imagine the words are balls of varying weights and sizes, for example, beach balls, cricket balls or even juggling balls. They will make decisions about the kind of ball each word might be and then 'throw' the last words in the speech to the opposite team, each team taking a word at a time.

▶ Ask pupils to apply the same exercise to the second speech, doing it at least twice, the second time with the imaginary balls. Ask pupils if the two experiences were different and in what way.

■ *How exactly are the last words of the two speeches different in sound and weight and meaning?*

■ *What do they tell us about how Macbeth feels in each case?*

3

Worksheet 20
▶ Pupils remain in their teams but work as a group rather than in a line. Tell them that they are each going to create a statue which represents the two Macbeths they have just encountered. Team A will be creating the Macbeth of the first speech and Team B the Macbeth from the second speech. Everyone in the statue will be a Macbeth but their group will shape itself in a way that represents the spirit of that speech (the first statue will probably be more upright, open and enquiring, the second more angular, irregular and closed). Either allow them two minutes to plan their statues or, for a more improvisational and intuitive response, allow no talking, count backward from ten and freeze them at the end of that time.

▶ Ask the pupils creating the Macbeth in Act 5 to remember their positions and to look at the Macbeth Act 1 statue. *What do you see? How would you describe this statue? Does it reflect your understanding of Macbeth at this point?* Tell the Macbeth Act 1 statue that you are going to clap your hands and when you do the statue should come to life and make sound. Ask the pupils observing to describe the movement and sounds they hear. Finally, ask the Macbeth Act 5 statue to reform, and repeat the same sequence.

▶ Plenary

▶ Ask:

■ *What have you understood about Macbeth's journey? Is it a happy or an unhappy journey?*

■ *How have you come to this conclusion?*

■ *What characteristics of the words Macbeth used in the two speeches gave you the clues?*

■ *What have you understood about how language creates character?*

► Homework

► Ask pupils to make **spider diagrams** ◩ for each of the speeches. At the centre should be a drawing representing Macbeth's emotional state for that speech. It can be very simple - stick figures will do well. The information surrounding the drawings should include:

■ A brief summary of what happened to cause this emotional state.

■ Three words to describe how Macbeth feels at this moment.

■ Words and phrases from the text which are especially valuable clues.

■ Thought balloons to show what he is thinking.

■ A sentence or two to describe what he is likely to do next (or what he does do if they already know the play).

Act 1 Scene 3

Stay, you imperfect speakers: tell me more.
By Sinel's death I know I am Thane of Glamis,
But how of Cawdor? The Thane of Cawdor lives,
A prosperous gentleman: and to be king
Stands not within the prospect of belief,
No more than to be Cawdor. Say from whence
You owe this strange intelligence or why
Upon this blasted heath you stop our way
With such prophetic greeting? Speak, I charge you.

▶ Notes

'Stay': wait

'imperfect speakers': Macbeth means the Weird Sisters who have, in his opinion, given him only part of the information he wants

'Sinel's death': Sinel was Macbeth's father. Macbeth has therefore already inherited the title of Thane of Glamis

'prospect of belief': possibility of believing

'strange intelligence': strange information

'blasted heath': open land battered by rain and wind

'I charge you': I order you

Act 5 Scene 3 l. 34-67 (edited)

I'll fight till from my bones my flesh be hacked.
Give me my armour. I'll put it on.
Send out more horses: skirr the country round:
Hang those that talk of fear. Give me mine armour. -
Come, put mine armour on: give me my staff. -
Seyton, send out. Doctor, the thanes fly from me. –
Pull't off, I say....
Bring it after me.-
I will not be afraid of death and bane,
Till Birnam Forest come to Dunsinane.

▶ Notes

'skirr': scour

'send out': referring to Macbeth's earlier order to send out more men on horseback to discover where the soldiers of the opposing army are located

'dispatch': hurry up

'Seyton': the name of Macbeth's servant

'Pull't off': pull off my armour

'bane': destruction

Act 1 Scene 3

Use the questions and instructions in italics to prompt pupils to speak the speech in unison.

Teacher: *Macbeth, you look amazed by what the Weird Sisters have just said! Speak to them again! Don't let them leave!*
Pupils: Stay, you imperfect speakers: tell me more.

Teacher: *Go on.*
Pupils: By Sinel's death I know I am Thane of Glamis,

Teacher: *Yes, you are. But not Thane of Cawdor.*
Pupils: But how of Cawdor?

Teacher: *Why not Cawdor?*
Pupils: The Thane of Cawdor lives,
A prosperous gentleman:

Teacher: *What about being King?*
Pupils: ...and to be King
Stands not within the prospect of belief,
No more than to be Cawdor.

Teacher: *What else would you like to ask them?*
Pupils: Say from whence
You owe this strange intelligence...

Teacher: *Anything else?*
Pupils: ...or why
Upon this blasted heath you stop our way
With such prophetic greeting?

Teacher: *Why aren't they answering you?*
Pupils: Speak, I charge you.

MACBETH
LESSON 11: TELLING OFFSTAGE STORIES

Key Objective

To gain a new perspective on the main plot of the play by exploring other stories which happen offstage.

KS3

5.2 Understanding and responding to ideas, viewpoints, themes and purposes in texts

8.1 Developing viewpoint, voice and ideas

KS2

Speaking, Listening and Responding, Group Discussion and Interaction, Drama, Understanding and Interpreting Texts, Engaging and Responding to Texts

LESSON DESCRIPTION

Pupils create their own versions of the story of *Macbeth*, from the perspective of a character of their choice.

Preparation and Resources

You will need:

► A hall or drama studio, or classroom with tables pushed back

► Chairs: one per pupil

► **Resource Sheet 7**

► **Worksheet 21:** one per group

► **Worksheet 22:** one per pupil

 A lot of the story and action of *Macbeth* is reported but not seen in the play. Some incidents are hinted at or can be imagined (as was the case in Lesson 5 with the offstage murder of Duncan); some characters are only glimpsed rather than seen in full. A rich bed of dramatic possibilities is offered by these off-stage stories; the incidents that we hear about but do not see, and the characters who only appear briefly, all offer different points of view on the main narrative. Our interpretations of them, as performers and audience, enrich and enliven the play. Any of them can be used as the starting point for other stories or for a short devised piece.

 Worksheet 21 is provided for younger or less able pupils.

LESSON STRUCTURE

▶ Starter Activity

Resource Sheet 7: Macbeth Fruit Salad

▶ This exercise is a variation on a drama game called fruit salad or fruit bowl. One person stands in the middle and everyone else sits on chairs in a circle. At certain moments some or all of the group have to leave their chair and find a different one to sit on. One person will be left without a chair and becomes the new person in the middle. To start the game, ask pupils to sit in a circle on chairs. You stand in the centre and go around the circle giving each pupil one of the names at the top of the sheet: Macbeth, Lady Macbeth, Banquo, Duncan, Witch, or Macduff. Keep repeating names until all the pupils have been given one.

▶ Then read aloud the story from Resource Sheet 7. Every time you mention one of the character names in bold, all the pupils with that name should stand up and move to another chair. When you say the word 'Murder' the entire group should stand up and change seats. Each time you call out a name you should also try to sit down on one of the chairs, so that there is one pupil left standing in the centre without a seat. You continue to read the story from your chair or wherever you are in the circle. (Alternatively you could adapt this resource into a *Whoosh!* ☒)

▶ Main Activity

▶ Divide pupils into groups of three or four. Tell them that each group is going to create a new retelling of the story (or part of the story) of Macbeth. In Shakespeare's version, we get the story primarily from Macbeth's point of view, but this is a chance to see the story from another character's perspective.

▶ First, each group needs to decide from whose point of view they are going to tell the story. Some possible options are:

■ One of the other key characters, such as Macduff, Banquo or Lady Macbeth (who shares Macbeth's point of view at the beginning of the play but disappears from view in the final two acts).

■ One of the minor characters, for example, Seyton (Macbeth's servant), one of the Murderers, or Lennox.

■ An important character who only has a short life within the play, such as King Duncan.

■ Inventing a new character of their own, for example, a fellow soldier of Macbeth's who stays in the army, a court painter or balladeer, an English soldier who marches from Birnam Wood to Dunsinane, the cook at Dunsinane Castle.

■ A character who is dead, for example, Banquo's Ghost.

Ask each group to discuss the options and to choose a character.

▶ Worksheet 21: Creating your character

Younger or less able pupils may find it helpful to develop their story using the questions on Worksheet 21 before moving onto the next activity in the sequence.

▶ Ask pupils in their small groups to tell the story from their chosen character's point of view. Within the groups, each pupil takes a turn at telling the story, working from the beginning to the end. Explain that you will time the exercise so that pupils have one or two minutes to tell their part of the story. They should speak in the first person, for example, *'And then I went to the castle...'*. If they get stuck, other members of the group should ask questions to prompt them, for example, *'What could you see?' 'Who else was there?'* The resulting work will be a mixture of the story as it is in the play, and invented story which pupils imagine.

▶ Ask the groups to think about their chosen character and explore more specific reasons and contexts for them telling their story. Ask them to decide:

■ *Where* the character is when they are telling their story.

■ *Whether* their character is alive or dead.

■ *When* the character is telling the story: in the present action of *Macbeth*, or looking back at it.

■ *Who* the character is telling the story to and why.

Suggested examples include:

■ The witches telling the story of Macbeth to an ambitious young soldier years later.

■ Malcolm recalling the battle of Dunsinane in an anniversary speech.

■ Banquo's Ghost, explaining to his son Fleance what has happened and why he was murdered.

■ Lady Macbeth, just before she takes her own life, explaining to her doctors why she can't sleep.

▶ Ask each group to create a short scene which sets the context for their story and allows their chosen character to speak the first couple of lines of their tale.

Worksheet 22: Offstage moments from the story

▶ Ask pupils to read over the list of offstage moments from *Macbeth* along with the accompanying quotes. (The quotes are generally a comment about the moment being referred to.) Ask pupils to decide:

■ Which moment could fit within their storytelling context. (For example, if they have chosen the frame of the Witches telling the story of Macbeth to an ambitious soldier, a group might choose to work on Macbeth's moment of victory in the battle, or the Witches before they first meet with Macbeth.)

■ Which character speaks the accompanying quote.

▶ Ask groups to discuss how they would structure a performance around their chosen moment, including the storytelling context. Ask them first of all to choose one defining freeze frame for their piece, then to improvise a short scene that begins with this freeze frame, and ends with the quote that accompanies their chosen moment.

Finally, pupils *showback* ⟡ their scene to the rest of the class. Share the plenary discussion questions with the group before the performances.

▶ Plenary

▶ Ask:

■ *How did creating these 'off-stage' scenes change your understanding of the story of Macbeth?*

■ *How did it change the way you think about the characters' journeys through the play?*

▶ Macbeth fruit salad

Macbeth

Lady Macbeth

Banquo

Duncan

Witch

Macduff

Murder (*entire group change seats*)

The play begins with the brief appearance of three **Witches**, then moves to a military camp where the Scottish **King Duncan** hears the news that his generals, **Macbeth** and **Banquo**, have defeated two invading armies. **Macbeth** and **Banquo** encounter the **Witches**, who predict that **Macbeth** will be made Thane of Cawdor and eventually King of Scotland. They also predict that **Banquo** will father a line of Scottish kings, although Banquo will never be King himself. The **Witches** vanish, but some of **King Duncan's** men come to tell **Macbeth** that he has just been named Thane of Cawdor. **Macbeth** writes to his wife to share his news with her, and his uncertainty about what it means. He tells her that he is on his way home and that the King is coming to visit them that night.

Lady Macbeth does not share her husband's uncertainty. She decides they should **murder Duncan** and make her husband King. While **Duncan** is asleep, **Macbeth murders** him, egged on by his wife, who cannot kill the sleeping King herself as he looks so much like her father. When the King´s death is discovered the next morning by **Macduff**, **Macbeth** easily assumes the kingship. **Duncan's** sons Malcolm and Donalbain flee to England and Ireland respectively, fearing that their father´s killer will **murder** them as well.

Fearing the **Witches**' prophecy that **Banquo's** heirs will seize the throne, the new King **Macbeth** hires a group of men to kill **Banquo** and his son Fleance, but Fleance escapes into the night. **Macbeth** is furious: his troubled mind is further distressed at a banquet that night, when he is visited by **Banquo's** ghost. When he sees the ghost, he talks wildly and is obviously upset. **Lady Macbeth** tries to soothe him and tells the guests that this is just a sickness he has had since childhood.

Macbeth goes to visit the **Witches**. He is told he must beware of **Macduff** but that he is incapable of being harmed by any man born of woman; and that he will be safe until Birnam Wood comes to Dunsinane Castle. **Macbeth** is relieved and feels secure, because he knows that all men are born of women and that forests cannot move. When he learns that **Macduff** has fled to England to join Malcolm, he orders the murder of Lady Macduff and her children.

On hearing the news of his family's slaughter, **Macduff** is stricken with grief and vows revenge, joining Prince Malcolm, **Duncan's** son, who has succeeded in raising an army in England. **Lady Macbeth**, meanwhile, sleepwalks and thinks she sees bloodstains on her hands. As his enemies approach, **Macbeth** receives news that his wife has killed herself, and is then numb with fear when he learns the English army are camouflaged with tree boughs cut from Birnam Wood, fulfilling half of the **Witches**' prophecy: Birnam Wood is on the move. On the battlefield, **Macbeth** encounters the vengeful **Macduff**, who declares that he was not '*of woman born*' but instead had a caesarean birth and was from his mother's womb '*untimely ripped*'. The two fight but the tyrant **Macbeth** is killed by the noble **Macduff**. Malcolm becomes King of Scotland, like his father **Duncan** before him, bringing an end to this time of unease and **murder!**

Creating your character

1 Who are you?

2 What is your relationship to the Macbeths?

3 Where does your story begin?

4 Where are you when you are telling your story?

5 What are the most exciting things that happened to you?

6 How do you feel at the end of your story?

Offstage moments

1 Macbeth at the moment of victory in battle
Unseamed him from the nave to th'chops,
And fixed his head upon our battlements

2 The witches in the hours before they meet Macbeth in Act 1 Scene 3
Here I have a pilot's thumb,
Wreck'd as homeward he did come

3 The conversation of King Duncan's guards as they stand on watch.
His spongy officers

4 The murder of King Duncan and his guards.
One cried 'God bless us' and 'Amen' the other

5 The execution of Cawdor
Go pronounce his present death,
And with his former title greet Macbeth.

6 Lady Macbeth poisoning the guards before the murder of King Duncan
His two chamberlains
Will I with wine and wassail so convince

7 Lady Macbeth and Macbeth trying to sleep; Lady Macbeth sleepwalking
You lack the season of all natures, sleep

8 Lady Macduff alone with her children, fearing discovery
All is the fear and nothing is the love

9 The murderers waiting for Banquo and Fleance
I am one, my liege,
Whom the vile blows and buffets of the world
Hath so incensed that I am reckless what
I do to spite the world

10 Lady Macbeth preparing for the banquet or clearing up after it has gone so badly
The fit is momentary

MACBETH

Key Objective

To review the play's action and to decide who or what is ultimately responsible for Macbeth's downfall.

KS3	KS2
4.1 Using different dramatic approaches to explore ideas, texts and issues	Listening and Responding, Group Discussion and Interaction, Drama, Understanding and Interpreting Texts and Engaging and Responding to Texts
5.2 Understanding and responding to ideas, viewpoints, themes and purposes in texts	

LESSON DESCRIPTION

Pupils rehearse and deliver the messages Macbeth receives in the course of the play, before deciding who or what is responsible for his downfall.

Preparation and Resources

You will need:

▶ A hall or drama studio, or classroom with tables pushed back

▶ A whiteboard or flipchart

▶ **Worksheet 23:** one per pupil

TN In the course of the play Macbeth receives many warnings and messages, for example, prophecies from the witches and information from his servants and messengers. The witches' prophecies bolster his confidence and his ambitions but the factual messages brought to him often tell of danger, as his enemies move against him. Malcolm, Duncan's son, has been raising an army in England. Macduff, a powerful Scottish lord, has joined him to fight against Macbeth. Macbeth also hears news of the death of his wife, when she commits suicide.

As pupils near the end of their experiential journey through the play it can be useful to review all this information – to revisit the tide of fortune that brings about Macbeth's downfall. At its most energetic, this lesson needs an open space, but it can also be adapted to a conventional classroom with desks. If you are using a conventional classroom, position Macbeth at the front of the class or in the centre of the room and have pupils leave their desks one at a time to deliver their messages, returning immediately to their desks. Each message should be delivered with energy and be accompanied by an appropriate gesture.

▶ Starter Activity

▶ Tell pupils that they are going to explore the many messages Macbeth receives during the course of the play. As a warm-up, ask them to think of examples of good and bad news and explore how it feels to be on the receiving end of these messages. Give them a context – school life, for instance – and ask them what kinds of news they would like to hear (that the school football team has won an important match; that a snow day has been declared; that a school trip is planned; that the school will be rebuilt...) and what kinds of news they would be unhappy to receive (there will be a test tomorrow; their favourite teacher is leaving; the school is moving to a new site...) Write up their suggestions.

▶ Tell pupils they are going to create *freeze frames* ◨ with their faces and bodies which show how they feel about some of these events. Give them a selection of the list they have compiled and after each one give them a brisk count of five in which to create their freeze frame. Encourage expressiveness:

■ *Can you make that 50% bigger? 100% bigger?*

▶ Main Activity

Worksheet 23: Bringing news to Macbeth

▶ Distribute Worksheet 23. Tell pupils that they are going to work in role as messengers, delivering to Macbeth much of the important news, both good and bad, that he receives during the play. At the end you will be asking them to what extent they think Macbeth caused his own downfall.

▶ Appoint a Macbeth or a cluster of Macbeths. With younger pupils you may prefer to play Macbeth yourself. The Macbeth(s) should be given their lines (at the end of the sequence on the worksheet) and told to become as familiar as possible with them. If the role is shared out, pupils should plan how they will deliver the speech.

▶ Share out the 'messenger' lines from page one of the worksheet. With younger or less confident pupils you could assign two pupils to each line and ask them to deliver it together. It doesn't matter if some pupils have more than one line, as long as all lines are assigned. Give the last line ('*Macduff was from his mother's womb untimely ripped*') to all pupils: they will all confront Macbeth and deliver that final line.

▶ Give pupils five minutes to become as familiar with their lines as possible. Suggest different ways of saying the line, for example, whispering, shouting, slowly, quickly, until they are comfortable saying the line without reading it.

▶ With pupils in a circle, run the lines in sequence, encouraging pupils to deliver their lines to you rather than looking at the worksheet and to speak them expressively.

2

► Ask pupils to spread out through the space so that they are equidistant from one another and no one is touching anyone else. Place the Macbeth(s) in the middle of the space. Explain that the messengers will be taking their lines to Macbeth in the order on the worksheet. They should deliver them with as much purpose and energy as possible, kneeling or bowing before or after they speak if that seems appropriate for the line. Once they have delivered their line they freeze.

► Remind them that everyone will be speaking the final 'messenger' line and should encircle Macbeth to do that.

► Tell pupils that when you say, 'Deliver the news,' the speaker of the first line should go up to Macbeth, then the speaker of the second line and so on until all the news has been delivered. The messengers who are not speaking continue to move rapidly through the room. When all the messages have been delivered and the 'messengers' have encircled Macbeth and delivered their final piece of news, Macbeth begins to speak.

► **To start the exercise, encourage pupils to walk briskly about the room, constantly changing direction, always looking to walk into the open space, and staying equidistant from one another.** When the energy is quite high, cue the first line: 'Deliver the news!' and run the whole sequence through to the Macbeth(s) protesting their fate in the final speech. Ask pupils what they did well and what could be improved, then run the exercise again.

► Plenary

► Ask:

■ How would it feel to receive all this news over the course of a few months?

■ What are Macbeth's crimes – can you list them?

■ To what extent do you think Macbeth has brought about his own downfall? Is anyone else responsible for what happens to him?

■ How do you feel about the news that Lady Macbeth is dead? How do you think Macbeth reacts to this news?

■ Why does Macbeth believe the Weird Sisters?

■ How typical of Macbeth is his response to the final piece of news?

► Homework

► Ask pupils to prepare arguments for and against the idea: 'The Weird Sisters caused Macbeth's downfall – in the end, it's their fault.' They should list three points under each heading, 'For' and 'Against', supported by evidence from the text and an explanation. Alternatively, if you don't want to set homework, you could move this into the plenary activity and give mini whiteboards to your pupils asking them to write one reason for and against the idea with a quote and explanation. They could share it with a partner and then show the class.

Bringing the News

1 All hail, Macbeth: hail to thee, Thane of Glamis!

2 All Hail, Macbeth: hail to thee, Thane of Cawdor!

3 All hail, Macbeth, that shalt be King hereafter!

4 He bade me, from him, call thee Thane of Cawdor.
Hail, most worthy Thane!

5 Ring the alarum bell. Murder and Treason!
Our royal master's murdered.

6 My lord, his throat is cut; that I did for him.

7 Most royal sir – Fleance is scaped.

8 Macbeth, Macbeth, Macbeth, beware Macduff!
Beware the Thane of Fife!

9 None of woman born/Shall harm Macbeth.

10 Macbeth shall never vanquished be, until
Great Birnam Wood to High Dunsinane Hill
Shall come against him.

11 Macduff is fled to England.

12 There is ten thousand/Soldiers, Sir.

13 The English force, so please you.

14 All is confirmed, my lord, which was reported.

15 She is troubled with thick-coming fancies
That keep her from her rest.

16 The Queen, my lord, is dead.

17 Gracious my lord, I should report that which
I say I saw,/But know not how to do't.

18 The wood began to move.

19 I say, a moving grove.

20 Macduff was from his mother's womb/
Untimely ripped.

MACBETH: I will not yield
To kiss the ground before young Malcolm's feet
And to be baited with the rabble's curse.
Though Birnan Wood be come to Dunsinane
And thou opposed, being of no woman born,
Yet I will try the last. Before my body
I throw my warlike shield. Lay on, Macduff;
And damned be him that first cries, 'Hold, enough!'

MACBETH

Key Objective

To reflect on the rise and fall of *Macbeth* and to explore how power and ambition corrupts.

KS3	KS2
4.1 Using different dramatic approaches to explore ideas, texts and issues	Speaking, Listening and Responding, Group Discussion and Interaction, Drama, Understanding and Interpreting Texts, Engaging and Responding to texts
4.2 Understanding and responding to ideas, viewpoints, themes and purposes in texts	

LESSON DESCRIPTION

Pupils use lines of text to reflect on the rise and fall of Macbeth. They create sculptures of Macbeth and decide how Lady Macbeth and Macbeth will be remembered after their deaths.

Preparation and Resources

You will need:

- A hall or drama studio, or classroom with tables pushed back
- **Worksheet 24:** one per pupil
- **Worksheet 25:** one per pupil

TN The Elizabethans placed great importance on honour and reputation, as their belief in the Great Chain of Being illustrates. The chain was a visual metaphor, popular in Western culture for over 1000 years, for a structured philosophical ranking of all forms of life. At the top of the chain sat the divine being, God to the Elizabethans, and at the bottom was something akin to Hell – evil, the realm of the powers of darkness. In the middle was humankind, ranked from kings to slaves. Women were ranked slightly below men, but both men and women could fall from their positions into the realm of the animals through acts of misbehaviour ranging from irresponsibility to inhumanity.

According to this structure the Macbeths have fallen so low that they are described by other characters in the play in terms referring to the lowest order of all, to Hell. '*Turn, hellhound, turn,*' says Macduff to Macbeth, and Malcolm refers to them in his final speech as '*this dead butcher and his fiend-like queen*'. During the course of the play, Macbeth transforms from a valiant hero into a power-crazed, bloodthirsty butcher, and one of the big questions posed by the play is why this change happens. Does ambition and the thirst for power corrupt? You can ask your pupils this question as a way to highlight the relevance of *Macbeth* to current events. It is possible to draw analogies between the character of Macbeth and real-life political leaders. Certainly many recent productions have set the play in a contemporary setting that relates to the idea of a great leader being corrupted by power.

1

▶ Starter Activity

▶ Divide pupils into groups of five or six. Give each group one of the following lines from the play (it doesn't matter if more than one group has the same line):

- *'Look like th'innocent flower, / But be the serpent under't'*

- *'A heavy summons lies like lead upon me'*

- *'Glamis hath murdered sleep'*

- *'Witchcraft celebrates'*

▶ They use this line to make an image. Count down from ten. When you reach zero, the group must be frozen in their image.

1

▶ Main Activity

Worksheet 24: The rise and fall of Macbeth

▶ Distribute Worksheet 24 and tell pupils they will focus on the section labelled 'The fall of Macbeth'. Ask pupils to stand in two lines about six feet apart and facing one another. Label one line 'A' and the other 'B'. Pupils in line A 'throw' the first insult on the list at pupils in line B. Pupils in line B retaliate with the next insult. By 'throw' we mean call out with energy, hurl the words at each other as if it's a slanging match.

▶ Now ask pupils to imagine that the insults are balls of varying sizes and weights – when they throw the word or phrase they should throw it as a ball. They should make instinctive choices about the weight and size of the ball.

▶ Ask pupils what they noticed about the kinds of balls they were throwing and therefore about the sounds of the insults. Do the sounds of the words support their meanings?

2

Worksheet 24

▶ Pupils partner with the person opposite them in the line. Each person chooses two or three words on the insults list. Pupils in Line A close their eyes and pupils in Line B visit their partners and create a mini-**soundscape** ◪ with the two or three insults they have chosen. You may wish to model this first with a volunteer pupil. The visiting pupil whispers the selected insults in the ears of his/ her partner as they circle them. Encourage them to be inventive and expressive. Suggest that they repeat words several times, find different ways of saying them, make the most of the sounds of the words and use non-verbal sounds to reinforce the idea of the insult.

▶ An alternative approach would be to ask all members of Line A to sit on the floor and close their eyes and for Line B pupils to circle them, whispering to the group as a whole the various insults individuals have chosen. Again, encourage them to use a range of techniques for making the soundscape more effective.

▶ Pupils then swap roles and repeat the exercise. Ask pupils how it felt to be surrounded by insults.

▶ Now repeat the sequence using the list of words in the section entitled 'The Rise of Macbeth' on Worksheet 23, first throwing the words, then throwing them as balls, and finally making mini-**soundscapes** 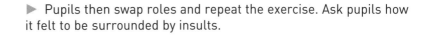 in pairs or as two groups. Ask pupils how it felt to be bathed in compliments.

Worksheet 24

▶ *Sculpting* Divide pupils into pairs – A is the sculptor and B is the clay.

▶ First, pupil A sculpts his partner into an image of Macbeth when he is the rising star. The sculptor may feed in lines from 'The Rise of Macbeth' section on Worksheet 24. If the person being sculpted feels that they want to alter themselves slightly in response to these lines, they can do so.

▶ Next, pupil A sculpts his/her partner into Macbeth during his downfall, again feeding in lines from 'The Fall of Macbeth' section of Worksheet 24.

▶ Pupil B, now a sculpture of Macbeth, tries moving between the two positions. Ask the pupils how it makes them feel. *Do any lines or sounds come to mind as you change position?* If so, they should voice them.

Worksheet 25: Finding out about Lady Macbeth

▶ Divide pupils into new pairs and ask them to read through the words on Worksheet 25 that are either said by Lady Macbeth or said about her. Ask each pair to make a quick memorial statue of the couple after their deaths, as opposed to the living ones they have just made of Macbeth. In death, Lady Macbeth is referred to as a *'fiend-like Queen'* and Macbeth a *'dead butcher'* with a *'cursed head'*.

▶ Plenary

▶ Ask pupils what this exercise tells them about Macbeth's journey from the beginning to the end of the play.

■ *How (and why) does Macbeth change as a character?*

■ *How do other characters' views of Macbeth change?*

■ *How does the audience's view of Macbeth and Lady Macbeth change?*

▶ Homework

▶ Ask pupils to imagine that they are journalists writing newspaper articles about what happens in Scotland at the time the play *Macbeth* takes place. They are to invent headlines for the following stories:

■ **1** An article published at the end of the play, reporting the final events.

■ **2** An article published at the beginning of the play, about Macbeth's victory against the Norwegians.

The Fall of Macbeth

BUTCHER
HELL-HOUND
DEVIL
ABHORRED TYRANT
FIEND
MONSTER
USURPER'S CURSED HEAD
BLACK MACBETH
BLOODY MACBETH
AVARICIOUS
DECEITFUL
MALICIOUS
DEVILISH MACBETH
HELL-KITE
SMACKING OF EVERY SIN
DEVIL DAMNED IN EVIL

The Rise of Macbeth

VALIANT COUSIN
WORTHY GENTLEMAN
BRAVE MACBETH
WORTHY THANE
PEERLESS KINSMAN
MY GOOD LORD
WORTHIEST COUSIN
MY WORTHY CAWDOR
GREAT GLAMIS
FULL O'THE MILK OF HUMAN KINDNESS

Lady Macbeth

DEAREST PARTNER OF GREATNESS

DEAREST LOVE

THE INNOCENT FLOWER WHILE BEING THE SERPENT UNDER'T

DIREST CRUELTY

FIEND-LIKE QUEEN

A MIDSUMMER NIGHT'S DREAM

A MIDSUMMER NIGHT'S DREAM

The following sequence of work suggests lesson plans for working on *A Midsummer Night's Dream*. Some of the lesson plans are linked but all of them can stand alone. You could use the lessons in the sequence offered here, or pull out single lessons to add to an existing scheme of work.

The lessons take a multi-sensory, multi-disciplinary approach to exploring the **world(s) of the play** ◻ as *A Midsummer Night's Dream* is arguably the text most suited to a multiple intelligences approach.

You will be able to deliver most of this work in your own classroom with the tables and chairs pushed back. Some lessons require a larger space to work in.

Display suggestions

The work in this unit can be mapped using a classroom display which shows the four groups of characters (court, lovers, fairies, mechanicals). The display can be added to with work completed throughout the sequence and by the end will include:

- Character profiles

- Theatre set designs

- Character relationships

- Fairy research

- An exploration of language

Title photograph: RSC Production of *A Midsummer Night's Dream* (2008)
Photographer **John Haynes**

CONTENTS

A MIDSUMMER NIGHT'S DREAM
LESSON 1: DISCOVERING THE FOUR WORLDS OF THE PLAY

Key Objective

To introduce the play and its four contrasting worlds.

KS3

4.1 Using different dramatic approaches to explore ideas, texts and issues

5.2 Understanding and responding to ideas, viewpoints,

KS2

Listening and Responding, Group Discussion and Interaction, Drama, Understanding and Interpreting Texts, Engaging and Responding to Texts

LESSON DESCRIPTION

Pupils create the worlds of the court, the mechanicals, the lovers and the fairy kingdom and discuss their potential interactions.

Preparation and Resources

You will need:

▶ A hall or drama studio, or classroom with tables pushed back

▶ Chairs for all pupils in a circle or have pupils sit on the floor when they need to

▶ A whiteboard or flipchart

▶ **Worksheet 1:** one per member of the world of the court group/s

▶ **Worksheet 2:** one per member of the world of the fairy kingdom group/s

▶ **Worksheet 3:** one per member of the world of the mechanicals groups

▶ **Worksheet 4:** one per member of the world of the lovers group/s

 It is understandable that *A Midsummer Night's Dream* is often taught in Years 5, 6, 7 and 8, with its irresistible combination of magical fairies, young lovers, hilarious transformations and breathless activity. However, the complicated storyline can be confusing. The structure of the play is quite unlike the linear format of *Macbeth* for example. In *A Midsummer Night's Dream*, four very different worlds collide and it is this that creates the central conflict and action of the play. First we meet Theseus and Hippolyta and the rule-ridden world of the Athenian court. The lovers are dragged into the court and, as a consequence of its death threats, decide to run away to the nearby Athenian woods. Then we meet the mechanicals, rehearsing a play for the Duke's wedding, hopeful of being selected for performance. And finally, through Puck, Oberon and Titania, we are introduced to the magical world of the fairy kingdom. Thereafter, the action rapidly shifts between these four worlds, enmeshing them ever more tightly with one another.

This lesson is designed to help pupils understand the four worlds of the play. They will begin to appreciate how the language and actions of each world embody their distinctive culture, just as in their own lives what they say and do in one context creates a 'world' distinct from many others they inhabit.

LESSON STRUCTURE

▶ Starter Activity

▶ Pupils sit in a circle. Ask them to think of times and places where they behave quite differently – for example in a school classroom, at home or when out with their friends. List suggestions on a flipchart or whiteboard. Now ask:

■ *What makes each of these 'worlds' different from the rest?*

■ *Are there different rules or expectations in each?*

■ *Do you speak differently? Do you wear different clothes?*

■ *How do you feel in these different 'world's'?*

▶ Explain that the class will be exploring a play that is similarly made up of very different 'worlds', each with their own rules of behaviour. Tell the group that one way we can establish rules of behaviour is through imagining how different characters might greet each other. Position pairs around the space and give them a five-second countdown to make each of the following *freeze frames* ◘ of characters greeting each other:

■ workmen

■ two friends meeting to run away together

■ a fairy king and queen

■ courtiers

As each freeze frame is created, pick a few and ask the pairs to describe their thinking.

▶ Main Activity

▶ **Worksheets 1, 2, 3, 4: The four *worlds of the play* ◘**
Ask each pair to join with another to form groups of four, assign each of them one of the four worlds and distribute the worksheets accordingly (more than one group may have the same world). First, ask groups to match the five or six events listed with the appropriate line of text.

▶ Now ask groups to make a series of snapshots for the story of their world, one for each event listed on the worksheet. Each snapshot begins as a *freeze frame* ◘, which comes to life for a few seconds and speaks its line of text before freezing again. All members of the group must be involved in each snapshot. The lines may be spoken by one person or several; pupils should use the line in whatever way they feel best captures the spirit of the situation. There can be a brief pause between each image. Alternatively, pupils may move in slow motion from the ending of one freeze frame to the beginning of the next.

 ► Run the image sequences in turn. Each time, ask:

■ *How are people behaving in this world?*

■ *How would you feel about being in this place?*

■ *Which of the four worlds do you think this is and why?*

► Plenary

 ► Ask:

■ *What are the main differences between these four worlds?*

■ *How do you imagine these four very different worlds will relate to one another in A Midsummer Night's Dream? What storyline could draw them all together?*

► Homework

► Ask pupils to create a list of four rules that young people have to abide by in the court. They should use information from the court world and the lovers to inform their thinking. If you are following the lessons in sequence, these rules will help set up the next lesson which examines one of the central dilemmas at the beginning of the play.

World of the Athenian Court of Duke Theseus

Here are some of the things that happen in this world:

- The Duke describes his courtship of his bride-to-be.

- Great celebrations are planned in honour of the Duke's marriage.

- The Duke makes an important legal decision when a daughter refuses to marry the man her father has chosen for her.

- The Duke goes hunting.

- A silly play is performed at a royal wedding.

Here are some of the things people say in the court. Match each of them to one of the listed events:

- *'Stir up the Athenian youth to merriments.'*

- *'Hippolyta, I wooed thee with my sword.'*

- *'To you your father should be as a god.'*

- *'My love shall hear the music of my hounds.'*

- *'This is the silliest stuff that e'er I heard.'*

Now, starting with a freeze frame, bring each event to life for up to ten seconds, including the matching line of text.

World of the Fairy Kingdom

Here are some of the things that happen in this world:

- The King and Queen of the Fairies quarrel.
- A fairy puts some magic juice in the lovers' eyes while they lie asleep in the forest.
- The King plays a trick on the Queen.
- The Queen falls in love with a donkey.
- The Queen comes to her senses.
- The King and Queen of the Fairies make up.

Here are some of the things members of the fairy kingdom say. Match each of them to one of the listed events:

- *'Ill met by moonlight, proud Titania.'*
- *'O, how I love thee! How I dote on thee!'*
- *'My Oberon, what visions have I seen! Methought I was enamoured of an ass.'*
- *'Come, my Queen, take hands with me.'*
- *'Wake when some vile thing is near!'*
- *'Churl, upon thy eyes I throw All the power this charm doth owe.'*

Now, starting with a freeze frame, bring each event to life for up to ten seconds, including the matching line of text.

World of the Mechanicals

Here are some of the things that happen in this world:

- Six workmen – mechanicals as they are sometimes called – rehearse a play to celebrate the Duke's wedding.
- One of the mechanicals, called Bottom, wants to play all the parts, especially the lion.
- A fairy uses magic to give Bottom a donkey's head.
- The Fairy Queen falls in love with Bottom and has her fairies wait on him.
- The mechanicals think that the Duke likes their play and ask if he wants to see some more entertainment.

Here are some of the things the mechanicals say. Match each of them to one of the listed events:

- *'I will make the Duke say, "Let him roar again."'*
- *'Methinks I have a great desire to a bottle of hay.'*
- *'O Bottom, thou art changed!'*
- *'Meet me in the palace wood – there we will rehearse.'*
- *'Will it please you to see the epilogue, or to hear a Bergomask dance between two of our company?'*

Now, starting with a freeze frame, bring each event to life for up to ten seconds, including the matching line of text.

► **Notes**

'**Bergomask**': a rough form of country dancing

World of the Lovers

Here are some of the things that happen in this world.

- A girl disobeys her father to marry the man she loves.
- Two lovers plan to run away to a forest.
- A fairy puts magic juice in one of the lovers' eyes while they sleep.
- Under a magic spell, one of the lovers falls madly in love with his girlfriend's best friend.
- Everyone marries happily in the end.

Here are some of the things the lovers say. Match each of them to one of the listed events:

- *'The course of true love never did run smooth.'*
- *'Tomorrow truly will I meet with thee.'*
- *'Not Hermia but Helena I love.'*
- *'Flower of this purple dye,*
  Hit with Cupid's archery.'
- *'Here come the lovers, full of joy and mirth.'*

Now, starting with a freeze frame, bring each event to life for up to ten seconds, including the matching line of text.

A MIDSUMMER NIGHT'S DREAM

LESSON 2: INVESTIGATING CHARACTER MOTIVATION: ACT 1 SCENE 1

Key Objective

To understand the circumstances of Act 1 Scene 1.

To understand that the play can be seen from different points of view.

KS3	KS2
3.2 Taking roles in group discussion	Speaking, Listening and Responding, Group Discussion and Interaction, Drama, Understanding and Interpreting Texts, Engaging and Responding to Texts.
4.1 Using different dramatic approaches to explore ideas, texts and issues	

LESSON DESCRIPTION

Using the drama convention *Voices in the head* , pupils consider what motivates the characters in Act 1 Scene 1.

Preparation and Resources

You will need:

▶ A hall or drama studio, or classroom with tables pushed back

▶ Chairs: enough for everyone in the biggest circles you can make in the available space

▶ A cloak

▶ **Worksheet 5:** one per pupil

▶ Pencils: one per pupil

▶ **Worksheet 6:** 16 copies

▶ **Worksheet 7:** 4 A3 size copies (one per group)

▶ **Worksheet 8:** 2 copies

▶ **Worksheet 9:** one per pupil

TN Many of Shakespeare's plays start with a complex dilemma. *Voices in the head* is an effective *ensemble* ▢ technique through which to explore a dilemma from different points of view. It asks pupils to 'stand in the shoes' of a character and argue from their viewpoint. During rehearsals, actors will often explore their character's motivations and relationships using improvisation techniques. This sequence emulates that process to enable students to establish the relationships at the beginning of the play.

 Inevitably, pupils will bring their own ideas of what is right and wrong into their exploration of the dilemma, and younger or less able pupils will particularly tend to do this. It is important to note that one of the objectives of the lesson is simply to understand the circumstances of Act 1 Scene 1; the exercise will allow pupils to draw parallels between their own life experience and that of the characters. Older or more able pupils should also understand that the values of the society in which the play happens are different to their own world and bring this into their arguments. You might want to build on pupils' understanding of the speech on Worksheet 5 by working with the whole group on an *ensemble reading* ▢ of Egeus' speech from the scene, by *imaging* ▢ the words, or by asking *interpolated questions* ▢, adopting the point of view of Duke Theseus.

▶ Starter Activity

▶ Explain that the story of *A Midsummer Night's Dream* happens in a place called Athens. The Duke of Athens is called Theseus. One day, a rich citizen of Athens called Egeus comes to see Duke Theseus because he has a problem. He brings with him his teenage daughter Hermia and two Athenian young men called Demetrius and Lysander. In Athens it is against the law for a daughter to disobey her father, or to have a boyfriend without her father's permission.

Worksheet 5: Act 1 Scene 1, Egeus' speech

▶ Divide the pupils into four equal sized groups and label them A, B, C or D. Give each group a section of Egeus' speech on Worksheet 5. Ask pupils to choose and underline three key words in their section of the speech. They should choose the words that particularly stand out for them or that they think are important because they show Egeus' attitude to what he is describing (for example, in section A, they might choose *vexation, complaint, bewitched.*) Pupils then pick a gesture to emphasise the words they have chosen (for example, they could punch a fist into their hands on *complaint* to emphasise the meaning of the word.)

▶ The teacher reads the speech slowly through. As each word is spoken pupils add the gestures they have chosen. (You might want to read through the speech more than once.) Ask pupils to reflect on the following questions.

- *What is the situation that Egeus is describing in this section?*

- *Which words stood out for you in your section and why?*

- *How does Egeus feel about Lysander/Demetrius/his daughter? How did the actions and sounds add to your understanding of how Egeus feels?*

- *Why has Egeus brought them to see Duke Theseus?*

- *What does Athenian law say is the penalty for a daughter who will not marry the man her father has arranged?*

▶ Main Activity

Worksheet 6 and 7: Meeting the characters

▶ Explain that Hermia has a best friend called Helena.

▶ Pupils return to their small groups. Give each group a marker pen, Worksheet 6 and an A3 version of Worksheet 7 with the character name for that group written at the top (for example, Group A 'Demetrius'). Ask each group to choose a scribe. Pupils read aloud the facts on the worksheet about the society in which the play takes place and the facts about their character.

▶ Explain that the character they have been exploring will now have the opportunity to talk to Duke Theseus and try to persuade him to adopt their point of view. In order to prepare for this, the scribe will write down the group's responses to the following:

WANTS : What does their character want?
LAW: Is their character acting lawfully or unlawfully? How does their character feel about the law?
ARGUMENT: What could their character say to the Duke to persuade him to their point of view? What is their character's strongest argument? How will their character start their argument? How will they make sure this argument is heard?
TACTICS : How could their character influence the Duke? Flatter him? Reason with him? Threaten him?

▶ Each group nominates a spokesperson, the 'mouthpiece' of the character. The other members of the group are the 'Voices in the head' of their character. They form a close group behind their 'mouthpiece' and whisper into their ear what they should say next. The 'mouthpiece' is not allowed to speak unless the 'voices' give them something to say, although they can ask the 'voices' for advice. The 'voices' can only whisper in their 'mouthpiece's' ear, they are not allowed to speak to Duke Theseus directly.

▶ Arrange the groups in the four corners, facing the centre of the room. Explain that you will take on the role of Duke Theseus, wearing a cloak to signify the character. You will **improvise** a conversation with each group in turn, starting with group A. The rest of the pupils can sit down until the Duke speaks to them, at which point they will stand.

▶ Improvising whilst wearing the cloak, approach Group A and address them as if they are Demetrius and you are Duke Theseus. (See **Teaching in role** .) Ask 'Demetrius' what he thinks you should do about Egeus' request. Ask questions and make comments as the Duke which make the pupils think hard about their character and what motivates them. (For example, *Why are you interested in Hermia if she loves Lysander? Is it only her father's money you are interested in?*) Provoke an emotional response by adopting a challenging tone. (For example, *What makes you think you're so special? Lysander is rich as well.*) Don't be easily persuaded, (for example, *What can you say to me that will make me change my mind?*) and give the pupils opportunities to use all of the tactics they have discussed (for example, *Is there anything else you can say to make me see things your way?*) Direct all your questions and comments to the 'mouthpiece' and wait for the 'voices' to give the 'mouthpiece' a response. Finish each improvisation by asking the group to sit down.

▶ Move on to the next group, addressing them by their character name to start the next improvisation

▶ As a conclusion to the activity, you might want to ask the person acting as the mouthpiece for Hermia to speak Hermia's lines on Worksheet 8 and you can respond as Theseus setting out Hermia's choices: to die or to live the life of a nun.

▶ Then take off the cloak and sit the pupils down in a large circle.

▶ Plenary

▶ As a whole group complete Worksheet 7 for Theseus. Add the other completed character worksheets to a display with Theseus in the centre. *Where do all the other characters fit around him?*

▶ Ask:

■ *Who do you have the most sympathy with in Act 1 Scene 1 and why?*

■ *What do you think about the Athenian attitude to marriage? Why do you think such an attitude existed?*

▶ Homework

Worksheet 9: Character relationships
▶ Ask pupils to create a poster showing the links between the characters explored in this lesson. They can either develop their own key for Worksheet 9 or use the worksheet and existing key as a basis for their designs. Their posters should illustrate what themes link the characters to each other; pupils can think about who is linked by Love, Family, Friendship and Unrequited Love as well as by who has power over whom.

Act 1 Scene 1

EGEUS

GROUP A:
Full of vexation come I, with complaint
Against my child, my daughter Hermia.
Stand forth, Demetrius. My noble lord,
This man hath my consent to marry her.
Stand forth, Lysander. And my gracious duke,
This man hath bewitched the bosom of my child.-

GROUP B:
Thou, thou, Lysander, thou hast given her rhymes,
And interchanged love-tokens with my child.
Thou hast by moonlight at her window sung,
And stol'n the impression of her fantasy
With bracelets of thy hair, rings, gauds, conceits.

GROUP C:
With cunning hast thou filched my daughter's heart,
Turned her obedience, which is due to me,
To stubborn harshness. - And, my gracious duke,
Be it so she will not here before your grace
Consent to marry with Demetrius,

GROUP D:
I beg the ancient privilege of Athens:
As she is mine, I may dispose of her;
Which shall be either to this gentleman
Or to her death, according to our law.

Meeting the characters

This is a society where *your father should be as a god* and the law states that daughters must marry whomever their fathers choose for them. The penalty for disobedience is death or a life as a nun. Theseus, the Duke of Athens has the last word on the law. Young men traditionally ask the Duke for permission to marry.

A: DEMETRIUS

- Has Egeus' consent to marry Hermia.
- Is a worthy gentleman.
- Has plenty of money. Will get more money by marrying Hermia.
- Has previously asked Helena to be his girlfriend, and she still loves him. Duke Theseus and all Athens know this.

B: LYSANDER

- Has secretly exchanged love tokens with Hermia and loves her.
- Has asked Hermia to be his girlfriend without her father's permission, and knows that it is against the law.
- Is a worthy gentleman.
- Has plenty of money.

C: HELENA

- Demetrius has been treating Helena as his girlfriend, which everyone in Athens knows.
- Loves Demetrius and wants to marry him.
- Wishes she was like Hermia so that Demetrius would love her.
- Has been best friends with Hermia since they were children and knows that Hermia loves Lysander.

D: HERMIA

- Has accepted secret gifts and attention from Lysander without her father's permission.
- Loves Lysander and wants to marry him.
- Will not marry someone she does not love.
- Has been best friends with Helena since they were children and knows that Helena loves Demetrius.

Character Name: ....

ARGUMENTS (What will I say?)

TACTICS (How will I say it?)

WANTS (What do I want?)

LAW (How does the law affect me?)

Act 1 Scene 1

THESEUS: What say you, Hermia? Be advised, fair maid,
To you your father should be as a god,
One that composed your beauties, yea, and one
To whom you are but as a form in wax
By him imprinted and within his power
To leave the figure or disfigure it.
Demetrius is a worthy gentleman.

HERMIA: So is Lysander.

THESEUS: In himself he is.
But in this kind, wanting your father's voice,
The other must be held the worthier.

HERMIA: I would my father looked but with my eyes.

THESEUS: Rather your eyes must with his judgement look.

HERMIA: I do entreat your grace to pardon me.
I know not by what power I am made bold,
Nor how it may concern my modesty
In such a presence here to plead my thoughts:
But I beseech your grace that I may know
The worst that may befall me in this case,
If I refuse to wed Demetrius.

THESEUS: Either to die the death or to abjure
Forever the society of men.

Character Relationships

Link the characters using different coloured pens or collage materials to represent the types of relationship they have with each other. Either work from this sheet or draw your own.

Egeus

Theseus

Hermia

Lysander

Helena

Demetrius

▶ **Key**

In love with:

Related to:

In charge of:

Friends with:

A MIDSUMMER NIGHT'S DREAM
LESSON 3: INVESTIGATING A PAIR OF LOVERS

Key Objective

To understand the lovers' dilemma which drives the story forward.

To strengthen connections between the play and pupils' own lives and experiences.

KS3	KS2
4.1 Using different dramatic approaches to explore ideas, texts and issues	Listening and Responding, Drama, Understanding and Interpreting Texts, Engaging and Responding to Texts
5.2 Understanding and responding to ideas, viewpoints, themes and purposes in texts	

LESSON DESCRIPTION

Pupils use a range of short, practical activities to explore the relationship between Helena and Demetrius.

Preparation and Resources

You will need:

▶ A hall or drama studio, or classroom with tables pushed back

▶ **Worksheet 10:** one per pupil

▶ Small balls (for example tennis or juggling balls): one for every two pupils – or use crumpled-up newspaper

 Hermia and Lysander decide their only option is to run away together through the Athenian woods. On the other side of the woods lives Lysander's elderly aunt whom they can shelter with while they arrange their marriage away from the strict laws of Athens. They tell Helena of their plans and she tells Demetrius in order to gain favour with him. Demetrius sets off in pursuit of his runaway fiancée and Helena follows after him so that all four lovers end up in the woods, home of the fairy kingdom.

This lesson uses a series of tried and tested scene study approaches to explore the troubled relationship between Helena and Demetrius. The active strategies are all highly transferable to other texts and provide students with safe boundaries in which to explore a range of interpretive choices.

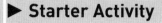

LESSON STRUCTURE

▶ Starter Activity

▶ Pupils form a circle.

▶ Introduce the rhythm of **iambic pentameter** ◘ to the group by asking pupils to run very fast on the spot for 30 seconds and then vocalise the rhythm of their heart beat. De DUM, de DUM, de DUM, de DUM, de DUM. Explain that this is one of the main rhythms that Shakespeare uses in his writing, i.e. the lines are often written using a structure that equates to five sets of heart beats.

▶ Ask pupils to stamp out the rhythm of an iambic line on the spot, one unstressed and one stressed stamp. Then ask them to stamp out the rhythm to a count "And ONE and TWO and THREE and FOUR and FIVE".

▶ Either share, or ask pupils to think of, phrases they use that are in that rhythm. *You KNOW you MAKE a LOVely CUP of TEA.*

▶ Explain to pupils that the iambic rhythm is very suited to the exchange of compliments or insults.

▶ Ask pupils to use the iambic rhythm and create one insult and one compliment each. For example:
Insult: *Will YOU get LOST, I REAlly HATE your GUTS*
Compliment: *I LIKE the WAY you've DONE your HAIR toDAY*

▶ Ask pupils to walk around the room and on a signal from you (for example, a clap) they meet another pupil and exchange their compliments with each other. Repeat this three or four times. Then ask pupils to exchange insults and again repeat three or four times with new partners. Finally, ask pupils to respond in the opposite way – if their partner gives them a compliment they need to insult them.

▶ Ask pupils how it feels to receive an insult when they've complimented their partner and vice versa. Explain that in this lesson they are going to work on a scene in which one of the characters is always complimenting the other and telling him how much she is in love with him and only gets insults in return.

▶ Main Activity

Worksheet 10: Act 2 Scene 1, Demetrius and Helena
▶ Pupils sit or stand in a circle and do an **ensemble reading** ◘ of the scene.

▶ Ask pupils to find a partner. In pairs, the class work through each of the following activities in turn:

- **five point chase** ◘

- **one word dialogues** ◘

- **choral characters** ◘

▶ Ask pupils to reflect on their discoveries. What have they found out about Helena and Demetrius and their relationship from applying these different techniques to the scene?

 ▶ In pairs, pupils now read the scene again but this time ask them to choose one word or phrase from the other character's preceding speech to repeat before speaking lines. For example, Helena might choose to repeat 'no more' from Demetrius's first speech before saying her line: 'You draw me, you hard-hearted adamant.'

▶ Keeping in pairs, give each Demetrius a small ball or crumpled-up piece of newspaper. Explain that the speaker of the line has the ball but by the end of each of his/her speeches must have given it to the other character. Speakers should focus on how they give the object to their partner. Does Demetrius slap it into Helena's hand or gently place it there? How does Helena give it back?

 ▶ Choose two or three contrasting versions of the scene to show to the whole class.

▶ Plenary

▶ Ask pupils for words which describe how Helena feels during this scene. Then do the same for Demetrius. Ask:

■ *Why does Helena continue to pursue Demetrius?*

■ *Why might Demetrius have transferred his affections from Helena to Hermia?*

■ *Does this scene feel familiar to you in terms of your own lives? Is this something that we might see happen today or not?*

▶ Homework

▶ Ask pupils to imagine that they are agony aunts and Helena and Demetrius have written in separately explaining their dilemmas and asking for help. They should compose the letter from one of the two characters asking for advice, and then the response that they would offer as an agony aunt.

Act 2 Scene 1

DEMETRIUS: I love thee not, therefore pursue me not.
Hence, get thee gone, and follow me no more.

HELENA: You draw me, you hard-hearted adamant.

DEMETRIUS: Do I entice you? Do I speak you fair?
Or rather do I not in plainest truth
Tell you I do not nor I cannot love you?

HELENA: And even for that do I love you the more.

DEMETRIUS: Tempt not too much the hatred of my spirit;
For I am sick when I do look on thee.

HELENA: And I am sick when I look not on you.

DEMETRIUS: I'll run from thee, and hide me in the brakes,
And leave thee to the mercy of wild beasts.

HELENA: The wildest hath not such a heart as you.

DEMETRIUS: I will not stay thy questions, let me go;
Of if thou follow me, do not believe
But I shall do thee mischief in the wood.

HELENA: I'll follow thee, and make a heaven of hell,
To die upon the hand I love so well.

▶ **Notes**

'adamant': very hard stone   'brakes': bushes

A MIDSUMMER NIGHT'S DREAM
LESSON 4: INVESTIGATING OBERON AND TITANIA

Key Objective

To understand the cause of the argument between Oberon and Titania in Act 2 Scene 1.

KS3

5.1 Developing and adapting active reading skills and strategies

4.2 Developing, adapting and responding to dramatic techniques, conventions and styles

KS2

Speaking, Listening and Responding, Group Discussion and Interaction, Drama, Understanding and Interpreting Texts, Engaging and Responding to Texts

LESSON DESCRIPTION

Pupils investigate the cause of Titania and Oberon's argument. They bring the scene to life and explore the *backstory* behind the argument using the reported action in Titania's speech.

This is the first in a sequence of four lessons that explore the Athenian woods and the fairy world.

Preparation and Resources

You will need:

► A hall or drama studio, or classroom with tables pushed back

► Chairs: enough for everyone in the biggest circle possible in the available space

► A lightweight piece of white cloth, about the size of a cot sheet

► **Worksheet 11:** one per pupil

► **Worksheet 12:** one per pupil

TN In the play we move quickly between the four different worlds. Soon after the initial scenes in the court Shakespeare moves us to the Athenian woods, home of the fairy kingdom. There are disputes and power struggles here just as there are in the world of the court (and mechanicals). Oberon and Titania are king and queen of the fairies, magical, otherworldly creatures, but they are also a reflection of the other king and queen, Theseus and Hippolyta (the parts are often doubled) and they have some very human qualities. This lesson introduces the key dispute between Titania and Oberon and invites pupils to empathise with the characters to understand their points of view.

LESSON STRUCTURE

▶ Starter Activity

Worksheet 11: Act 2 Scene 1, Titania and Oberon

▶ Explain that you are now going to take a closer look at the fairy world, where all is not well. The queen of the fairies, Titania, and the king of the fairies, Oberon, have been arguing. Oberon has asked Titania to give him *'a little changeling boy'* that she has looked after since he was a baby. Ask the pupils if they know what a 'changeling' is. Pupils brought up with fairy tales may have come across changelings – usually the term refers to a fairy child being swapped for a human child. In this case, there is no mention of a fairy child left with humans, but the boy is a human child who has been brought into the fairy world and so has 'exchanged' one world for another. Oberon wants the boy to be his page. Titania has refused and they are both very angry with each other. Although Titania is avoiding Oberon, they come across each other in the forest and we are going to look at what they say.

▶ Divide pupils into pairs. Distribute the worksheet and ask them to label themselves A and B. Explain that A will be Oberon and B will be Titania. Pupils then do a **scene study ▣** sequence which includes the following activities:
Scene study – *Back to back reading*
Scene study – *Whispered reading*
Scene study – *Sharing the words across space*
Scene study – *Experimenting with movement*

▶ In addition, pupils could do a **five point chase ▣**

▶ Ask the pupils to discuss with their partner all the things they have found out about the characters by doing the exercises. Explain that they are now free to speak the words and move as they think the characters would in relation to each other. There is no right way of doing it. They should do what feels right to them, and create their own version of the scene.

▶ Sit pupils down in the circle with their partners. Choose three or four volunteer pairs to perform their version of the scene in the centre of the circle. After each one pick out any significant differences/similarities between the scenes and ask:

■ *What does it make us think of the character if she/he says that line like that?*

■ *How serious have these two actors made the argument? How could you tell?*

■ *How did they feel about each other? How could you tell?*

■ *Why might this child have caused such big arguments between Titania and Oberon – why might they both want him so much?*

Pupils may come up with interesting and valid answers of their own here. From the text, the only clue we have is Oberon's jealousy, but it may be that Oberon is trying to rescue the boy from Titania who is becoming over-protective of him as he grows up or perhaps she is neglecting other duties because of him. We do know more about Titania's reasons which are explored in the main activity.

▶ Main Activity

▶ Explain that you have so far been looking at an edited version of the scene between Titania and Oberon, but that in the full scene, Titania has a lot more to say. She explains why the boy is so important to her. We are now going to explore the **backstory** ⟴, looking at who the boy is and what he means to Titania.

▶ Sit pupils in a circle and ask them to imagine that in the middle of the circle is a beautiful beach. Ask:

■ *What do we think of when we imagine a beach?*

■ *What is the temperature like?*

■ *What is under our feet?*

■ *What is the sky like?*

■ *What can we hear?*

■ *What is the sea like?*

Explain that, out at sea, boats are sailing by. Ask:

■ *What do the boats look like?*

■ *Where is the horizon in relation to our beach?*

Choose two pupils to sit in the middle of the circle as if on the beach. Explain that they are very good friends and they are relaxing and gossiping together. Ask:

■ *How would they be sitting?*

■ *What would they be doing?*

▶ Ask the two pupils on the 'beach' to show what is happening, while you tell the story.

▶ Explain that one of the characters is very heavily pregnant and the other one is her friend: Titania, queen of the fairies. Give the pregnant character a white cloth to use as they wish during the story. They are watching the boats sailing by and, to make Titania laugh, her pregnant friend is pretending to be a boat with her belly sticking out like the sail. The friend looks around the beach to find a present for Titania. Now freeze the two pupils in the middle as a picture, and ask the rest of the pupils: *What sort of things might she find on the beach to bring as gifts?* (For example, shells, crabs, a smooth piece of driftwood).

▶ Continue with an explanation and 'showing' of the friend finding and bringing the gifts that the pupils have suggested to the Queen. Freeze the two pupils in the middle again, and ask the rest of the pupils: *How might these two characters feel at this moment? What might they be thinking?*

Worksheet 12: Act 2 Scene 1, Titania's speech

▶ Ask the two pupils in the middle to re-join the circle. Distribute the worksheet and explain that this is how Titania, the queen, describes the scene. Pupils do **Ensemble reading** ◘, then repeat with pupils whispering the words as if passing on a shared secret to the next reader. Clarify any unfamiliar words. Ask:

■ *What country is the beach in?*

■ *What happens to the friend? What happens to her baby?*

▶ Ask the two pupils to return to the centre of the circle; the rest of the group **sculpt** ◘ them into a new freeze frame in which the friend is dead and Titania has the baby boy in her arms. Use the white cloth to represent the baby. Ask:

■ *How does the Queen feel about the loss of her friend?*

■ *Why is she holding the baby? How does she feel about the baby?*

▶ Ask the rest of the pupils to think of a promise that Titania makes to her friend about the baby. *What words would she use to make such a promise?* Ask for volunteers to make their promise. Each of them walks over to the freeze frame and puts a hand on Titania's shoulder as they speak the promise aloud. Choose three or four volunteers. Ask the pupil representing Titania to react to what she/he hears.

▶ Explain that pupils will do an **ensemble reading** ◘ of the speech again, but this time as if they are sharing a secret; the pupils in the centre of the circle will 'act out' what's happening as it is described. Ask the actors to try and show how the two characters feel. They start in their first freeze frame of two friends relaxing and gossiping on the beach. The sequence is performed as the speech is read. At the end of the speech, give the two 'performers' a round of applause.

▶ Plenary

▶ Ask:

■ *Why is the Indian boy so important to Titania?*

■ *Do you have any other thoughts about Oberon and why he might want to take the boy away from Titania?*

■ *How has acting out the words made them easier to understand?*

Act 2 Scene 1 (edited)

Enter Oberon, the King of Fairies, with his train, and Titania, the Queen, with hers.

OBERON: Ill met by moonlight, proud Titania.

TITANIA: What, jealous Oberon? Fairies, skip hence.
I have forsworn his bed and company.

OBERON: Why should Titania cross her Oberon?
I do but beg a little changeling boy
To be my henchman.

TITANIA: Set your heart at rest:
The fairy land buys not the child of me.

OBERON: Give me that boy.

TITANIA: Not for thy fairy kingdom. Fairies, away.

Exit Titania and her train.

OBERON: Well, go thy way: thou shalt not from this grove
Till I torment thee for this injury.

Titania, Act 2 Scene 1

His mother was a votress of my order,
And in the spicèd Indian air by night
Full often hath she gossiped by my side,
And sat with me on Neptune's yellow sands,
Marking th'embarkèd traders on the flood,
When we have laughed to see the sails conceive
And grow big-bellied with the wanton wind,
Which she, with pretty and with swimming gait
Following - her womb then rich with my young
squire -
Would imitate, and sail upon the land,
To fetch me trifles, and return again
As from a voyage, rich with merchandise.
But she, being mortal, of that boy did die:
And for her sake do I rear up her boy,
And for her sake I will not part with him.

► **Notes**

'**votress**': follower
'**marking**': watching
'**th'embarked traders**': sailing merchants

'**flood**': sea
'**wanton**': playful
'**swimming gait**': graceful movement

A MIDSUMMER NIGHT'S DREAM
LESSON 5: CLIMATE CHANGE - ELIZABETHAN STYLE

Key Objective

To understand the status of Oberon and Titania in Act 2 Scene 1 and the effects of their argument on the fairy and human worlds.

KS3	KS2
5.1 Developing and adapting active reading skills and strategies	Speaking, Listening and Responding, Group Discussion and Interaction, Drama, Understanding and Interpreting texts, Engaging and Responding to Texts
4.2 Developing, adapting and responding to dramatic techniques, conventions and styles	

LESSON DESCRIPTION

Pupils recap on their understanding of the dispute between Titania and Oberon. They then look at Titania's descriptions of the adverse weather conditions caused by their argument and explore the imagery in Shakespeare's language.

This is the second in a sequence of four lessons that explore the Athenian woods and the fairy world.

Preparation and Resources

You will need:

▶ A hall or drama studio, or classroom with tables pushed back

▶ Chairs: enough for everyone in the biggest circle possible in the available space

▶ **Worksheet 13:** one per pupil

▶ **Worksheet 14:** enough for a quarter of the group

▶ **Worksheet 15:** enough for a quarter of the group

▶ **Worksheet 16:** enough for a quarter of the group

▶ **Worksheet 17:** enough for a quarter of the group

▶ A supply of A3 or flipchart-sized paper and a collection of coloured pens and pencils

 This lesson tackles some of the most powerful language in *A Midsummer Night's Dream*, breaking down the images and creating visual representations to help pupils understand and appreciate the language Shakespeare uses as they explore the impact of the fairy argument on the human world. We learn through the speech that the human world is being badly affected by severe changes in the weather, brought on by Titania and Oberon's argument; the natural world is turned upside down. This is particularly useful information in terms of the design choices that pupils will be asked to think about in Lesson 7 but also reflects Elizabethan beliefs about the kinds of things that happen on Midsummer's Eve, which you might like to tell your pupils about.

(*Refer to the CD-ROM for an extended set of teacher notes explaining some of the most common Elizabethan beliefs about Midsummer's Eve and the fairy world.*)

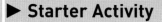

LESSON STRUCTURE

▶ Starter Activity

Worksheet 13: Act 2 Scene 1, Oberon and Titania

▶ Start with everyone sitting on chairs in a circle. Recap with pupils what we learnt about Oberon and Titania in the last lesson: who are they, what are they arguing about and why might this be? Explain to pupils that as a king and queen, Oberon and Titania each have a train of faithful followers and that these followers can help the audience to understand what is going on. Ask:

■ *How do you think the followers react to the argument?*

■ *Where do you think they are during the argument?*

▶ Ask pupils to come and sit at one end of the room to allow the largest stage space possible for the class to work in. Ask for volunteers to be Oberon and Titania. You will also need five pupils to be Oberon's train, five to be Titania's train and one to be the Indian boy in Titania's train. Everyone else will be the 'directors' who will remain seated, watching the action as it unfolds. Discuss where the characters should enter from and to in the stage space; negotiate two separate 'entrances' and mark them with chairs. Oberon and his train should go to one of these entrances and Titania and her train to the other. Ask the directors:

■ *Who comes in first? Is their train with them?*

■ *What mood are the characters in before they meet? Does this change when Oberon and Titania see each other?*

■ *How do the rest of Titania's train react to the Indian boy? (For example, they might be playing with him and then attempt to hide him as soon as they see Oberon.)*

■ *How do Titania and Oberon's followers react to one another?*

▶ Ask 'Titania' and 'Oberon' to play the scene while the directors watch carefully and decide what they think the followers and Indian boy should be doing during the scene, bearing in mind their thoughts about why Titania and Oberon are acting the way they are. Try out three or four ideas and negotiate which version is to be used.

▶ Finally, perform the scene.
Ask:

■ *What difference does it make to the scene when Oberon and Titania have their followers there?*

■ *Why do you think Shakespeare put the fairy 'train' into this scene?*

▶ Main Activity

Worksheets 14 - 17: Act 2 Scene 1, Titania's speech

▶ Explain that in the full version of this scene, Titania is worried about the effect that her argument with Oberon is having on the human world. She describes all the bad things that are happening, as a result of their anger, to all the ordinary people of the land who live outside the luxury of the Athenian palace.

▶ Divide pupils into four groups, and give each group a copy of one section of Titania's speech.

▶ In turn, ask the pupils in each group to read aloud the overview of what is being described in their section of speech, followed by Titania's words. Their task, as a group, is to create a storyboard of their section which includes the words themselves and images to illustrate the words. They should first discuss as a group what these images might be and then decide how best to share out the task. Encourage them to find out what any unusual words mean by using dictionaries.

▶ They can use the words themselves as pictures. For example, they could write *'contagious fog'* in letters that look like fog or clouds; or write the whole line in 'fog' writing as though it is falling from the sky to the land to illustrate how the fog *'falls in the land.'* They may like to use magazines or search on computers for suitable images.

▶ The displays could be worked on further for homework and ten minutes of a future lesson given to groups to put all their work together as a 'poster'for their group display. The work can then be displayed as a reminder of the deep impact that the fairy world has on humans, and as a visual reminder of the impact of Shakespeare's language. This work will also act as a stimulus for the next two lessons which explore the possible atmosphere and design of the Athenian woods.

▶ Plenary

■ *Did finding images for the words help you to understand Shakespeare's language?*

■ *Do Titania's words remind you of any weather conditions you have experienced?*

■ *Farming was many more people's livelihoods in Shakespeare's time and bad harvests meant famine and suffering. How affected by the weather do you think we are today?*

Act 2 Scene 1 (edited)

Enter Oberon, the King of Fairies, with his train, and Titania, the Queen, with hers.

OBERON: Ill met by moonlight, proud Titania.

TITANIA: What, jealous Oberon? Fairies, skip hence.
I have forsworn his bed and company.

OBERON: Why should Titania cross her Oberon?
I do but beg a little changeling boy
To be my henchman.

TITANIA: Set your heart at rest:
The fairy land buys not the child of me.

OBERON: Give me that boy and I will go with thee.

TITANIA: Not for thy fairy kingdom. Fairies, away.

Exit Titania and her train.

OBERON: Well, go thy way; thou shalt not from this grove
Till I torment thee for this injury.

Titania's speech: Group One

Titania describes how the whistling wind causes clouds and rainstorms that fill up the rivers and flood the land.

> Therefore the winds, piping to us in vain,
>
> As in revenge, have sucked up from the sea
>
> Contagious fogs, which falling in the land
>
> Hath every petty river made so proud
>
> That they have overborne their continents.

▶ **Notes**

'piping': whistling
'contagious': harmful
'petty': small

'proud': swollen
'overborne their continents': flooded

Titania's speech: Group Two

Titania describes how hard the farmers have worked, but the rain has rotted the crops in the fields. The sheep have been infected with disease and their dead bodies are being eaten by crows.

> The ox hath therefore stretched his yoke in vain,
>
> The ploughman lost his sweat, and the green corn
>
> Hath rotted ere his youth attained a beard.
>
> The fold stands empty in the drownéd field,
>
> And crows are fatted with the murrion flock.

▶ **Notes**

'**stretched**': pulled at
'**lost**': wasted
'**ere his youth attained a beard**': before developing any bristle or growth

'**fold**': animal pen
'**murrion**': infected

Titania's speech: Group Three

Titania describes the places where people play games and dance: no one can use them because the rain has made them so muddy. Although it's actually summer, humans need to wrap themselves up as if it is winter, the time of year when we traditionally hear hymns or carols.

The nine-men's morris is filled up with mud,

And the quaint mazes in the wanton green

For lack of tread are undistinguishable.

The human mortals want their winter here:

No night is now with hymn or carol blessed.

▶ **Notes**

'**nine men's morris**': area of ground marked out for a game involving nine pegs ('men')
'**quaint**': elaborate
'**wanton green**': lush grass, before developing any bristle or growth

'**want their winter here: No night is now with hymn or carol blessed**': though the weather is wintry there are no winter festivities like Christmas

Titania's speech: Group Four

Titania describes how their argument is creating damp air which makes people get colds; the bad weather is changing the seasons.

Therefore the moon, the governess of floods,

Pale in her anger, washes all the air,

That rheumatic diseases do abound.

And through this distemperature we see

The seasons alter.

▶ **Notes**

'**Therefore**': because of our dispute
'**floods**': tides
'**washes**': makes moist

'**rheumatic diseases**': illnesses such as colds
'**distemperature**': poor weather

Key Objective

To understand that the setting for Shakespeare's text may be interpreted in different ways.

To introduce the idea of mood or atmosphere.

KS3	KS2
4.1 Using different dramatic approaches to explore ideas, texts and issues	Group Discussion and Interaction, Drama, Understanding and Interpreting Texts, Engaging and Responding to Texts
4.2 Developing, adapting and responding to dramatic techniques, conventions and styles	

LESSON DESCRIPTION

Pupils are introduced to *soundscaping* techniques and use these to interpret the Athenian woods, home to the fairy kingdom.

This is the third in a sequence of four lessons that explore the Athenian woods and the fairy world.

Preparation and Resources

You will need:

▶ A hall or drama studio, or classroom with tables pushed back

▶ Chairs: for all pupils in a circle or have pupils sit on the floor when they need to

▶ A whiteboard or flipchart

▶ Completed storyboards of Titania's speech from Lesson 5

▶ Two contrasting images of forests or woodland (from a magazine or the internet)

▶ **Worksheet 18:** one per pupil

TN As is evident in the activities elsewhere in this book, one invaluable way to help young people feel a sense of ownership of Shakespeare is to explore with them the wide range of interpretative possibilities his plays offer. No element of a Shakespeare play has been more widely interpreted than the Athenian woods of *A Midsummer Night's Dream*. Victorian actor-managers used detailed perspective painting to reproduce hundreds of fairies in tutus and, for one famous production in 1900, real grass and real rabbits appeared on stage. Peter Brook rang the changes in 1970 when the fairies wore grey boiler suits and the trees were metal coils. Some woods have been dark and dangerous, others bejewelled and exotic. Soundscaping is a powerful platform through which pupils can explore some of the interpretive possibilities for the home of the fairy world.

This lesson would be an effective lead into Lesson 7. If you are following the lessons in sequence, it should also allow you to see evidence of prior learning about the historical context of the fairy world.

▶ Starter Activity

▶ Display the storyboards of Titania's speech from the previous lesson. Explain that during this lesson pupils will explore the atmosphere of the woods – what it might feel like to be in them. You might refer back to some of the images pupils have drawn, or some of the words that Titania speaks, during the course of the lesson.

▶ Invite pupils to suggest words which describe the atmosphere in the following settings:

■ A warm day at the seaside (for example, carefree, noisy, relaxed, exciting).

■ An assembly.

■ Break-time in the playground.

■ A football match.

■ The last day of school before the holidays.

▶ Revisit the seaside setting. Tell pupils it is no longer a warm day but a winter's night. Ask:

■ *What words would you now use to describe the atmosphere*?

▶ Ask pupils what they think the word 'atmosphere' means. Explain that they are now going to explore the different kinds of atmosphere the Athenian woods in *A Midsummer Night's Dream* might have. Show them images of two contrasting woods (from a magazine or the internet) and ask them for words to describe these. Collect the vocabulary the pupils develop by writing each word or phrase on a Post-it and attaching it to the picture.

▶ Explain that an important task for a director and designer of *A Midsummer Night's Dream* is to decide on the atmosphere of the woods in their production and then decide how to create that atmosphere. Pupils are now going to experiment with creating different kinds of woods that might be suitable for the play. You might want to revisit the four worlds work from Lesson 1 to remind pupils what happens in the woods.

▶ Main Activity

Worksheet 18: Sounds from an Athenian wood

▶ Pupils form a circle. Each pupil in turn speaks aloud one of the phrases on the worksheet. Encourage them to speak as expressively as possible, modelling this if necessary.

▶ Pupils speak the phrases on the worksheet a second time, this time making the most of any onomatopoeic words, for example, 'hissing snakes'. Then ask pupils to replace the words with pure sound: now the snakes simply hiss.

▶ Give pupils three words to describe a wood, for example cold, mysterious, dangerous. Explain that they are going to create a

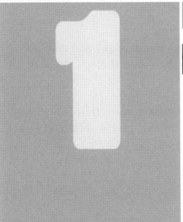

soundscape 🔳 of a wood with those qualities. Ask for a volunteer to make a first sound that will act as a trigger for other sounds in the wood (designate a second and third contributor if pupils seem shy at this point). Ideally all members of the class should participate in creating the soundscape.

▶ Tell pupils that they now have a group responsibility for creating the atmosphere of a wood which is cold, mysterious and dangerous, using only sounds. They must listen closely to one another so that the sounds work together to create a particular sense of place rather than just making a general noise. They may change their sound in the course of the soundscape and sounds may be of short or longer duration. Everything should contribute to make this cold, mysterious, dangerous wood as real as possible. Remind pupils that the trigger sound(s) will begin the soundscape and their contributions should follow.

▶ Tell pupils to shut their eyes and invite the first sound to begin. It is important they close their eyes because it removes a lot of the self-consciousness that might inhibit their contributions and allows their imaginations to travel to the place they are making. When the soundscape has lasted about 30 seconds to a minute, bring it to a close and ask pupils whether they think they were successful in creating this wood. Ask:

■ *What worked well? What could have been improved?*

▶ Now create a contrasting wood, for example, hot, tropical and relaxing. Again nominate someone to make the first sound with other pupils adding in. Ask pupils to reflect on what worked and what didn't.

▶ Now divide the class into groups of six to eight. Tell them they are going to use the same **soundscaping** 🔳 technique to make their own choices about the atmosphere of the Athenian woods in their production of *A Midsummer Night's Dream*. To help create their soundscape, they should decide on three words that describe the spirit of this wood. They should also decide on whether there is any element of magic within it. The woods are home to the fairies and pupils need to decide how much of an influence the fairy world has on the atmosphere of the woods. Explain that pupils will be performing their **soundscape** 🔳 for the rest of the class.

▶ Give groups five to ten minutes to prepare. Towards the end of this period ask them to decide where they want their audience to sit or stand (for example, everyone could sit in the middle of the space and be surrounded by the sounds). The audience will have their eyes shut. Encourage them to be inventive about how they use sound in relation to the audience.

▶ Designate a running order for the soundscapes and remind groups to tell their audiences where they want them to be. Run the soundscapes.

▶ Ask the pupils listening to the soundscapes to think about things they could see in their imaginations – make a note of these to help with the next lesson.

▶ Plenary

▶ After each soundscape, ask:

■ *What kind of a place was this?*

■ *What kind of fairies might inhabit this kind of wood? Who else lives here?*

■ *Would you want to visit such a place?*

■ *How would you feel if you were lost in this wood?*

▶ Finally, discuss the range of soundscape experiences they have just had. Does Shakespeare's play support all of these choices? Is this perhaps one reason why his plays are performed so often – because they offer such a wide choice of possibilities?

Sounds from an Athenian wood

- Playing on pipes
- A rushing brook
- Whistling wind
- Hissing snakes
- A strange sound never heard before
- A lullaby
- An owl hooting
- Fairies singing
- Someone whistling
- A wolf howling
- A bird singing
- Actors rehearsing
- Trees creaking
- Beating wings
- A child's laughter
- Bells
- Footsteps running
- A donkey braying
- Lovers laughing
- Whispers

Key Objective

To create a theatre design for the Athenian woods.

KS3	KS2
1.1 Developing active listening skills and strategies	Listening and Responding, Group Discussion and Interaction, Understanding and Interpreting Texts, Engaging and Responding to Texts
5.2 Understanding and responding to ideas, viewpoints, themes and purposes in texts	

LESSON DESCRIPTION

Pupils create a theatre design for the Athenian woods.

This is the last in a sequence of four lessons exploring the Athenian woods and the fairy kingdom.

Preparation and Resources

You will need:

▶ A classroom or art room with tables pushed back

▶ Two images from the CD-ROM of different kinds of woods

▶ **Worksheet 19:** one per pupil

▶ A bag of material scraps, coloured paper and card

▶ A whiteboard or flipchart

▶ A supply of A3 or flipchart-sized paper and a collection of coloured pens and pencils

In this lesson, pupils work together to create a design for the Athenian woods in their production of *A Midsummer Night's Dream*. Design approaches are a valuable way of helping pupils understand that there are no single 'right answers' when it comes to staging a Shakespeare play. A designer must know the play intimately before he or she can interpret it for an audience and they will always look to the text to provide the inspiration for their ideas. It is the job of the designer and director, working together with the actors, to interpret a particular Shakespeare play for a contemporary audience, so every production will be different. Pupils will need to draw on their prior knowledge of the fairy world in this lesson, particularly Lesson 5 and Titania's description of the impact of the fairy argument on the human world.

▶ The object exercise included in this lesson is sometimes used by actors and directors in the rehearsal room when devising a piece of theatre; it forces them to think quickly and imaginatively and shows pupils how one object can stand in for another on stage. This can involve abstract as well as literal images. Theatre designers will also use this technique when they are designing a play. They will find ways of suggesting a setting or environment rather than creating a literal representation of it.

▶ Starter Activity

▶ Put pupils into pairs and ask them to label themselves A and B. Pupils choose an object, from the room or their bag, which they would like to work with. The purpose of the exercise is to show that an object can be transformed into something entirely different Without speaking, A demonstrates the object to B and shows how it can become something different – for example, a plastic water bottle could be a microphone or a boat bobbing on the sea. B's task is to work out what the object has been transformed into and call it out when they know. They then swap so that B demonstrates to A something else that the object could be. This swapping should continue for two or three minutes with each partner demonstrating and the other guessing. To ensure the free flowing of ideas, a pupil can say 'pass' if they do not have any idea in mind when the object is handed to them. Ask:

■ *What ideas do you have for objects we could use to become trees or other things in the Athenian woods?*

▶ Main Activity

▶ Tell the class they are going to create a design for the Athenian woods, using pictures for inspiration. Remind pupils of their storyboard work on Titania's speech describing the changes that have taken place in the human world due to the conflict in the fairy world. Pupils will need to consider whether the wood in which the fairies live is affected in the same way as the rest of the world by Titania and Oberon's argument. To help them create their design, they will look at pictures of different kinds of woods.

▶ Divide the class into two groups and distribute copies of 'Woodlands by day' from the CD-ROM to half the class and copies of 'Moonlit wood' to the other half. Each pupil should spend a couple of minutes looking at their picture, taking in as much detail as possible.

▶ Pupils sit on the floor with some paper and a pencil in front of them. Tell them that they should listen to the following prompt questions, think of their answers and write them down.

■ *Think of as many words as you can to describe your picture.*

■ *What can you see? What colours and textures are there?*

■ *How does the picture make you feel?*

■ *If you were going to rename the picture, what would you call it?*

■ *What time of day is it? How can you tell?*

▶ Ask pupils to talk to someone else who looked at the same picture as them and share their responses.

▶ Now ask pupils to partner with someone who looked at the other picture and take them on a **Guided Imaginary Journey ▷** through their wood. They should use the ideas and words that were captured in the last exercise. After they have each had a turn, pupils return to their original picture groups and discuss whether the journeys they went on, or were describing, have given them any new ideas for the woods in *A Midsummer Night's Dream*.

▶ In their picture groups ask pupils to find a partner and explain that each pair will now create a theatre design for the Athenian woods in *A Midsummer Nights' Dream*.

▶ Introduce pupils to the concept of a mood board. Explain that a mood board is like a collage and designers often use them to capture the mood and atmosphere of the play they are designing. Mood boards also help to create a colour palette that designers will use for the sets and costumes. Ask pupils to choose two or three colours that they want to use in their design for the woods, and to collect some material scraps using these colours. They should think about texture as well as shade. The collage should not contain any literal representation of trees or people in the wood, but should instead be a patchwork of all the colours and textures that they think represents their wood. As further inspiration, they could look at other images such as Gustav Klimt's 'Fir Forest' or 'In the Forest' by Gustave Courbet, both available to view on the Internet.

▶ Ask pairs to draw a design for their Athenian wood on a large sheet of flipchart paper using coloured pens. The primary challenge is to capture the spirit of their wood as they have planned it, rather than providing a very realistic drawing. The most important question they need to consider at this stage is whether their wood is magical or not. Is it the fairies alone that provide the magic or is there something enchanted about the woods themselves? As they start work, ask pupils to think back to the exercise at the beginning of the lesson. How might they use objects to suggest a wood on stage as opposed to creating a literal wood? Give groups at least twenty minutes to complete the drawing.

▶ Finally ask pupils to answer the questions on Worksheet 19. Their answers should relate to the woods they have created so far.

▶ Plenary

▶ Ask some of the pairs to take the rest of the class on a tour of their mood boards and designs using Worksheet 19 as a prompt. If there is time, pupils could bring some of the choices to life in the classroom. After each presentation ask other students to think about the similarities and differences between their designs.

▶ Homework

▶ Ask pupils to do some individual research online about set designs for productions of *A Midsummer Night's Dream* (www.rsc.org.uk/explore). Ask them to find a stage design that most reflects their idea of the woods. Pupils could print off images and these pictures could then be attached to the mood board and used in a display. Ask pupils to find set designs for the scenes in the world of the court as well. Can they find images for the wood and the court that complement each other in some way? For example, a very bare, stark design for the formal setting of the court compared with a very colourful and explosive design for the informal setting of the woods.

Designing the Athenian woods

1. Choose three words to describe the spirit of your Athenian woods. Think about: What kind of a place is it? How would it feel to go there?

2. Is your wood magical or not? Why?

3. How do you hope your design will make the audience feel about the woods? Scared, excited, enchanted, intrigued?

4. What words/phrases/images from the text have inspired your design of the Athenian woods?

5. How have you used your knowledge of the context in which Shakespeare wrote *A Midsummer Night's Dream* to inform your choices?

A MIDSUMMER NIGHT'S DREAM
LESSON 8: DISCOVERING CHARACTERS THROUGH LANGUAGE

Key Objective

To understand how vocabulary, rhythm, and the sounds of words help to create the character who speaks them.

KS3

4.2 Developing, adapting and responding to dramatic techniques, conventions and styles

6.2 Analysing how writers' use of linguistic and literary features shapes and influences meaning

KS2

Drama, Understanding and Interpreting Texts and Engaging and Responding to Texts

LESSON DESCRIPTION

Pupils explore Shakespeare's poetry in practical, physical ways and discover how two contrasting characters, Theseus and Oberon, are created through Shakespeare's very different language choices.

Preparation and Resources

You will need:

▶ A hall or drama studio, or classroom with tables pushed back

▶ Chairs: for all pupils in a circle

▶ Blank paper and pencil: one per pupil

▶ **Worksheet 20/20a:** one per pupil

▶ **Resource Sheet 1/1a**

 There is a tradition of the same actor playing both Theseus and Oberon and this is likely to have been the case in Shakespeare's time. Shakespeare would have written the parts with a particular actor in mind. He would have thought about the similarities of the characters: their authority, their attraction to strong women, their sense of justice and fairness, perhaps their arrogance and jealousy. But he would also have thought about how being a supernatural creature would make Oberon different. And he wrote the difference into the words he gives each character. He creates breathing patterns for them and rhythms which suggest the way they move. In the two speeches used here as examples, Theseus and Oberon are both in work mode dealing with the lovers; Theseus is in his court proclaiming the law of Athens on Hermia, while Oberon is using his powers to ensure a happy ending for Helena and Demetrius. This lesson allows pupils to physically explore these different 'professional' speeches and how the way they are written helps an actor to discover more about the character he is playing.

 Worksheet 20a provides an alternative edit of the speeches for younger or less able pupils.

▶ Starter Activity

▶ Give pupils two minutes to write down five of the words or phrases they use most in their everyday speech. Then ask them to choose a particular kind of leader and write down five words or phrases they imagine that person might use most in their everyday speech, for example, the Queen, a football captain, a headteacher etc.

▶ Ask pupils to volunteer some of the words and phrases from both lists. Ask:

■ *How are the two lists different? What does this tell you about the speakers?* Discuss how words define the kind of world we live in and who we are as people.

▶ Tell pupils that they are now going to investigate the words of two characters, two leaders from *A Midsummer Night's Dream* (one from the Athenian court and one from the fairy kingdom). They are going to see if they can tell from the words the characters use what they are like. They will be language detectives.

▶ Main Activity

Worksheet 20/20a/Resource Sheet 1/1a: Who speaks like this?

▶ *Interpolated questions* ⟨⟩ Tell pupils that they are all Duke Theseus and they are about to pronounce judgment on Hermia, whose father has brought her to court because she refuses to marry the man he has chosen as her future husband. After using interpolated questions ask:

■ *What kind of leader do you think Duke Theseus is from speaking his words? Why?*

▶ Now ask pupils to imagine they are Hermia. Duke Theseus is about to tell her what will happen to her if she does not obey her father. Read through Theseus' speech slowly having asked them to echo or repeat after you all the words which would worry pupils if they were Hermia. Ask:

■ *Which words particularly worried you? Why?*

■ *Do you think Duke Theseus will keep his word and put you to death if you continue to disobey your father's wishes?*

■ *As Hermia, what kind of leader do you think Duke Theseus is from hearing these words?*

Encourage pupils to support their responses with evidence from the text.

▶ Beat through the rhythm of the speech with pupils, referring to Shakespeare's use of *iambic pentameter* ⟨⟩. They should hit their knees or the floor on every stressed syllable. *How well does Theseus's speech fit the rhythm?* With the full text on Worksheet 19, it is not an easy fit. There are feminine endings (where the number of syllables in the line is more than the regular ten of a pentameter rhythm) and the stress does not always fall in the right place for an iambic rhythm. (This last point can be found on Worksheet 19a too with the word 'either'.) These disruptions tell us something about Theseus; perhaps that he is wrestling with his conscience to impose a law that he knows is unfair; perhaps he is distracted by thoughts of his own marriage; perhaps the irregularites are calculated to give more weight to his words as they force people to listen more carefully.

▶ Repeat the exercise with Oberon's speech. How well does this speech fit the rhythm? (This is a classic iambic pentameter speech with a very regular rhythm.) *What does this suggest about Oberon?* The rhythm gives a lightness of touch; perhaps Oberon is more comfortable and assured in his power than Theseus; perhaps he is freer to do what he wants rather than what the law requires; perhaps his magic means he doesn't have to be so clever with words.

▶ Use **Punctuation shift** ⟲ first with Theseus' speech. Explain to pupils that they are now going to 'walk' Theseus's speech so that they can better understand what it is like to be him. The rule is that every time they come to a punctuation mark they must change direction. Model this using the first two or three lines. Explain that this is done as an individual journey; younger or less confident pupils may work in pairs, linking arms to ensure they move in the same direction at the same time. When they have finished the speech they should stand still.

▶ Ask:

■ *How did the speech make you feel?*

■ *What did you notice about the rhythm?*

■ *What words would you now use to describe Theseus?*

▶ Pupils then use **punctuation shift** ⟲ with Oberon's speech. When they are finished ask:

■ *How did the speech make you feel?*

■ *What did you notice about the rhythm?*

■ *What words would you now use to describe Oberon?*

■ *How is he different from Theseus?*

Worksheet 20/20a: Who speaks like this?

▶ Pupils form two lines facing one another, A and B. Explain that often, in poetry, the first and last words of the lines of verse are especially important. They are now going to look at the last words of the two speeches.

▶ Firstly pupils will concentrate on Theseus's speech. Line A says the last word of the speech ('*abjure*') to Line B and Line B says the last word of the second line ('*men*') to Line A. This continues until they come to the end of the speech. (It's often possible to instinctively grasp the meaning of a speech through looking at the last words of the verse lines in this way.)

▶ Still retaining a focus on the last words, ask pupils to imagine that each word is a ball of a particular size and weight. They should make quick, instinctive choices about what kind of ball a particular word is as they are 'throwing' it. Is it a tennis ball, or a large, light beach ball, or a small hard cricket ball? The way they 'throw' the words should reflect the kind of ball they are using. Ask:

■ *What kinds of words does Theseus use? How would you describe his vocabulary?*

■ *Do you notice anything about this collection of last words?*

▶ Now do the same with Oberon's speech. Ask if they notice anything special about the words Oberon uses (all are simple and monosyllabic – the word 'throws' will probably be short and sharp). He uses rhyming words indicating a playfulness in his magic. What difference might having magical powers make to his language?

▶ Tell pupils to put their worksheets aside but to remain in their two groups. Explain that they are going to make two statues which capture and celebrate the spirits of the two characters. Line A will create Theseus and Line B Oberon. Everyone will be a Theseus or an Oberon but their group will also shape itself in a way which represents that character (for example, Theseus might be upright and quite symmetrical while the statue of Oberon may be more angular and irregular). Either allow them two minutes to plan their statues or, for a more improvisational and intuitive response, allow no talking, count backward from ten and freeze them at the end of that time.

▶ Ask the pupils creating Oberon to remember their positions but to relax and look at the Theseus statue. Ask:

■ *What do you see?*

■ *How would you describe this statue?*

■ *Does it represent Theseus to you? In what way?*

Tell the Theseus statue that you are now going to clap your hands and when you do the statue should come to life and make sounds. Ask the observing group to describe the movement and sounds they hear.

▶ Now ask the Oberon statue to reform and repeat the sequence above.

▶ If pupils are confident enough the two statues could encounter one another. How do they feel about each other?

▶ Plenary

▶ Ask pupils to review the words they have chosen to describe Theseus and Oberon. Write these on a whiteboard or flipchart. Ask:

■ *Who is more powerful, Oberon or Theseus?*

■ *What has influenced your sense of who is more powerful?*

■ *What have you learnt through the lesson about the similarities and differences between Theseus and Oberon?*

▶ Homework

▶ Ask pupils to research fairies and bring in pictures and facts about belief in fairies and their powers. You might want to direct them to research anything more they can find out about belief in fairies in Shakespeare's time. To prepare for the next lesson you could ask them to specifically research Robin Goodfellow.

Who speaks like this?

Act 1 Scene 1

THESEUS: Either to die the death, or to abjure
For ever the society of men.
Therefore, fair Hermia, question your desires,
Know of your youth, examine well your blood,
Whether, if you yield not to your father's choice,
You can endure the livery of a nun,
For aye to be in shady cloister mewed,
To live a barren sister all your life,
Chanting faint hymns to the cold fruitless moon.
Thrice blesséd they that master so their blood
To undergo such maiden pilgrimage;
But earthlier happy is the rose distilled
Than that which withering on the virgin thorn,
Grows, lives and dies in single blessedness.

Act 3 Scene 2

OBERON: About the wood go swifter than the wind,
And Helena of Athens look thou find.
All fancy-sick she is and pale of cheer
With sighs of love, that costs the fresh blood dear.
By some illusion see thou bring her here.
I'll charm his eyes against she doth appear.

Who speaks like this?

Act 1 Scene 1

THESEUS: Take time to pause, and by the next new moon –
Upon that day either prepare to die
For disobedience to your father's will,
Or else to wed Demetrius, as he would.

Act 3 Scene 2

OBERON: About the wood go swifter than the wind,
And Helena of Athens look thou find.
All fancy-sick she is, and pale of cheer
With sighs of love that cost the fresh blood dear.
By some illusion see thou bring her here.
I'll charm his eyes against she do appear.

Interpolated questions

Use the questions in **_bold italics_** below to prompt pupils to speak the speech in unison.

Teacher: **_Duke Theseus, what will happen to me if I refuse to obey my father's wish for me to marry Demetrius?_**
Pupils: Either to die the death, or to abjure
For ever the society of men.

Teacher: **_What shall I do?_**
Pupils: Therefore, fair Hermia, question your desires,

Teacher: **_What else?_**
Pupils: Know of your youth, examine well your blood,

Teacher: **_Why?_**
Pupils: Whether, if you yield not to your father's choice,

Teacher: **_What will happen?_**
Pupils: You can endure the livery of a nun,

Teacher: **_How do they live?_**
Pupils: For aye to be in shady cloister mewed,

Teacher: **_Don't they have families?_**
Pupils: To live a barren sister all your life,

Teacher: **_Doing what?_**
Pupils: Chanting faint hymns to the cold fruitless moon.

Teacher: **_I would never be able to marry?_**
Pupils: Thrice blesséd they that master so their blood,
To undergo such maiden pilgrimage,

Teacher: **_But?_**
Pupils: But earthlier happy is the rose distilled

Teacher: **_Than what?_**
Pupils: Than that which withering on the virgin thorn,

Teacher: **_Does what?_**
Pupils: Grows, lives and dies in single blessedness.

Interpolated questions

Use the questions in **bold italics** below to prompt pupils to speak the speech in unison.

Teacher: *Duke Theseus, what will happen to me if I refuse to obey my father's wish for me to marry Demetrius?*

Pupils: Take time to pause, and by the next new moon –

Teacher: *What will happen then?*

Pupils: Upon that day either prepare to die!

Teacher: *Why?*

Pupils: For disobedience to your father's will,

Teacher: *Is there another choice?*

Pupils: Or else to wed Demetrius, as he would.

A MIDSUMMER NIGHT'S DREAM
LESSON 9: INTERPRETING A CHARACTER: PUCK

Key Objective

To interpret the character of Puck.

KS3	KS2
4.1 Using different dramatic approaches to explore ideas, texts and issues	Speaking, Listening and Responding, Group Discussion and Interaction, Drama, Understanding and Interpreting Texts, Engaging and Responding to Texts
5.2 Understanding and responding to ideas, viewpoints, themes and purposes in texts	

LESSON DESCRIPTION

Pupils consider the character of Puck and make active interpretive choices about him, using clues in the text and researching the social and historical context.

Preparation and Resources

You will need:

▶ A hall or drama studio, or classroom with tables pushed back

▶ Chairs: enough for everyone in the biggest circle possible in the available space

▶ **Worksheet 21:** one per pupil

▶ **Worksheet 22:** one per pupil

▶ **Worksheet 23**

▶ Pencils: one per pupil

▶ A whiteboard or flipchart

 Like Titania and Oberon, Puck would have been a familiar concept to Shakespeare's audience but not a familiar character. Pucks were a type of small devil that could cause harm. On the other hand, Robin Goodfellow (as Puck is also known) was a more benign creature that could help with household chores but would also play tricks if he felt like it. Shakespeare seems to have drawn on various folkloric ideas and added some of his own to create Puck. Puck has been portrayed in many different ways over the years: he has been a young boy (and girl) and an old man; light and airy or solid and earthy, but in whatever guise he appears he has become one of Shakespeare's best known and most loved creations. Pupils can have great fun creating their very own version of Puck.

Shakespeare constantly juxtaposes the fairy world with the human world and strong comparisons can be drawn between them, with echoes of one world found in the other. By exploring the character of Puck it is possible to see both the power of the fairy world and the fallibility of it and, in turn, explore the impact of this fallibility on mere mortals.

 Younger or less able pupils, who are less inhibited and still 'play' unselfconsciously, might prefer to act out Puck's actions in the main exercise rather than making freeze frames.

LESSON STRUCTURE

▶ Starter Activity

▶ Explain that in *A Midsummer Night's Dream* the character of Puck is right-hand man to Oberon, the King of the Fairies. Ask pupils what characteristics they think a character called Puck might have. Write the responses on a whiteboard or flipchart. If pupils were set the homework task about Puck from Lesson 8, ask them to share their research findings.

Worksheet 21: Puck

▶ Pupils work in groups of four (labelling themselves A, B, C and D) to **sculpt ⟨⟩** Puck. A reads the character facts aloud, and C and D sculpt B into a statue that represents 'Puck'. A adjusts the statue if they can see any opportunities to add detail. Prompt pupils by asking:

■ *Where is Puck looking and why?*

■ *Does the face of your Puck show what kind of character he is?*

■ *Should Puck's body be relaxed or tense? Why?*

A, C and D copy the statue they have sculpted, so that all four members of the group can present the same image of Puck to their peers.

▶ Divide the class in half – performers and observers. Half the group are to present their 'Puck', making their statues when they hear the word *freeze!* Count down from five to *freeze*. Ask the observers what words they would use to describe Puck using clues from the statues. Add these words to the whiteboard or flipchart. Repeat with the other half of the group.

▶ Main Activity

Worksheet 22: Puck's story

▶ Explain that Puck influences every character in the play at one point or another and pupils are now going to tell his story.

▶ Working in the same groups of four, give them each a section from Worksheet 22 (some groups will have two sections of the story to work with). Explain that each group is going to tell an element of Puck's story. One person could be the narrator whilst the rest of the group creates all the people, places and things that are mentioned (using a mixture of mimes and **freeze frames ⟨⟩**). Each group needs to find a way of including the text (in italics) in their piece. They must also think carefully about their interpretation of Puck. Does he intentionally use magic to cause mischief? Each scene should finish with a **freeze frame ⟨⟩** of Puck which shows as clearly as possible his attitude to the situation he is in at that point in the story.

▶ Give groups ten minutes to work on their story sections. When everyone is ready, perform the story in sequence around the class.

Ask:

■ *What moments do you particularly remember from the story? Why did they stand out?*

■ *Do you think Puck intentionally uses magic to make mischief?*

■ *What more have we learnt about Puck from this exercise?*

■ *Which seems more powerful to you, the fairy world or the human world?*

Worksheet 23: Act 5 Scene 1, Puck's epilogue

▶ Explain that, at the end of the play, there is an 'epilogue'. After the action has finished, the story has been resolved and all the other characters have gone, Puck speaks directly to the audience. Use **Ensemble reading** 🗘 to introduce the speech on the worksheet. Afterwards, ask:

■ *Why do you think Shakespeare has Puck enter and speak directly to the audience in this way?*

■ *Does the line 'Else the Puck a liar call' make you trust Puck more or less?*

■ *Does it depend on how the line is said?*

▶ Ask all the pupils to say the word 'yes' aloud. Ask them if they know what that word means. Now ask one pupil to say 'yes' as if they have just won the lottery, and another to say 'yes' as if they have been asked to wash up and it's not really their turn. Ask, *Does the word 'yes' mean the same thing when said for these different purposes?* Meaning depends on the intention of the speaker, and any actor playing Puck has to decide whether or not he deliberately causes chaos and confusion for the humans in the play. For example, does he squeeze the love juice onto the wrong man's eyes for his own amusement, or is his intention to do what Oberon tells him to do and he simply makes a mistake?

▶ Ask pupils to work with a partner and find a way of speaking the epilogue together as Puck, thinking especially carefully about the line 'Else the Puck a liar call'. They can decide to speak the lines together or choose bits that each of them will say. They can use gestures to make their 'intention' clear. An audience should be able to tell whether they think Puck is an 'evil' spirit, a good spirit or a bit of both.

▶ Plenary

▶ Two or three pairs present their epilogue for the rest of the class. Discuss the similarities and differences between their interpretations. Ask:

■ *What kind of spirit do you think Puck is?*

■ *How can you tell?*

■ *Do you think an Elizabethan audience would have felt differently about the character than we do today? Why/why not?*

Puck

- He works for the King of the Fairies.

- He lives in the woods and can move very fast.

- He can change shape and become any object.

- He can make himself invisible.

- He is described as a hob-goblin.

- The magic he uses causes lots of trouble and confusion.

1. Puck meets one of Titania's Fairies in the forest

Puck comes to check whether the coast is clear for the arrival of Oberon and finds one of Titania's fairies. The Fairy recognizes Puck as Robin Goodfellow, a fairy that plays tricks on humans.

Fairy: Are you not he
That frights the maidens of the villagery?

Puck: Thou speak'st aright;
I am that merry wanderer of the night.

2. The Fairy and Puck argue over who should step aside, Titania or Oberon

Because Titania and Oberon have been having a terrible argument the Fairy and Puck know there will be trouble if they meet. They discover that Oberon and Titania are both due to be in the same part of the forest at the same time, and there is nothing they can do about it!

Puck: But, room, fairy! Here comes Oberon.

Fairy: And here my mistress. Would that he were gone!

3. Puck is sent to find a flower to put a spell on Titania

Oberon is very angry that Titania won't allow a little boy in her care to be his servant. He sends Puck to fetch a magic flower, the juice of which Oberon will squeeze on Titania's eyes while she is asleep. This juice will make her fall in love with the next thing she sees when she wakes up. Puck dashes off!

Puck: I'll put a girdle around about the earth
In forty minutes!

4. Puck returns with the flower and is given another job to do

Breathlessly Puck reappears with the magic flower. Oberon has been watching Helena chase Demetrius through the forest and feels sorry for her. He asks Puck to anoint Demetrius's eyes with the same flower so that he will fall in love with Helena. Puck has not seen Demetrius but Oberon tells him he will recognize him from the Athenian clothes he wears.

Oberon: Effect it with some care, that he may prove
More fond on her than she upon her love;
And look thou meet me ere the first cock crow.

Puck: Fear not my lord, your servant shall do so.

5. Puck mistakes Lysander for Demetrius

Searching the woods for Demetrius, Puck instead spies Lysander sleeping on the ground some distance from Hermia. He sees that they are wearing Athenian clothes and thinks he has found Demetrius. He puts the flower's juice on Lysander's eyes and leaves, feeling very pleased with himself. Unfortunately, Helena runs in, sees Lysander on the floor and shakes him from his sleep. He wakes up and falls instantly in love with her. He gets up and chases Helena through the woods, leaving Hermia asleep on the ground.

Puck: When thou wak'st, let love forbid
Sleep his seat on thy eyelid.
So, awake when I am gone;
For I must now to Oberon.

6. Puck spots the mechanicals rehearsing

Wandering near where Titania, the Fairy Queen, is sleeping, Puck spies the mechanicals, Bottom, Quince, Snug, Snout, Starveling and Flute, rehearsing their play. Quince is trying to direct but Bottom keeps taking over. The others are trying to work out how they will create a wall and a moon for their play. Puck is amused by their bad acting and decides to watch.

Puck: What, a play toward? I'll be an auditor,
An actor too perhaps, if I see cause.

7. Puck decides to play a trick on the actors and Titania

After watching the mechanicals rehearsing for a while Puck decides to play a trick on them. While Bottom is behind a tree waiting for his next cue, Puck changes Bottom's head into that of a donkey. This frightens the other mechanicals so much they run away. Just at that moment Titania awakes and, because of the spell Oberon has put on her, falls instantly in love with Bottom, just as Puck had planned.

Titania (to Bottom): I do love thee: therefore, go with me.
I'll give thee fairies to attend on thee.

8. Puck proudly tells Oberon what he has done....but then discovers his mistake

Puck proudly explains to Oberon that Titania is in love with a donkey and that he has put the love juice in the Athenian's eyes. Unfortunately, just at that moment, Demetrius and Helena arrive. Demetrius is tired of being chased by Helena through the woods and is clearly still not in love with her. Oberon is cross with Puck for having put the juice on the wrong man's eyes. He takes over and puts the juice on Demetrius's eyes whilst he's asleep. Just then Lysander arrives in pursuit of Helena. But he's closely followed by Hermia who's been searching for him through the woods. The noise wakes Demetrius and he falls instantly in love with Helena too. The four lovers fight because the flower's magic juice now means that both young men are in love with Helena. Oberon orders Puck to sort out the mess; he isn't sure whether Puck has been naughty on purpose or not.

Oberon: This is thy negligence. Still thou mistak'st,
Or else committ'st thy knaveries willfully.

Puck: Believe me, king of shadows, I mistook.
Did not you tell me I should know the man
By the Athenian garments he hath on?

9. Puck puts right his mistake and Oberon releases Titania from the spell

Oberon decides to release Titania from his spell and Puck is left to deal with the lovers. He gathers them all together using a magic spell and re-anoints their eyes, making sure they will each be in love with the right person when they wake up.

Puck: In your waking shall be shown.
Jack shall have Jill,
Naught shall go ill,
The man will have his mare again, and all shall be well.

10. The Fairies attend and bless the marriage

Theseus marries Hippolyta, Demetrius marries Helena and Lysander marries Hermia. Following their marriages, the three couples are entertained by the mechanicals' play. Puck clears the way for Oberon and Titania to bless the royal house.

Puck: Not a mouse
Shall disturb this hallowed house.
I am sent with broom before
To sweep the dust behind the door.

Puck: Act 5 Scene 1 (edited)

If we shadows have offended,
Think but this, and all is mended,
That you have but slumbered here,
While these visions did appear.
And this weak and idle theme,
No more yielding but a dream,
Gentles, do not reprehend.
If you pardon, we will mend.
Else the Puck a liar call.
So, goodnight unto you all.
Give me your hands, if we be friends,
And Robin shall restore amends.

▶ **Notes**

'mended': put right

'idle': foolish

'yielding but': real than

'Gentles': ladies and gentlemen

'reprehend': tell off

'mend': put it right

'Give me your hands': applaud

A MIDSUMMER NIGHT'S DREAM
LESSON 10: EXPLORING A MAGICAL TRANSFORMATION

Key Objective

To explore the theme of transformation through close study of Lysander and Hermia.

KS3

4.1 Using different dramatic approaches to explore ideas, texts and issues

5.2 Understanding and responding to ideas, viewpoints, themes and purposes in texts

KS2

Understanding and Interpreting Texts, Drama, Engaging and Responding to Texts, Speaking, Listening and Responding

LESSON DESCRIPTION

Pupils explore the relationship between Hermia and Lysander as it transforms from love to hate.

Preparation and Resources

You will need:

▶ A hall or drama studio, or classroom with tables pushed back

▶ **Resource Sheet 2**

▶ **Worksheet 24:** one per pupil

▶ A whiteboard or flipchart

TN This lesson should help your class discuss and understand what a theme is. Theme means more than simply 'topic' or 'subject matter'; themes are ideas which run throughout a play and create connections between different characters, events and scenes. Identifying themes can help us discover the big questions that lie at the heart of any story.

There are many themes running through *A Midsummer Night's Dream*. At the heart of the play is the theme of transformation. Shakespeare uses the setting of the Athenian woods to provide the perfect environment for radical changes to take place in characters' hearts, minds and even physical shape. From Bottom changing into an ass, to the destruction and subsequent rebirth of Hermia and Lysander's love, to Demetrius's change of heart as he 'remembers' his love for Helena, this play deals with many different kinds of transformation.

Themes are often linked with each other; in *A Midsummer Night's Dream* the theme of transformation is interwoven with the theme of love. The questions raised by this theme, such as *'What is the nature of true love?'* and *'Does the course of true love always run smooth?'* have no single answers, and so exploring them in the classroom can be a source of enjoyable debate. In this lesson, pupils will collectively create representations of two of the lovers in order to explore how they are transformed by love, by their surroundings, and by magic.

LESSON STRUCTURE

▶ Starter Activity

Resource Sheet 2: *A Midsummer Night's Dream Whoosh!*

▶ **Whoosh!** ◘ Pupils sit in a circle. Explain that they are all going to be involved in telling the story of Hermia and Lysander in the play, exploring how their relationship transforms from love to hate. You will tell the story and the pupils will be all of the people, places and things in the story. You will point to a pupil when it is their turn and they will stand up and come into the middle of the circle, making the shape of whoever or whatever has just been described. If they are a person, you might give them things to do or say. All the pupils have to do is listen to the story and react to what is being said.

▶ Explain that they will stay in the circle as part of the story until the circle gets too crowded. When that happens, you will say **'Whoosh!'** and wave your hands; this will be the cue for everybody who is up in the circle to return as quickly as they can to their places. (Refer to *Romeo and Juliet*, Lesson 4, for a more detailed description of a Whoosh!)

▶ After pupils have completed the Whoosh! ask:

■ *At what point in the story does Lysander change his feelings about Hermia?*

■ *Do you think his change of heart is permanent? Will the magic run out?*

■ *Who else experiences a transformation in the way they feel about each other in the play?*

Draw out responses from the pupils about the potential consequences of this transformation on both Hermia and Lysander.

▶ Main Activity

Worksheet 24: Character facts about Hermia and Lysander

▶ Explain that pupils are now going to explore Hermia and Lysander in more detail. Divide the class into six groups. Each group should take on one of the characters, either Hermia or Lysander. Ask them to refer to the list of character facts on the worksheet.

▶ Pupils use this information to make a group statue of their character. Encourage them to use their imaginations, their bodies and any available furniture in the room. Every person and therefore every character is multifaceted, and their statue could show the different sides of their character's personality. Help them to think about the best way of doing this. Ideas could include: a body with many heads; a row of chairs, each with a person sitting exactly the same but wearing a slightly different expression; or the journey of their character, from childhood to the end of the play. It is important that they decide as a group what sort of person Hermia or Lysander is, and how they are going to represent this collectively.

▶ In addition to the written facts, groups should now also focus on how each character behaves towards other people. Hermia begins the play by standing up to her father in front of the Duke. She then shows concern for her best friend, Helena; however, when she is in the wood and has been rejected by Lysander, she tries to attack Helena and can't believe that Lysander has deserted her. What about Lysander – how does he behave towards others? At the beginning of the play he is madly in love with Hermia, now he is madly in love with Helena. Ask the group to make another four statues, simpler than the previous ones, but again they could be abstract. These should reflect the following:

■ How others in the play see the character.

■ How the character feels about him/herself.

■ How the audience see the characters at the beginning of the play.

■ How the audience see the characters at the point we have reached in the story.

▶ Finally, each group takes the last two pictures (how the audience sees the character at the beginning of the play and at the point in the story we have reached) and finds a way of linking them together. They then **showback** to the rest of the class. One member of each group calls out selected facts from Worksheet 25, as if introducing the statue to an audience in a museum or art gallery. At the end of this, the character should animate briefly and speak their line, written in bold underneath the character facts. Ask the audience:

■ *To whom do you think the line was being addressed?*

▶ Plenary

▶ Ask the members of each group:

■ *Which words did you particularly want to emphasise after hearing yourself introduced?*

■ *What are the differences between the two pictures?*

■ *What has changed between the beginning of the play and this point in the story?*
If pupils do not know how the play ends, ask them to predict the outcomes for the transformations they have explored today, for example:

■ *What do you think the future holds for Hermia and Lysander?*

■ *If Puck undoes the magic and Lysander remembers his love for Hermia, will their relationship have changed?*

A Midsummer Night's Dream – Whoosh!

In the city of Athens, there is a beautiful young woman called **Hermia**, who has a best friend called **Helena**, who is also very beautiful. Helena used to have a boyfriend called **Demetrius**, who is rich and handsome, and Hermia has a boyfriend called **Lysander**, whom she loves with all her heart. Helena blows kisses to Demetrius (who ignores them), and Hermia blows kisses to Lysander (who returns them).

BUT Hermia lives with her father, **Egeus**, a very rich man who wants to make sure his daughter is married before he dies. He wants Hermia to marry Demetrius. (The same Demetrius who used to go out with Helena but has now decided he's in love with Hermia.) But Hermia folds her arms, stamps her foot and says *'I would my father look'd but with my eyes'* because she is in love with Lysander and determined to marry him. Hermia's father is very angry. He shakes his fist and says *'Scornful Lysander!'* Egeus warns Hermia that he will have her put to death unless she marries Demetrius and then storms out.

WHOOSH!

Hermia is very upset, and **Lysander** pats her on the back to comfort her. The two young lovers don't know what to do, until Lysander has an idea. He asks Hermia to run away with him. He says: *'I have a widow aunt, a dowager and she respects me as her only son. There, gentle Hermia, may I marry thee.'* He takes Hermia by the hand and they run away together into the woods (which is the quickest way to get to Lysander's aunt without being seen). The Athenian woods are full of **trees** that are twisted and spiky. Lysander and Hermia run through the trees until, exhausted, they find a place to hide and fall asleep. Meanwhile, back in Athens, **Helena** tells **Demetrius** that Hermia has run away with Lysander. She does this in the hope that it will make him like her again. But he pushes her away and says, *'Do I not in plainest truth tell you I do not nor I cannot love you?'* and he runs off into the woods to look for Hermia. Helena follows him, and they run in and out of the trees, but Helena cannot catch Demetrius. She declares, *'I'll follow thee and make a heaven of hell, To die upon the hand I love so well.'* Eventually, both exhausted and lost, they stop, drop to their knees and fall fast asleep.

WHOOSH!

Watching all of this is the Fairy King **Oberon**, who feels sorry for Helena. So he asks **Puck**, his servant, to sort it out with the help of a magic flower. He tells Puck where to find the flower: *'I know a bank where the wild thyme blows, Where oxlips and the nodding violet grows'*. Oberon tells Puck to put the magic juice from the flower onto **Demetrius's** eyes, so that he will fall in love with Helena, and everyone will be happy.

By now, night has fallen, and it is very spooky in the woods. Puck makes himself invisible, and he weaves his way through the trees. He finds **Lysander**, sleeping on the forest floor, with **Hermia** sleeping just a little way off. Puck mistakenly thinks she is Helena and so very carefully he squeezes the flower's juice onto Lysander's eyes. BUT oh no! in the darkness, he's got the wrong person. He should have squeezed the juice onto Demetrius's eyes! In a nearby part of the woods, Helena is still looking for Demetrius. She stumbles close by where Lysander and Hermia are sleeping, sees Lysander and shakes him awake. Because of the magic flower's juice, he falls instantly in love with her and proclaims, *'And run through fire I will for thy sweet sake. Transparent Helena!'* He goes down on one knee and asks Helena to marry him. Helena is really confused, and she runs away. Lysander chases after her, leaving Hermia asleep on the ground and all alone.

WHOOSH!

Oberon realises that Puck has put the magic juice onto the wrong Athenian's eyes. He searches the woods for **Demetrius** and finds him asleep on the ground. Then Oberon squeezes some of the magic flower's juice onto Demetrius's eyelids to make him fall in love with Helena. Just in time, because in runs **Helena**, chased by **Lysander**. Helena trips over Demetrius, who wakes up and falls instantly in love with her as well. He says, *'O Helena, goddess, nymph, perfect, divine!'* Both Lysander and Demetrius kneel down in front of Helena and, holding her hand, ask her to marry them. Now Helena really doesn't know what is happening. She thinks they must be deliberately trying to confuse her, and she doesn't believe that either of them really loves her. She tries to pull her hands away so she can escape, but they hold on tight, and she is trapped. She say's: *'O spite! O hell! I see you all are bent to set against me for your merriment'*

Meanwhile, on the other side of the forest, **Hermia** wakes up, realises she is all alone, and is very frightened. She jumps up and runs through the trees until eventually she finds the other three. She goes to **Lysander**, but he pushes her away and says, *'Not Hermia, but Helena I love'*. Hermia is really angry. She clenches her fists, screams, and, marching up to Helena points her finger at her and shouts, *'You juggler, you canker-blossom, / You thief of love!'* Helena is really confused! She replies *'Good Hermia, do not be so bitter with me. / I evermore did love you Hermia,'* But Hermia gets angrier and angrier until all four of them have their fists up, ready to fight each other! It's all Puck's fault! **Oberon**, seeing what has happened, is very angry and instructs Puck to sort it out!

Character facts

Hermia

- She is the only child of a strict father (Egeus).
- She has been friends with Helena since they were young.
- She is physically small but has a big temper.
- Her father wants her to marry Demetrius.
- She has been given a warning that if she does not marry Demetrius she will be put to death.
- She shows great courage in standing up to her father in front of the Duke.
- She loves Lysander and agrees to run away with him so that they can marry in secret.
- She cannot believe it when Lysander declares his love for Helena and she tries to scratch Helena's eyes out.

O hell! To choose love by another's eyes.
Act 1 Scene 1

Lysander

- He loves Hermia.
- He is of the same social status as Demetrius.
- He is disliked by Egeus, who accuses him of stealing his daughter's heart.
- He argues that he is as worthy a potential husband as Demetrius.
- He suggests to Hermia that they run away together and go to live with his aunt so that they can be married outside the laws of Athens.
- Puck puts magic juice in his eyes, making him fall in love with Helena.
- Puck reverses the spell and Lysander falls back in love with Hermia.

I am, my lord, as well derived as he,
As well possessed: my love is more than his.
Act 1, Scene 1

Key Objective

To stage Act 3 Scene 2 and deepen understanding of the interpretive choices available in playing the scene.

KS3

4.1 Using different dramatic approaches to explore ideas, texts and issues

5.2 Understanding and responding to ideas, viewpoints, themes and purposes in texts

KS2

Speaking, Listening and Responding, Drama, Understanding and Interpreting Texts, Engaging and Responding to Texts

LESSON DESCRIPTION

Pupils explore the text and action in Act 3 Scene 2 and devise different strategies for staging the scene.

Preparation and Resources

You will need:

▶ A hall or drama studio, or classroom with tables pushed back

▶ 8 sheets of A3 paper with 'Wants, Tactics, Emotions' written at the top of each

▶ **Worksheet 25/25a:** one per pupil

TN This scene, which takes place in the woods between the four lovers, is notoriously difficult to stage. One of the ways we can get to grips with staging scenes like this is through thinking about **wants** and **tactics** . Often an actor will work with their director on deciding what their character wants in a particular scene along with the different kinds of tactics they are going to use to get it. This can be a good way of making the language specific; we speak because we have a strong need for something. If you consider what each character wants in this scene, you will see that their goals are incompatible. For example, Demetrius and Lysander might both want to stay close to Helena; Helena probably wants them to stop mocking her and to run away; Hermia wants to be close to Lysander having found him after a long search. This tangle of conflicting wants can help us untangle the problem of putting the scene on its feet.

 Worksheet 25a provides an alternative edit of Act 3 Scene 2 for younger or less able pupils.

▶ Starter Activity

▶ Pass a clap around the circle, going as fast as possible. Then roll an imaginary ball around the circle in the other direction; pupils have to jump over it as fast as they can. Encourage them to focus so that when they get the clap and the ball at the same time, they are able to pass both on. When they have got the hang of this, add in other rules, for example:

■ When you say 'change' the clap and the ball must change direction.

■ One pupil makes eye contact with another across the circle so that the ball can be picked up and thrown to that person, who must then place it back on the floor and roll it on to the next person.

■ A pupil claps twice, makes eye contact with someone opposite and, through doing so, can pass the clap across the circle.

▶ Explain to pupils that they are now going to work on staging one of the most challenging scenes in *A Midsummer Night's Dream*. It's full of action and pace and requires quick thinking. This starter activity should have given everyone the right kind of energy level to start working on the scene.

Worksheet 25/25a: Act 3 Scene 2

▶ Pupils remain in the circle and do an ***ensemble reading*** ◲ of Act 3 Scene 2. Previous lessons should have established the story so far; however, it is worth reminding pupils what is happening in this scene. As Lysander and Demetrius lie sleeping in different parts of the wood, Oberon and Puck anoint their eyes with the juice of a magic flower which makes them fall in love with the first person they see. Both of them wake up and see Helena and fall madly in love with her. They chase her through the woods, getting more distraught and desperate as she rejects them and shows only disbelief in response to their sudden and, to her, inexplicable affection. Hermia then enters and the boys' rejection of her adds to the general confusion and fuels Hermia's fiery temperament.

▶ After looking at the scene, ask the group questions about each character, such as:

■ *How does Helena feel when Demetrius declares his love for her?*

■ *What does Helena want to do: stay and argue with them, run away, or something else?*

■ *How does Helena feel when Hermia first enters?*

■ *Why does she come to believe that Hermia is also part of the plot?*

There is no one right answer to these questions and it is only through discussion that the group will begin to develop a strong sense of what each of the characters is thinking and feeling in this scene. They should highlight any quotes from the text that they find especially useful.

▶ Main Activity

Worksheet 25/25a: Act 3 Scene 2

▶ Explain to the group they are now going to bring this complex scene to life. To help them, they will use an approach that an actor might take when rehearsing the scene with their director. Explore with the group the following definitions for the terms *setting*, **wants** ⟡, **tactics** ⟡, and *emotion* in relation to this scene.

Setting – Where and when is the scene set? In Act 3 Scene 2 (the scene on their worksheet) what time of day is it? What is the temperature? Is it a relaxed, playful, happy atmosphere, or a tense, threatening, violent one? For older/more able pupils, discuss how each character has found themselves in this particular situation.

Wants – From each character's point of view, what do they want in this scene? Why do they want it? How much do they want it? How long have they wanted it for? For example, Demetrius wants Helena to know he loves her; Lysander wants Helena to know he loves her; Helena wants to escape; Hermia wants Lysander to comfort her.

Tactics – How will each character try to get what they want; what tactics will they use? Are they going to beg, plead with or persuade other people in the scene, in order to get what they want? For example, if Demetrius wants Helena to know that he loves her, he might flatter her, caress her, implore her, beg her.

Emotion – How are the characters feeling? Does this change during the scene, and if so, when exactly? How does it affect their actions and what they want? How do these feelings contribute to the situation?

▶ Decide as a whole group what the setting for the scene will be, for example; *They are in the woods, it is dark. The only light coming though the tall trees is from the moon. The ground is slightly damp and uneven, there are treacherous roots to trip over, and all around is the sound of strange birds hooting and animals scurrying. There is a strong smell of wild flowers and damp wood.* You might want to look back at the designs the group created in Lesson 7. Alternatively you might want to use a whiteboard to create a sequence of pictures from which pupils can choose their setting. Ask:

■ *What difference might the setting make to the performance of a scene?*

▶ Divide the class into eight groups and ask them to refer to the scene on the worksheet. Explain that each group will focus on one of the characters in Act 3 Scene 2, either Lysander, Demetrius, Helena or Hermia (ideally you'll have two groups working on each character). Establish the setting they will use for their scene (this can be the one you have all agreed on as a class in the previous activity). Now give each group an A3 sheet of paper with their character name and *wants*, *tactics* and *emotion* written at the top. Ask them to look through what their character says in the scene and write down what they think their character wants in the scene, what **three** tactics they might use to get it and how they're feeling.

▶ Ask for one volunteer from each character group and choose four of them to form the first group of characters to play the scene with the wants and tactics they have chosen. Then ask the next four to perform with their chosen wants and tactics. Ask the pupils watching both versions of the scene to try and work out what each character wanted and the tactics they were using to get it. Ask:

■ *What did you think worked best? What could be improved?*

■ *Were you able to tell what each character wanted? What tactics did they use to get what they wanted?*

■ *Are the actors establishing their setting clearly? Is the audience 'seeing' where they are?*

■ *Were you able to tell how the characters were feeling?*

▶ Divide the class into new groups of four, and ask them all to have a go at playing their different wants and tactics as they read through the scene.

▶ Finally, ask pupils to devise some strategies for staging this scene. What reactions will help make the text clearer? Each group should devise two simple physical rules to help play the scene, for example:

■ Every time Helena steps towards the exit, both young men take a step towards her.

■ Every time Hermia takes a step towards Lysander, Lysander takes a step back and Demetrius takes a step nearer Helena.

■ Every time Hermia addresses Helena, Helena ducks or cowers.

■ Every time Helena speaks, Hermia pulls a face to the audience.

▶ Ask groups to apply their physical rules to the scene and to rehearse it ready to show. They then **showback** ⟨⟩ their work and invite the audience to spot the physical rules that the group have decided on.

▶ Plenary

▶ Ask:

■ *What new information about the lovers did you discover?*

■ *Of the different interpretations of the characters that you saw, which did you feel was most effective? Why? What evidence from the text can you use to support your answer?*

■ *Some critics of A Midsummer Night's Dream have said that all the lovers are too alike as characters. What do you think of this? What differences between them did you discover or imagine?*

Act 3 Scene 2 (edited)

Demetrius is asleep on the floor. Lysander is declaring his love to Helena.

LYSANDER: Why should you think that I should woo in scorn?

HELENA: These vows are Hermia's. Will you give her o'er?

LYSANDER: Demetrius loves her, and he loves not you you.

DEMETRIUS: *[Awaking]* O Helen, goddess, nymph, perfect, divine!
To what, my love, shall I compare thine eyne?

HELENA: O spite! O hell! I see you all are bent
To set against me for your merriment:
You both are rivals, and love Hermia;
And now both rivals to mock Helena.

LYSANDER: You are unkind, Demetrius; be not so,
For you love Hermia; this you know I know.

DEMETRIUS: Lysander, keep thy Hermia, I will none:
If e'er I loved her, all that love is gone.
Look, where thy love comes, yonder is thy dear.

Enter HERMIA

HERMIA: Why unkindly didst thou leave me so?

LYSANDER: Why should he stay, whom love doth press to go?

HERMIA: What love could press Lysander from my side?

LYSANDER: Fair Helena, who more engilds the night
Than all yon fiery oes and eyes of light.

HERMIA: You speak not as you think; it cannot be.

HELENA: Lo, she is one of this confed'racy!
Now I perceive they have conjoined all three
To fashion this false sport in spite of me.

HERMIA: I am amazèd at your passionate words.
I scorn you not; it seems that you scorn me.

HELENA: Have you not set Lysander, as in scorn,
To follow me and praise my eyes and face?
And made your other love, Demetrius,
To call me goddess, nymph, divine and rare,
Precious, celestial?

HERMIA: I understand not what you mean by this.

DEMETRIUS: *(to Helena)* I say I love thee more than he can do.

LYSANDER: If thou say so, withdraw, and prove it too.

DEMETRIUS: Quick, come!

HERMIA: Lysander, whereto tends all this?

LYSANDER: Hang off, thou cat, thou burr, vile thing, let loose,
Or I will shake thee from me like a serpent!

HERMIA: Why are you grown so rude?
Do you not jest?

LYSANDER: Be certain, nothing truer: 'tis no jest
That I do hate thee and love Helena.

HERMIA: O me!
(*to Helena*) You thief of love!

HELENA: I pray you, though you mock me, gentlemen,
Let her not hurt me; let her not strike me.

HERMIA: Why, get you gone: who is't that hinders you?

HELENA: A foolish heart, that I leave here behind.

HERMIA: What, with Lysander?

HELENA: With Demetrius.
I will not trust you, I,
Nor longer stay in your curst company.
Your hands than mine are quicker for a fray,
My legs are longer, though, to run away.

[Exit]

Act 3 Scene 2 (edited)

Demetrius is asleep on the floor. Lysander is declaring his love to Helena.

LYSANDER: *(to Helena talking about Hermia)* Demetrius loves her, and he loves not you.

DEMETRIUS: *[Awaking]* O Helen, goddess, nymph, perfect, divine!

HELENA: O spite! O hell! I see you all are bent
To set against me for your merriment:

LYSANDER: You are unkind, Demetrius; be not so,
For you love Hermia; this you know I know;

DEMETRIUS: Lysander, keep thy Hermia; I will none.

[Enter HERMIA]

HERMIA: Why unkindly didst thou leave me so?
What love could press Lysander from my side?

LYSANDER: My love, my life, my soul, fair Helena!

HERMIA: You speak not as you think; it cannot be.

HELENA: Lo, she is one of this confed'racy!
Now I perceive they have conjoined all three
To fashion this false sport in spite of me.

DEMETRIUS: *(to Helena)* I say I love thee more than he can do.

LYSANDER: If thou say so, withdraw, and prove it too.

DEMETRIUS: Quick, come!

HERMIA: *(to Lysander)* Why are you grown so rude?

LYSANDER: *(about Hermia)* What, should I hurt her, strike her, kill her dead?
Although I hate her, I'll not harm her so.

HERMIA: Hate me! Wherefore?
Am not I Hermia? Are not you Lysander?

LYSANDER: 'Tis no jest
That I do hate thee and love Helena.

A MIDSUMMER NIGHT'S DREAM
LESSON 12: INTRODUCING THE MECHANICALS

Key Objective

To gain a deeper understanding of the mechanicals.

KS3

4.1 Using different dramatic approaches to explore ideas, texts and issues

5.2 Understanding and responding to ideas, viewpoints, themes and purposes in texts

KS2

Understanding and Interpreting Texts, Drama, Engaging and Responding to Text, Speaking, Listening and Responding

LESSON DESCRIPTION

Pupils use a physical approach to create the characters of the mechanicals and determine their personalities.

Preparation and Resources

You will need:

▶ A hall or drama studio, or classroom with tables pushed back

▶ **Worksheet 26/26a:** one per pupil

 The mechanicals, the *'hempen home-spuns'*, as Puck describes them, are a brilliantly comic, odd assortment of people who will deliver the entertainment for Theseus and Hippolyta's wedding celebration. While Shakespeare sometimes seems to patronise the mechanicals by turning them into figures of fun, he also portrays them with great affection. Bottom is pompous and overblown, tripping himself up with his over-ambition, while dim-witted Snug asks for the lion's part to be written out for him, despite the fact he is told it is *'nothing but roaring'*.

Mechanical literally means 'men who do manual labour', and we quickly discover that back in the real world of Athens, each of these 'actors' has a trade. Exploring their trades gives us an intriguing window into Elizabethan England, where such things as bellows-menders and weavers were common professions; although this play is set in Greece, the world of the mechanicals has a distinctly English 'rustic' feel.

In the play, the mechanicals represent the most corporeal, earthy side of life, in contrast to the ethereal world of the fairies, the formal world of the court and the tempestuous world of the lovers. This lesson uses a physical approach to enable pupils to inhabit the mechanicals from the inside and directly appreciate this contrast.

 Worksheet 26a provides an alternative edit of Act 3 Scene 1 for younger or less able pupils.

▶ Starter Activity

▶ The characters of the mechanicals are:

■ **Peter Quince, the Carpenter:** makes furniture

■ **Bottom, the Weaver:** makes cloth

■ **Francis Flute, the Bellows-mender:** repairs bellows, which are used to increase the flow of air to a fire

■ **Robin Starveling, the Tailor:** makes clothes

■ **Tom Snout, the Tinker:** mends household items such as pots and pans

■ **Snug, the Joiner:** a skilled carpenter, who makes fittings such as cupboards and stairs which involve 'joints' of wood

Discuss with the class what they think each of the jobs entails. Ask:

■ *Are some more familiar to us today than others?*

■ *Do people still do these jobs?*

▶ Assign a job to each pupil (weaver, carpenter, joiner etc.) and ask them to stand in the space and create a repetitive action that demonstrates what their job entails. Ask them to walk around the space at a steady pace, repeating their action, whilst keeping an even spread of bodies throughout the space. If there is a gap they should move into it; ask them to imagine that any bit of floor without a body on it is dying, and in order to save it they must calmly walk into the space.

▶ When they are walking calmly at an even pace and rhythm, ask pupils to imagine they are the mechanical who does that job of work. Tell them that they are at work, finishing off their tasks for the day, and soon they will leave their workplace and head off into the woods for rehearsals. Ask them to think about the job they do and how long they have been doing it. Remember that all the jobs involve manual work: *What parts of the body do they use the most in their jobs? Are there parts of their bodies that feel particularly tired after a day's work?* Ask them to feel where there is any tension or fatigue, and to see how this affects the way they walk.

▶ Main Activity

Worksheet 26/26a: Act 3 Scene 1, the mechanicals
▶ The mechanicals in *A Midsummer Night's Dream*, and the characters they portray in the 'play within a play', are comedic: clearly drawn, with simple motivations. This activity looks at creating characters from a physical starting point. Read through the scene on the worksheet using **ensemble reading** ◪.

▶ Pupils get into pairs and label themselves A and B. The As sit on the floor while the Bs stand up. The As watch their partners

carefully. Ask Bs to start moving around the space allowing one part of their body to lead them as they walk: their head, their elbow, their knees. They should each make a very specific choice about which body part is leading them. (Alternatively you could call out different body parts for them to try.) At first they try and make this look as natural as possible, then, on a cue from you, they push this very slightly so that they exaggerate the shape and pace of their walk according to the part of the body they are following. On a second cue, they push it more so that their walk becomes over-the-top, cartoonish, even slightly grotesque.

▶ The As now stand up and walk behind their partners and mimic them. They should try to copy exactly what their partners are doing: how they move their arms and legs as they walk; how they place their feet on the ground, the position of their head, etc. Ask B to step out and look at their partner's copy of their walk. *What do they think? Is it funny or sad? What sort of people do they see?* As should keep walking in the space.

▶ The As start making eye contact with other people in the space and begin to greet them. How does their walk and stature affect their voice? Ask them to stop and exchange pleasantries with other pupils: *What do they say? Is their choice of words informed by their new physicality? Have they started to imagine a life story for themselves?*

▶ Ask pupils to relax, come back and sit in a circle and discuss what creating a character in this way is like. *How might it be useful for the mechanicals?*

▶ Working in groups of six, ask pupils to look again at the scene on Worksheet 26/26a, where the mechanicals discuss the play and the fact that the lion may frighten the women. Each member of the group should play a part. Ask them to decide on a way of walking and standing for their character. *Which part of the body does he lead with? Think about where he might have tension in his body, or have developed muscles, as a result of his job.* Once they are fully comfortable in their new physicality and feel as if they can remember and hold it, try playing the scene and see what happens.

▶ Plenary

▶ Ask:

■ *Did the physical approach to creating a character make it easier to bring the scene to life? Why?*

■ *What new sense of the mechanicals do you gain from approaching them in this way?*

■ *Remember Puck is going to enter at the end of the scene – what will he see? How do you think he, as an ethereal spirit, might view the mechanicals? What words might he use to describe them?*

■ *What do you think Puck's description of the mechanicals as 'hempen home-spuns' means?*

▶ Homework

▶ Draw a caricature of your character and label it with things you know about the character. These character studies could form part of your display. You might also want to ask pupils to costume their character as their character in the play – how would Bottom dress as Pyramus? Ask students to remember that they wouldn't have lots of money for props etc so they would have had to find most of the materials for their costumes.

Act 3 Scene 1

The wood.
Enter BOTTOM, QUINCE, SNUG, FLUTE, SNOUT and
STARVELING

QUINCE: Here's a marvellous convenient place for our rehearsal. This green plot shall be our stage, this hawthorn-brake our tiring-house, and we will do it in action as we will do it before the duke.

BOTTOM: There are things in this comedy of Pyramus and Thisby that will never please. First, Pyramus must draw a sword to kill himself; which the ladies cannot abide. How answer you that?

STARVELING: I believe we must leave the killing out, when all is done.

SNOUT: Will not the ladies be afeard of the lion?

STARVELING: I fear it, I promise you.

BOTTOM: Masters, you ought to consider with yourselves, to bring in – God shield us! – a lion among ladies is a most dreadful thing. For there is not a more fearful wild-fowl than your lion living. And we ought to look to it.

SNOUT: Therefore a prologue must tell he is not a lion.

QUINCE: Well, it shall be so. But there is two hard things: that is, to bring the moonlight into a chamber, for you know Pyramus and Thisbe meet by moonlight.

BOTTOM: Why, then may you leave a casement of the great chamber window, where we play, open, and the moon may shine in at the casement.

QUINCE: Ay, or else one must come in with a bush of thorns and a lantern, and say he comes to disfigure, or to present, the person of Moonshine. Then there is another thing: we must have a wall in the great chamber; for Pyramus and Thisbe, says the story, did talk through the chink of a wall.

SNOUT: You can never bring in a wall. What say you, Bottom?

BOTTOM: Some man or other must present Wall: and let him have some plaster, or some loam, or some rough-cast about him, to signify wall; or let him hold his fingers thus; and through that cranny shall Pyramus and Thisbe whisper.

QUINCE: If that may be, then all is well. Come, sit down, every mother's son, and rehearse your parts. Pyramus, you begin: when you have spoken your speech, enter into that brake, and so every one according to his cue.

Enter PUCK behind

PUCK: What hempen home-spuns have we swagg'ring here,
So near the cradle of the fairy queen?

Act 3 Scene 1 (edited)

The wood.
Enter BOTTOM, QUINCE, SNUG, FLUTE, SNOUT and
STARVELING

QUINCE: Here's a marvellous convenient place for our rehearsal.

BOTTOM: There are things in this comedy of Pyramus and Thisby that will never please. First, Pyramus must draw a sword to kill himself; which the ladies cannot abide.

STARVELING: I believe we must leave the killing out, when all is done.

SNOUT: Will not the ladies be afeard of the lion?

STARVELING: I fear it, I promise you.

BOTTOM: God shield us! A lion among ladies, is a most dreadful thing;

SNOUT: Therefore a prologue must tell he is not a lion.

QUINCE: Well it shall be so. But there is two hard things: that is, to bring the moonlight into a chamber, for you know Pyramus and Thisbe meet by moonlight.
Then, there is another thing: we must have a wall in the great chamber; for Pyramus and Thisbe, says the story, did talk through the chink of a wall.

SNOUT: You can never bring in a wall. What say you, Bottom?

BOTTOM: Some man or other must present Wall: and let him have some plaster, or some loam, or some rough-cast about him, to signify wall; or let him hold his fingers thus; and through that cranny shall Pyramus and Thisbe whisper.

Enter PUCK behind

PUCK: What hempen home-spuns have we swagg'ring here.
So near the cradle of the fairy queen?

A MIDSUMMER NIGHT'S DREAM
LESSON 13: EXPLORING THE 'PLAY WITHIN A PLAY'

Key Objective

To explore the 'play within the play' ('*The most lamentable comedy and most cruel death of Pyramus and Thisbe*'); its manner of delivery, and its relationship to *A Midsummer Night's Dream* as a whole.

KS3

4.1 Using different dramatic approaches to explore ideas, texts and issues

5.2 Understanding and responding to ideas, viewpoints, themes and purposes in texts

KS2

Listening and Responding, Group Discussion and Interaction, Drama, Understanding and Interpreting Texts and Engaging and Responding to Texts

LESSON DESCRIPTION

Pupils put themselves in the position of the mechanicals and explore the practical requirements of putting on a play, by producing and performing the Prologue of '*Pyramus and Thisbe*'.

Preparation and Resources

You will need:

▶ A hall or drama studio, or classroom with tables pushed back

▶ **Worksheet 27:** one per pupil

▶ **Worksheet 28:** one per group of six students

▶ Plot points summary on six pieces of card (see Starter Activity)

▶ Art and craft materials, for example cardboard, paint, crayons, scissors and fabric

TN The mechanicals, since they all have 'day jobs' and are putting on the play in their spare time, can be described as an amateur theatre group. In the UK today there are thousands of amateur theatre groups who meet in village halls, club rooms, theatres, pubs, etc. People's motives for giving up their free time in order to do this – to make new friends, to have fun, to learn new skills, to entertain etc. – may not be very different from those of the mechanicals in *A Midsummer Night's Dream*. Whatever the motives, it does seem that people are driven to make drama. You could use this lesson to discuss with your class the reasons why people throughout history have been determined to tell stories and make theatre.

The use of the play within a play adds to the overall theatricality of *A Midsummer Night's Dream*. Shakespeare understood the power of drama to make people think and reflect. Most famously, in *Hamlet* we see Prince Hamlet arranging a play that will reveal his stepfather's dark secret: '*The play's the thing / Wherein I'll catch the conscience of the king.*' In *A Midsummer Night's Dream* the mechanicals choose to highlight the theme of love in their play. How does this affect the audience's view of the love stories in the wider play? Does the love between Hippolyta and Theseus, Oberon and Titania, Lysander and Hermia, Demetrius and Helena seem more or less real in comparison with that of Pyramus and Thisbe? These are just some of the questions we can explore through working on '*The most lamentable comedy and most cruel death of Pyramus and Thisbe*'.

LESSON STRUCTURE

▶ Starter Activity

▶ Pupils sit in a circle. Ask:

■ *Have you ever been in a play?*

■ *What was your experience of performing?*

■ *What did you do to prepare for the play?*

▶ Pupils have already (in Lesson 11) met the mechanicals who are putting on a play for Theseus and Hippolyta's wedding, and have seen them rehearsing in the woods. Now introduce the story of the 'play within a play'. The play is a kind of melodrama: this means that the plot and action are much more important than the characters, and the emotions are broad, extreme and clearly drawn. Tell pupils the story of Pyramus and Thisbe using six large pieces of card or paper with one of the following plot points on each:

1. Pyramus and Thisbe are young lovers, who are forbidden from seeing each other by their parents.

2. They live next door to one another. There is a wall that runs between their two gardens and in this wall is a crack, where the lovers talk and arrange a midnight meeting.

3. Thisbe arrives first but, when she gets to their meeting place, she sees a lion nearby. Scared, she runs away, dropping her scarf in the process.

4. The lion picks up the piece of cloth in his mouth and drops it again, leaving it marked with blood stains.

5. When Pyramus arrives, he sees the lion's footsteps and the bloody scarf, assumes the lion has killed Thisbe and kills himself in grief.

6. Thisbe comes back, sees the dead Pyramus with her bloodied scarf, realises what has happened, and kills herself too.

▶ Split the class into six groups. Explain that they are now going to perform a silent movie version of 'Pyramus and Thisbe'. Each group will have a section of the story to work on and then the whole class will perform it in sequence. Explain that, because they are in silence, the acting in silent movies must be big and bold. Give each group one of the large cards with the plot point on it. Ask them to find a way of presenting the card to the audience first: for example, they could dance on with it, they could scroll it horizontally across the stage, and they could make a tableau with the card displayed at the centre. Next, ask each group to act out the plot point written on their card with five or six seconds of action. Remember, the action has to be bold and over the top – this is no place for subtlety! Remind pupils that Flute, a young man, is playing Thisbe and that he doesn't really want to play a woman's part.

▶ Pupils *showback* ◘ their work. Ask groups to remember what they've done as they'll be using this work again later in the lesson.

▶ Main Activity

Worksheet 27: Act 5 Scene 1

▶ Now divide the class into groups of six and do an **ensemble reading** ◨ of the prologue. Explain that a prologue was a popular device in Elizabethan theatre where the audience were told about the play there were going to see. In this prologue, Peter Quince tells the audience about Pyramus and Thisbe to prepare them for the tragedy. Ask pupils what they would need if they were going to stage *'The most Lamentable Comedy and Most Tragical Death of Pyramus and Thisbe'*. Remind pupils that everything the mechanicals used would have to be made and carried to the palace!

They should concentrate on the **props** ◨ and costumes that are essential for telling the story, and should ensure that each character has one object (either a prop or piece of costume) which represents them. Remind groups of the characters:

Quince, the Carpenter – Prologue
Snug, the Joiner – Lion
Bottom, the Weaver – Pyramus
Flute, the Bellows-mender – Thisbe
Snout, the Tinker – Wall
Starveling, the Tailor – Moonshine

▶ **Props and costume-making:** Now ask groups to make one object for each character. Some possible ideas are:

■ Card, coloured pens and wool, to make a simple lion mask for Snug.

■ Recycled cereal boxes to make a wall for Snout.

■ A cuddly toy for a dog.

■ A balloon for the moon.

■ A colourful piece of cloth for Thisbe's scarf, a cape for Pyramus.

■ a scroll of paper for the Prologue.

▶ **Casting:** Ask each group to cast the play, with each member of the group playing one of the parts. First, pupils should make a statue of their character and have a line to speak (distribute Worksheet 28 which contains text spoken by each character in the 'play within the play'.) The character should speak this line and use it to show off their prop/costume.

▶ **Rehearsal:** Ask each group to present their statues, lines and props to the rest of the class. Compare and contrast the choices. Ask the whole group why they made the decisions they did. Decide if certain versions of the characters would work better in new groups; if so, mix the groups up. (For easy comparison, you can line up all the versions of one character next to each other.)

▶ **Performance:** In groups, combine the silent movie techniques, the statues and their props or costumes to create a performance of the prologue from *'The most lamentable comedy and most cruel death of Pyramus and Thisbe'*. The pupil playing Peter Quince could be the narrator whilst the others stand in a line as statues, only coming alive when they are introduced. Alternatively, pupils could break down the prologue so that they each introduce themselves or one of the other characters.

► Plenary

► Ask:

■ *What would happen to A Midsummer Night's Dream as a whole if the 'play within a play' was presented seriously, rather than as a comedy?*

■ *Why is it meant to be funny?*

■ *How does the story of the 'play within a play' reflect the story of the play as a whole? Can you see any connections between the story of Pyramus and Thisbe, and the story of A Midsummer Night's Dream?*

■ *Why do you think Shakespeare included a 'play within a play' in A Midsummer Night's Dream?*

Act 5 Scene 1:

Prologue to 'The most lamentable comedy and most cruel death of Pyramus and Thisbe'

Gentles, perchance you wonder at this show,
But wonder on, till truth make all things plain.
This man is Pyramus, if you would know;
This beauteous lady Thisbe is certain.

This man with lime and rough-cast doth present
Wall, that vile Wall which did these lovers sunder.
And through Wall's chink, poor souls, they are content
To whisper. At the which let no man wonder.
This man, with lantern, dog, and bush of thorn,
Presenteth Moonshine. For, if you will know,
By moonshine did these lovers think no scorn
To meet at Ninus' tomb, there, there to woo.

This grisly beast, which Lion hight by name,
The trusty Thisbe, coming first by night,
Did scare away, or rather did affright.
And as she fled, her mantle she did fall,
Which Lion vile with bloody mouth did stain.
Anon comes Pyramus, sweet youth and tall,
And finds his trusty Thisbe's mantle slain;
Whereat, with blade, with bloody blameful blade,
He bravely broached his boiling bloody breast.
And Thisbe, tarrying in mulberry shade,
His dagger drew, and died. For all the rest,
Let Lion, Moonshine, Wall, and lovers twain
At large discourse, while here they do remain.

Prologue: Our true intent is. All for your delight

Wall: That I, one Snout by name, present a wall.

Pyramus: I fear my Thisbe's promise is forgot.

Thisbe: My love thou art, my love I think.

Lion: When lion rough in wildest rage doth roar.

Moonshine: Myself the man i'th'moon doth seem to be.

ROMEO AND JULIET

ROMEO AND JULIET

This chapter suggests single lesson plans for working on *Romeo and Juliet*, which you can use as and when you think they are appropriate. Some of the lesson plans are linked but all of them can stand alone. You could use the lessons in the sequence offered here, or if you prefer you can pull out single lessons to add to an existing scheme of work. Each lesson plan models an approach which you can transfer and apply to any of Shakespeare's plays.

You will be able to deliver most of this work in your own classroom with the tables and chairs pushed back. Some lessons may require a larger space to work in.

Title photograph: RSC Production of *Romeo and Juliet* (2006)
Photographer **Ellie Kurttz**

CONTENTS

ROMEO AND JULIET
LESSON 1: EXPLORING THE PROLOGUE

Key Objective

To introduce the action of the play.

To explore the dramatic technique and convention of prologues.

KS3

4.2 Developing, adapting and responding to dramatic techniques, conventions and styles

5.2 Understanding and responding to ideas, viewpoints, themes and purposes in texts

KS2

Listening and Responding, Group Discussion and Interaction, Drama, Understanding and Interpreting Texts and Engaging and Responding to Texts

LESSON DESCRIPTION

As an introduction to *Romeo and Juliet*, pupils translate and bring to life the Prologue.

Preparation and Resources

You will need:

▶ A hall or drama studio, or classroom with tables pushed back

▶ Enough chairs for everyone in the biggest circle you can make in the available space

▶ A whiteboard or flipchart

▶ **Worksheet 1:** one per pupil

▶ **Worksheet 2:** one per pupil

 Prologues, epilogues and choruses were among a variety of dramatic conventions used by the Elizabethan playwrights. Others included masques, soliloquies, songs, dumb-shows and the five-part play structure. The bare stage of the Elizabethan theatre is one explanation for the popularity of prologues and choruses, inviting audiences to use their imaginations in travelling to distant times and places. Even so, why would Shakespeare want to give the game away in the first fourteen lines of the play? And what is the effect of this choice on his theatre audiences? This lesson asks pupils to consider these questions after they have gathered all the information available from the Prologue about the action of the play. And it is all there: the death of the two young protagonists, the family feud, the power of fate, children defying parents to find their own path, the clash between duty and love. The Prologue is, of course, a sonnet, and you may wish to explore the characteristics of this verse form as an extension activity.

 Although notes are provided on the Prologue worksheet, with younger or less able pupils, you may want to work through the more difficult language with them at the end of the starter exercise.

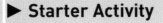

LESSON STRUCTURE

▶ Starter Activity

▶ Start with pupils sitting in a circle. Tell them they are going to be detectives looking for clues to the storyline of *Romeo and Juliet*. As a first step you will read them the opening lines of the play and will want them to echo, or repeat after you, any words they think are especially important. How much information can they discover just from listening? Pupils close their eyes while you read, in order to give their full attention to the words.

▶ Tell pupils they are now going to create some of the words and phrases they echoed. Ask them to push back the chairs, find a partner and spread out through the space so that all pairs are equidistant from one another. Everyone needs a good amount of space around them. Tell them they have a count of five to create ***freeze frames*** ◨ of:

■ *'two households'*

■ *'two foes'*

■ *'star-crossed lovers'*

■ *'death-marked love'*

■ *'parents' rage'*

■ Ask pupils what they have discovered so far about what happens in the play. Record their insights on a whiteboard or flipchart.

▶ Main Activity

Worksheet 1: The Prologue
▶ Divide the class into groups of four or five. Allocate two successive lines of the Prologue to each group until all seven pairs of lines have been assigned. Ask the groups to translate their two lines into their own words, using the notes on the worksheet to help. Tell them to be prepared to speak their lines aloud so that a part of the group speaks the original text and the others speak the modern version.

▶ Groups ***showback*** ◨ their work so that the whole class get to hear the prologue lines alongside the modern paraphrase.

▶ Now ask each group to create a sequence of actions which tell the story of their two lines from the prologue. The sequence should begin and end in a ***freeze frame*** ◨ and Shakespeare's lines should be spoken during the action. Groups can choose one person or the whole group to say the lines during the sequence of actions. Give pupils about five minutes to prepare their pieces, then position the groups around the space in speech order so that the Prologue runs in sequence.

▶ Plenary

Worksheet 2: Recording your discoveries

▶ Pupils continue working in the same small groups. Ask them to record on Worksheet 2 what they have discovered about the story of *Romeo and Juliet*, the characters in it and why they think Shakespeare chose to give us the ending of the play in the first fourteen lines. To prompt their written work, ask:

■ *What effect does it have on the audience if they know what happens before the action of the play starts?*

■ *For example, how might they feel when Romeo and Juliet die, just as the prologue has told us?*

▶ Pupils share their thoughts with the rest of the group.

▶ Homework

▶ Ask pupils to design a poster for a production of *Romeo and Juliet* based on what they have learnt from the Prologue. What images from the prologue would they use to base their design around? If appropriate, ask them to accompany the poster with a paragraph explaining their choices.

The Prologue

CHORUS:

Two households, both alike in dignity,

In fair Verona, where we lay our scene,

From ancient grudge break to new mutiny,

Where civil blood makes civil hands unclean.

From forth the fatal loins of these two foes

A pair of star-crossed lovers take their life,

Whose misadventured piteous overthrows;

Doth with their death bury their parents' strife.

The fearful passage of their death-marked love;

And the continuance of their parents' rage,

Which, but their children's end, nought could remove,

Is now the two hours' traffic of our stage;

The which if you with patient ears attend,

What here shall miss, our toil shall strive to mend.

► **Notes**

'**dignity**': social standing and importance

'**ancient grudge**': a quarrel passed down through generations

'**civil**': involving ordinary citizens, not the military or police

'**fatal loins**': from parents whose actions kill their children

'**whose misadventured piteous overthrows**': whose tragic ending

'**but**': except for

'**traffic**': activity or business

'**what here shall miss**': what is left out here

'**mend**': fix or repair

The Prologue to *Romeo and Juliet*

Now that you have investigated the Prologue to Shakespeare's *Romeo and Juliet*, what clues did you find that tell you what will happen in the story? Record your discoveries below, together with information about the way the Prologue is put together and how you feel about the story of this play.

1 List all the facts that you've discovered about the story of *Romeo and Juliet*. For example, who are the main characters? What causes the tragedy? Why? What happens in the end?

2 What have you noticed about the way the Prologue is written? Why do you think Shakespeare wrote it this way?

3 How do you feel about being given so much information about the story at the start of the play? Why might Shakespeare have chosen to do this?

ROMEO AND JULIET
LESSON 2 : AN ACTOR'S APPROACH TO ACT 1 SCENE 1

Key Objective

To introduce the **world of the play** .

To explore the language and action of Act 1 Scene 1.

KS3	KS2
4.2 Developing, adapting and responding to dramatic techniques, conventions and styles	Speaking, Listening and Responding, Group Discussion and Interaction, Drama, Understanding and Interpreting Texts, Engaging and Responding to Texts
6.2 Analysing how writers' use of linguistic and literary features shapes and influences meaning	

LESSON DESCRIPTION

Pupils and teacher enact sections of Act 1 Scene 1.

Preparation and Resources

You will need:

▶ A hall or drama studio, or classroom with tables pushed back

▶ Enough chairs for everyone laid out in the biggest circle possible

▶ A cloak

▶ **Resource Sheet 1:** displayed on a whiteboard, flipchart paper or sugar paper on the wall

▶ **Resource Sheet 2:** Prince Escalus' speech from Act 1 Scene 1. Learn this speech in advance if possible or read from the resource sheet

▶ **Worksheet 3:** one per pupil

TN In working through the text of *Romeo and Juliet*, we discover that Verona is a place with a very clear set of expectations. Respect for the social hierarchy, for the church, for one's elders, for one's parents, are facts of life in this world. In this first scene of the play, the audience is invited into the sub-culture that threatens the stability of the city. We see how the young people of Verona challenge the dominant culture with their own way of talking, with their own gestural language. The play wrestles with the question of identity, a question that is as relevant now as it was when Shakespeare wrote the play. We know it is urban, hot and a place in which '*ancient grudge*' breaks to '*new mutiny*': all things that could be true of a place in the Mediterranean 500 years ago, or places like Birmingham, Kabul or Dover now. Verona is a close community, claustrophobic even. It is of paramount importance to be included in society. Exclusion is unthinkable. Every community experiences the tensions that Shakespeare explores in the play to a greater or lesser degree, so the young people you work with can imagine the **world of the play** with direct relevance to their own lives.

1

'According to the social code of the time, it is the duty of the young to obey the old.'
RSC Shakespeare Complete Works: Edited Jonathan Bate and Eric Rasmussen, 2007

'There is no world without Verona walls'
Act 3 Scene 3

▶ Starter Activity

▶ Pupils form a circle. Work through the following as a whole class, allowing a minute for each:

■ Pupils walk around the space, avoiding eye contact with each other.

■ Pupils now make eye contact as they pass each other.

■ Pupils make and hold eye contact with another pupil.

■ Pupils join up with their eye contact partner. This person is in their gang.

■ Pupils walk around with their gang partner, making sure that everybody else in the room understands they are together.

■ Gang partners regard everybody else in the room as a potential enemy, and show their 'enemies' how they feel about them using just eye contact.

▶ As the partners continue moving, ask them to listen and respond to this information:

■ *They are in a place called Verona where there are rival gangs – the Capulets and the Montagues. They have always hated each other.*

■ *They are in the market place, the public space in the centre of Verona. Fighting is against the law. It is hot.*

2

▶ Stop the exercise, ask each pair of pupils to join another pair and sit down in groups of four. Ask:

■ *How did you feel during the eye contact exercises?*

■ *How did you behave?*

■ *What happened to your body language and facial expressions when you heard who you were and about the circumstances you were in? What happened to the way you used the space – how close did you get to other people? How far away did you want to be?*

1

▶ Main Activity

Worksheet 3: Act 1 Scene 1

▶ Explain to pupils that one pair in each group will be Capulets – Samson and Gregory, and one pair will be Montagues – Abraham and Balthasar (a non-speaking part in this edit). Pupils decide who will be which character within their group. They read the script aloud to each other.

 ▶ Ask:
■ *Does it make sense?*

■ *Is it always clear who is talking to whom? Which lines are confusing?*

■ *What do you think is happening in the line 'I will frown as I pass by them'?*

■ *What does 'bite your thumb' mean?* Demonstrate the biting thumb gesture and explain that this is the worst insult in Verona. Ask pupils if they can think of insulting gestures that are used today. Biting your thumb is the equivalent.

■ *What does 'Draw if you be men' mean?* (Draw your weapons to prove you are men.)

 ▶ In their small groups, pupils read through the script again, this time moving as they speak and remembering their discoveries from the previous activities, using their eyes, faces and bodies as well as the words to communicate. The Capulets and Montagues must start the scene some distance apart and move towards each other, imagining it is the market place of Verona.

▶ *Blocking* ⟨⟩: Pupils discuss exactly how they think the scene should be played and set agreed movements and positioning for the scene. Explain that there is no right way of doing this and they should do what feels right to them. Give pupils at least five minutes to block their scene.

Resource Sheet 1: Fighting Talk

 ▶ Display the words on Resource Sheet 1. Tell pupils that they do not have any actual weapons to use in the scene, but that they will instead use words as weapons. Explain that the words on display are insults used by different characters throughout the play. On a count of three, ask them to call out the words on Resource Sheet 1, making the most of each insult.

▶ Ask pupils to repeat the exercise, this time making the most of the sounds in the words (for example, exaggerating the vowels in the word *Liar!* or the consonants in the word *Ratcatcher!*).

▶ Explain that pupils will simultaneously 'perform' Act 1 Scene 1 as a whole class using Worksheet 3, but when they get to the end of the scene they will start to *improvise* ⟨⟩ using the 'Fighting Talk' insults from Resource Sheet 1. There is one rule: they must not physically touch each other. Show them the cloak and explain that it belongs to another character in the play. Tell pupils that you will be in the scene as that character, and that when they see you wearing the cloak they should react to you as that character.

Resource Sheet 2: Prince Escalus

 ▶ *Teaching in role* ⟨⟩: Pupils perform their scenes simultaneously. Once every group has reached the 'Fighting Talk' and is improvising, put the cloak on, walk into the centre of the room, and use your disciplinary voice to deliver Prince Escalus' speech, bringing the action to a halt.

▶ Take off the cloak and ask pupils to sit back down in the circle with the 'gang' partner they have been working with.

► Plenary

► Pupils discuss with their partner:

■ *What have we found out about the character who intervened?*

■ *Why did he intervene in the conflict?*

■ *What did he say and why?*

■ *How did we feel?*

■ *How did he feel? How did we know?*

■ *What is the new law that he has imposed? What does 'on pain of death' mean?* (The death penalty has been imposed.)

■ *Why do we think Shakespeare chose this moment for Prince Escalus to enter the scene?*

■ *What does it feel like to be part of a gang?*

■ *Why do we think the Capulets and Montagues are enemies?*

► Pairs feed back their findings to the whole group.

Worksheet 3: Act 1 Scene 1

► Pupils think again about the words used in the scene. Ask:

■ *Why is the word 'sir' repeated so often in the scene?* (It is a polite term used as an insult, sarcastically.)

■ *Why is 'bite your thumb' repeated?* (To give the characters a chance to repeat the physical insult, pretending that they are simply clarifying.)

■ *What clues did you find in the words which told you where to move?*

■ *Could a similar argument happen today?*

■ *Where and in what circumstances today might an argument like this happen?*

Resource Sheet 2: Prince Escalus

► Display Prince Escalus' words. Ask:

■ *Which words reveal who he is and what his relationship is with the citizens involved in the scene?*

■ *Which words reveal how he feels?*

■ *Why does he repeat the death penalty in the speech?*

▶ Homework

▶ Ask pupils to write an explanation of why Shakespeare chose to set the first scene of *Romeo and Juliet* in the marketplace of Verona. It should cover:

■ A description of the scene.

■ An explanation of why Shakespeare uses repetition in the scene.

■ An explanation of how Shakespeare structures the scene to create dramatic tension.

■ An explanation of where they would choose to set the scene if they were staging a production of the play for today, and why.

Act 1 Scene 1 (edited)

GREGORY: I will frown as I pass by, and let them take it as they list.

SAMPSON: Nay, as they dare. I will bite my thumb at them, which is a disgrace to them if they bear it.

ABRAHAM: Do you bite your thumb at us, sir?

SAMPSON: I do bite my thumb, sir.

ABRAHAM: Do you bite your thumb at us, sir?

SAMPSON: Is the law of our side, if I say ay?

GREGORY: No.

SAMPSON: No, sir, I do not bite my thumb at you, sir, but I bite my thumb, sir.

GREGORY: Do you quarrel, sir?

ABRAHAM: Quarrel sir? No, sir.

SAMPSON: If you do, sir, I am for you. I serve as good a man as you.

ABRAHAM: No better?

SAMPSON: Yes, better.

ABRAHAM: You lie.

SAMPSON: Draw, if you be men.

Fighting Talk

VILLAIN	DOG
RATCATCHER	SLAVE
ROGUE	COWARD
SCURVY KNAVE	BEAST
LIAR	FOOL

Act 1 Scene 1 (edited)

PRINCE ESCALUS:

Rebellious subjects, enemies to peace,

Profaners of this neighbour-stained steel-

Will they not hear? – What, ho! You men, you beasts,

Throw your mistempered weapons to the ground,

And hear the sentence of your movéd prince.

Three civil brawls, bred of an airy word,

By thee, Old Capulet, and Montague,

Have thrice disturbed the quiet of our streets.

If ever you disturb our streets again,

Your lives shall pay the forfeit of the peace.

Once more, on pain of death, all men depart.

▶ **Notes**

'Profaners of this neighbour-stained steel': you spoil your swords by staining them with your neighbours blood

'mistempered': created for the wrong reasons

'moved': angry

'pay the forfeit of the peace': be the price for spoiling the peace

---

ROMEO AND JULIET
LESSON 3: EXPLORING A KEY THEME: LAW AND ORDER

Key Objective

To explore the theme of law and order in the play.

KS3	KS2
3.1 Developing and adapting discussion skills and strategies in formal and informal contexts	Speaking, Listening and Responding, Group Discussion and Interaction, Drama

LESSON DESCRIPTION

This is an **In-role meeting** ◌ in which pupils and teacher debate law and order. Pupils should be aware of the long-standing feud between the Capulets and the Montagues, that fighting on the streets is against the law of Verona and that Prince Escalus is in charge of law and order in the city.

Preparation and Resources

You will need:

▶ A cloak

▶ **Resource Sheet 3:** cut up into the separate roles and placed in a hat

▶ **Worksheet 4:** one copy

▶ A circle of chairs (this is not essential. The lesson can be delivered in a traditional classroom layout)

▶ A whiteboard or flipchart

TN In this sequence pupils are invited to imagine the everyday lives and concerns of the people of Verona by adopting a point of view on a difficult dilemma. They address the question, *'What can be done to stop the violence on Verona's streets?'* but in so doing they will be addressing the same question for contemporary culture. The teacher's role here is high status. As Prince Escalus talking to his citizens, you will have the same, if not more, authority over the group as you do out of role. If you decide to delegate the chairing of the meeting to a pupil in-role, it is important to choose someone who has presence in the group. This will not necessarily be the most academic pupil. It is useful to choose a pupil who has the respect of their peers. Delegating the authority of the role can offer a pupil who has limited written skills but good oracy skills an opportunity to prove what they can achieve.

LESSON STRUCTURE

1

▶ Starter Activity

▶ Pupils recap on what they have discovered about the situation in Verona. Ask:

■ *Who is the feud between?*

■ *What is against the law?*

■ *Who is in charge of the city?*

2

Resource Sheet 3: In role categories
▶ Pupils work in groups of three. One member per group pulls a role for their group from the hat. Pupils use the following questions to discuss their role, imagining that they are in the story.

■ *How old are they?*

■ *What is their relationship with each other?*

■ *Is one of them in charge?*

■ *How does the conflict between the Capulets and Montagues affect their lives?*

▶ Tell the pupils that they come each week to the marketplace in Verona on market day. They should decide on a reason for this visit: is it to buy food? For work? To meet friends?

1

▶ Main Activity

Worksheet 4: A public meeting notice
▶ Each small group of three introduces themselves in role, and explains why they usually come to the market place. Display the worksheet on the whiteboard or flipchart and explain that this is posted on the marketplace wall. Ask pupils what the meeting is about and where and when it will take place.

▶ In their small groups, pupils discuss in-role why they want to attend the meeting.

▶ Explain that you will take on the role of Prince Escalus, and that you will wear the cloak to symbolise that character. Go into a corner, put on the cloak, adopt the role of Prince Escalus and turn back to the class to open the public meeting.

'To know our further pleasure in this case. To old Free-town, our common judgement place.'
Act 1 Scene 1

▶ ***Teaching in-role*** ◖: Prince Escalus thanks the citizens for coming to the meeting. He invites each group of citizens to say why they have come, then explains that he needs their help and advice. Recently, the violence on the streets of Verona has escalated and it is affecting the lives of innocent, law-abiding citizens. He needs the citizens to recommend three measures that he should put into place in order to stop the fighting. The Prince invites initial suggestions (and may go on to chair the rest of the meeting).

▶ If there are limited ideas from the group, suggest possibilities.

A curfew? A weapons amnesty? Increasing fines? Community service? Closing down the marketplace?

▶ After a short time the Prince can delegate another member of the group to take on the role of chair, and leave the meeting on the premise of having important business elsewhere, but setting a strict time limit for his return when the citizens must make their recommendations. After five minutes, you return in-role as the Prince, take the recommendations of the group and promise to consider them.

▶ Take off the cloak and explain that the meeting is over.

▶ Plenary

▶ Out of role, ask the pupils:

■ *Why do you think that 'ancient grudge' has broken to 'new mutiny' in Verona?* (quote from The Prologue)

■ *Do you think Prince Escalus will find a peaceful solution? Why / Why not?*

■ *Does the situation in Verona remind you of any events in the news?*

■ *What effect does conflict have on a community?*

■ *Why do you think Shakespeare wrote this play? What did he want us to think about?*

▶ Ask pupils to write down one recommendation from the meeting that they think will help reduce violence on the streets. These could be displayed in the classroom under the heading 'What the citizens of Verona think'.

ROMEO AND JULIET
RESOURCE SHEET 3

GROUP ONE
You are a poor family whose business is trading at the market.

GROUP TWO
You are a group of local elderly people.

GROUP THREE
You are Prince Escalus' men, a group of law enforcement officers.

GROUP FOUR
You are a group of teenagers who do not belong to either the Capulet or the Montague household.

GROUP FIVE
You are a family who run a place to eat and drink in the marketplace.

GROUP SIX
You are a group of servants in the Capulet household.

GROUP SEVEN
You are a family whose son has been killed in a street fight.

GROUP EIGHT
You are a family whose business is weapons-making.

GROUP NINE
You are a group of servants in the Montague household.

GROUP TEN
You are a group of teachers at the local school. You are responsible for the young people that you teach.

By Order of Prince Escalus

A PUBLIC MEETING

LAW AND ORDER ON OUR STREETS

How can we protect our city from violence?

TONIGHT 6pm

THE MARKET PLACE

The Prince invites all citizens of Verona to an open public meeting to discuss ways of tackling the rising number of street fights and violent crimes affecting our community. Attendees will be invited to contribute their ideas to the debate.

ROMEO AND JULIET
LESSON 4: AN ACTIVE APPROACH TO EXPLORING THE STORY

Key Objective

To understand and become familiar with the whole story of the play.

KS3

1.2 Understanding and responding to what speakers say in formal and informal contexts

5.2 Understanding and responding to ideas, viewpoints, themes and purposes in texts

KS2

Speaking, Listening and Responding, Group Discussion and Interaction, Drama, Understanding and Interpreting Texts

LESSON DESCRIPTION

The whole class are involved in enacting the story of the play.

Preparation and Resources

You will need:

▶ A hall or drama studio, or classroom with tables pushed back

▶ Enough chairs for everyone in the biggest circle you can make in the available space. Younger pupils may be more comfortable sitting on the floor

▶ **Resource Sheet 4:** You should be familiar with this in advance. It is particularly effective if you are able to learn it but not essential

TN The strategies used in this lesson can be used to tell the whole story or just a part of it. You could use these ideas to 'fill in' between one scene which you have studied in detail and another later in the play. You could use them to tell *backstory* . You could also use them as introductory or revision activities.

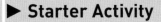

LESSON STRUCTURE

▶ Starter Activity

▶ Pupils sit in a circle. Explain that they are all going to be involved in telling the whole story of the play: you will tell the story and the pupils will be all of the different people and things in the story. You will point to a pupil when it is their turn and they will stand up and come into the middle of the circle, making the shape of whoever or whatever has just been described. If they are a person, you might give them things to do or say. All the pupils have to do is listen to the story and react to what is being said.

▶ To ensure they understand what to do, use the following as an example. Ask them if anyone can think of a place where things happen in the *Romeo and Juliet* story and take suggestions, for example *a balcony*. Then point to three pupils and ask them to come and make the shape of the balcony. Nominate two further pupils to be Romeo and Juliet to demonstrate how the balcony can be used. For example, 'Romeo' could kneel underneath one side whilst 'Juliet' leans out over the other. Explain that pupils will stay in the circle as part of the story until the circle gets too crowded. When that happens, you will say **'Whoosh!' ⟨⟩** and wave your hands; this will be the cue for everybody who is in the circle to return as quickly as they can to their places. Demonstrate this with the pupils who are the balcony and Romeo and Juliet.

▶ Main Activity

▶ Resource Sheet 4: Romeo and Juliet *Whoosh* ⟨⟩
Tell the story with energy and pace. Nominate pupils sequentially round the circle, regardless of gender, to come up for their turn. Every character or object that is highlighted in bold in the text is the thing the pupil/s will come into the circle to create. Any direct speech in bold italics is first said by you, then repeated by the pupil representing that character. At the end of the story, encourage pupils to give each other a big round of applause.

▶ Now ask pupils to work in groups of five or six. Tell them that they are illustrators but that they are only allowed to have one illustration for the whole story. Their task is to make that illustration together as a *freeze frame* ⟨⟩. Everyone in the group must be involved in it, but they do not have to be characters, they can also be things. They can choose what they think is the most important moment in the story, or they can choose to make an illustration showing what they think the story is about. Set a strict time limit in which they must make their freeze frame (5 mins). You can make this activity competitive if you think it will motivate pupils.

▶ Keep giving reminders of time to prompt pupils to make decisions and work together effectively. Encourage them to imagine an audience looking at their freeze frame, and the need for them to be able to see everything in the illustration.

▶ When each group has achieved a freeze frame, tell pupils that you will give a ten-second countdown and that all the groups will show their work simultaneously.

► Count down from ten and when you reach zero, remind the pupils to hold their positions. Congratulate the pupils when they achieve their freeze frames.

► Plenary

► Discuss the choices that each group made for their illustration *freeze frame* ⧉. As described in the common bank of activities, highlight key themes, ideas, characters, relationships and moments from the action of the play that the pupils have selected for their work.

Romeo and Juliet: WHOOSH!

Once upon a time in the city of Verona, there were two great families: the Capulets and the Montagues. On one side of the city lived **Lord Capulet**, who was rich and powerful. He lived with his wife **Lady Capulet**, who always stood by her man, and they had an only child – a daughter, **Juliet**, who was fourteen. Like most wealthy young girls of the time, Juliet spent most of her time at home, under the watchful eye of her parents, BUT the person she learnt most about the world from was her **Nurse**. The Nurse loved Juliet with all her heart: she had worked for the Capulets since Juliet was born, and she was more like a mum to Juliet than Lady Capulet was. These two whispered their secrets to each other and were the best of friends. The Capulets also had a nephew called **Tybalt** of whom they were very fond, despite his bad temper.

On the other side of town were **Lord and Lady Montague** and their son Romeo. **Romeo** was a lover, not a fighter. He sighed, and he dreamed of perfect love, and the only thing that could distract Romeo from romance were his mates, **Benvolio** and **Mercutio**, the lads. Verona's finest, they strutted around the streets together.

For as long as anyone could remember, the Capulets and the Montagues had hated one another. They scowled and shook their fists at each other. No-one knew what it was about, but the feud was deep and bitter.

WHOOSH!

One day this ancient grudge broke to new mutiny. A gang of **Capulets** and a gang of **Montagues** faced each other in the street. The Capulets shouted, *'Down with the Montagues'* and the Montagues shouted, *'Down with the Capulets!'* and they bit their thumbs at each other, which was the worst insult that you can imagine. And then they all drew out their swords, and cried, *'Cowards!'*.

Luckily, at that moment **Prince Escalus** arrived – he was in charge of law and order in the city. So, when he raised his hand, the street fell silent. As he walked between the warring families he declared, *'If ever you disturb our streets again, your lives shall pay the forfeit of the peace ... On pain of death, all men depart!'*

WHOOSH!

Meanwhile, **the Montagues** were worried about their son **Romeo**. He was depressed and moody, so they called on his cousin **Benvolio** to find out what the matter was, then hastily moved to a discreet distance and waited to find out what Benvolio could discover. Benvolio tried to cheer Romeo up, but Romeo was in love with a girl called **Rosaline**, who had sworn to become a nun. There was no way she was ever going to return Romeo's love. She would continue to turn her back on him. Benvolio said, *'Be ruled by me; forget to think of her!'* but Romeo simply shook his head and said, *'O, teach me how I should forget to think.'* And with a hand on his heart, and another on his brow, he wandered off.

WHOOSH!

ROMEO AND JULIET
RESOURCE SHEET 4: CONTINUED

Love and marriage were also in the thoughts of Verona's most eligible young bachelor, **Paris**. He was very rich, and he was Prince Escalus' nephew, so as he walked around the streets every young woman tried to catch his eye. But Paris made a deal with **Lord Capulet**. When Juliet was old enough she would be Paris' wife. They shook hands on this arrangement, and then Lord Capulet decided that he would throw a great big party where Paris and Juliet could be introduced. He sent for a servant, **Peter**, and gave him a long list of guests to invite.

Off Peter set to deliver the invitations. He turned the list one way and then the other, but he could not read, so he went out all around Verona, giving invitations to everyone. EVEN **Romeo** and his mates **Benvolio** and **Mercutio** got invited by mistake.

WHOOSH!

At the Capulets' house, **Juliet** was getting ready for the big night helped by her **Nurse**. In came her mother, **Lady Capulet**, who announced, *'The County Paris seeks you for his love!'* The Nurse was delighted but Juliet shrugged. She would wait to see what this Paris was like. In came **Lord Capulet** striding around the room, hosting the party, and welcoming the guest of honour, **Paris**. Paris approached Juliet and bowed, she curtsied and away they danced around the room. Meanwhile **Tybalt**, Juliet's cousin, acted as bouncer: he kept a close eye on everything, one hand on his sword. Things were going very well, until **Romeo**, **Benvolio** and **Mercutio** entered the party in disguise.

Tybalt recognised Romeo and drew out his sword, but Lord Capulet calmed him down, not wanting anything to spoil his daughter's big night. Across the crowded room, Romeo and Juliet spotted each other. They fell instantly in love, and moved towards each other. Their fingertips touched, and Romeo bent to kiss Juliet's hand. But suddenly, the Nurse was at Juliet's side, pulling her away, and Benvolio pulled Romeo away. The party was over.

WHOOSH!

But ... **Romeo** did not go home. Instead, he found his way to Juliet's bedroom window. High above him was a **balcony**. Soon, Juliet appeared and called out, *'O Romeo, Romeo, wherefore art thou Romeo?'* Romeo climbed up the balcony, went down on one knee and asked Juliet for *'The exchange of thy love's faithful vow for mine.'* Juliet, overjoyed, cried, *'If that thy bent of love be honourable, thy purpose marriage, I'll follow thee my lord throughout the world.'*

WHOOSH!

Next morning **Romeo** rushed to see his friend, the local priest, **Friar Laurence**. He begged the Friar to perform a secret wedding ceremony and the Friar, hoping that this might bring peace between the Montagues and Capulets, agreed. The wedding was on. **Juliet** and the **Nurse** sneaked out of the Capulet house, through the streets of Verona to the church, then Juliet knelt with Romeo in front of the Friar, with the Nurse acting as best woman. The Friar blessed their marriage, the nurse threw confetti, and the deed was done. Romeo and Juliet were married.

WHOOSH!

Later, on the streets of Verona, tensions were running high. **Benvolio** and **Mercutio** were out and about. It was hot and sticky and Benvolio could see that trouble was brewing. He said to Mercutio, *'The day is hot, the Capulets abroad, / And if we meet we shall not scape a brawl, / For now is the mad blood stirring.'*

Sure enough, along came **Tybalt** with his **gang** from one direction, and **Romeo** from another. Tybalt, still angry that Romeo had gatecrashed the party, drew his sword and challenged Romeo, saying, *'I hate hell, all Montagues, and thee!'*. But Romeo held out his hands in peace, and would not fight. Mercutio couldn't stand by and see his friend Romeo insulted, so he drew out his sword, and fought with Tybalt. Romeo tried desperately to stop them, but as he jumped in between them, Tybalt stabbed Mercutio under Romeo's arm, and Mercutio fell to the floor. Romeo desperately tried to help his friend but Mercutio, with his last breath, said, *'A plague on both your houses!'* and died!

Romeo leapt up with fury burning in his heart. Now he faced Tybalt and drew out his sword. Back and forth they parried, until Romeo stabbed Tybalt right through the heart and Tybalt fell to the floor, dead. There was a moment of disbelieving silence, then Romeo ran away. Just at that moment, in came **Prince Escalus** with his **police officers**. The officers took hold of all the young men. In ran **Lord and Lady Capulet** and **Lord and Lady Montague**. They gasped in horror when they saw the bodies of Mercutio and Tybalt. Lady Capulet turned to the Prince and cried bitterly, *'I beg for justice, which thou, Prince, must give! Romeo slew Tybalt, Romeo must not live!'* But Benvolio fell on his knees and told the Prince what had happened, and the Prince, hearing how Romeo had tried not to fight, was merciful. He declared, *'For that offence, immediately we do exile him hence.'* Lady Montague was so upset at the thought of never seeing her son again, she died of grief.

WHOOSH!

Back at Juliet's house, **Juliet** was pacing up and down in her room, waiting for Romeo, when in came the **Nurse** with the terrible news: *'Tybalt is killed, and Romeo is banished.'* Juliet was horrified: she wept, then sent the Nurse to find Romeo. The nurse went straight to **Friar Laurence** and found **Romeo**. Once again, in secret, the Friar and the Nurse arranged for Romeo to climb up to Juliet's window. (Ssh!) Then they tiptoed away, leaving Romeo and Juliet to enjoy their wedding night.

WHOOSH!

Next morning, **Romeo** and **Juliet** were lying in each other's arms, saying a last tearful goodbye, when there was a knock at the door. Romeo leapt up, climbed out through the window and down the balcony as quickly as he could, and ran off to exile in Mantua. In burst **Lady Capulet** and the **Nurse**. Lady Capulet pulled her daughter to her feet, dried her tears and told her that it had been arranged for her to marry Paris next Thursday.

Juliet stamped her foot and said *'No!'* but then in came her father, **Lord Capulet**. When he heard that Juliet had refused Paris, he was incredibly angry. He went up to Juliet, as close as he could, and jabbed a finger into her face, warning her: *'An you be mine, I'll give you to my friend. An you be not, hang, beg, starve, die in the streets!'* Then he stormed out, closely followed by Lady Capulet and the Nurse. Juliet was alone. She went to see the **Friar**, who came up with a cunning plan. Into a little bottle, he put a pinch of herbs. He gave it a shake and handed it to Juliet. It was a sleeping potion that was so strong, it would make her appear dead. The Friar wrote a letter to Romeo explaining the plan and asking him to come and take Juliet away to Mantua. The Friar then gave the letter to another **priest** to take to Romeo in Mantua.

WHOOSH!

That night, **Juliet** went to her bedroom alone. She took out the bottle, swigged the sleeping potion and fell, as if dead, to the floor. Next morning, the day of the wedding, the **Nurse** came to wake the bride-to-be. She shook Juliet gently, then more vigorously, but she could not wake her and cried *'O woeful day!'* In came **Lady Capulet**, **Paris**, **Lord Capulet** and the **Friar**. They gasped, and shook Juliet, but no one could wake her. She was surely dead! So, they lifted her up to take her to her funeral.

WHOOSH!

Meanwhile the **priest** carrying the letter for Romeo was suspected of having the plague and was kept from travelling by **two armed guards**. They would not let him leave and the letter was never delivered to Romeo. Meanwhile, in Mantua, **Romeo** was sitting sighing and pining for his wife when in came his servant **Balthasar** to tell him the news that Juliet was dead. Romeo was devastated, so much so that he wanted to die. He bought a tiny bottle of deadly poison, which he put in his pocket, then set off back to Verona to the tomb where Juliet lay.

WHOOSH!

At the tomb lay **Juliet**, as still as stone, mourned by **Paris**, who knelt by her body and wept. In came **Romeo**. They drew swords and fought until Paris was wounded and died. Then Romeo reached into his pocket and pulled out his little bottle of poison; drinking it down, he kissed Juliet one last time, and cried, *'Thus with a kiss, I die'*. Moments later, Juliet stirred and awoke. When she saw Romeo dead, she pulled out his dagger and stabbed herself. Just then, in rushed **Friar Laurence, the Prince, Lord and Lady Capulet**, and **Lord Montague**. As one, they drew back in horror. The Prince was first to speak. He stepped forward, saying, *'Where be these enemies? Capulet? Montague? See, what a scourge is laid upon your hate ... all are punished.'* Lord Capulet held out his hand to Lord Montague. They shook hands and made peace. Then, **all Verona** stood to pay their respects to the young lovers as the Prince declared,

'For never was a story of more woe,
Than this of Juliet and her Romeo.'

THE END

ROMEO AND JULIET
LESSON 5: STAGING ACT 1 SCENE 5

Key Objective

To understand how staging choices affect our interpretation of Act 1 Scene 5.

LESSON DESCRIPTION

Pupils stage the Capulets' party, Act 1 Scene 5. They should be aware of who the characters in the play are and of the relationships between them.

Preparation and Resources

This lesson is complex and requires thorough preparation for effective classroom management. You will need:

▶ A hall or drama studio, or classroom with tables pushed back

▶ Chairs: enough for everyone, arranged along three sides of the room

▶ Props: a table and five chairs, a tablecloth, candlesticks, a wine bottle, five plates

▶ **Resource Sheet 5:** You could cut these lines up into individual texts to be given out to the pupils, or simply speak the lines for individual pupils to repeat

▶ **Worksheet 5:** six copies

▶ **Worksheet 6:** twenty copies

▶ **Worksheet 7:** one per pupil

▶ Pencils: one per pupil

▶ Plenary questions displayed on a whiteboard, flipchart or sugar paper on the wall

 There are many scenes like this one in Shakespeare's plays: public events, which involve multiple characters, during which an important private conversation takes place. In order for pupils to make a constructive set of choices about *staging* ◌ a scene, and be able to write about those choices, they must have the opportunity to work with a group of their peers to explore the interpretive possibilities. It is only by setting up the scene and speaking the lines with all the relevant characters present that we can understand the complexity of staging such a scene. This sequence is a transferable approach, which involves the whole class, and enables pupils to:

▶ Discover what it feels like to be in the scene.

▶ Understand how theatre practice brings the scene to life for an audience.

▶ Solve the staging challenges.

▶ Understand the risks that Romeo and Juliet take in their first meeting.

It might be useful for pupils to know at this point that in Elizabethan society, women had secondary status to men and their primary role was to be a wife and mother. Most marriages in high society were arranged and it was legal to marry from the age of twelve, although many women did not marry until they were older.

LESSON STRUCTURE

▶ Starter Activity

▶ Pupils sit on the chairs. The chairs represent three walls of the room where the party takes place. Explain that Lord Capulet holds a party in order for his daughter, Juliet, to meet Paris, the rich relative of Prince Escalus. Lord Capulet has arranged for Juliet to marry Paris.

▶ Divide the pupils into three groups. Group One (six pupils) are actors playing the Capulets and Paris; Group Two (seven pupils) are directors; and Group Three (the rest of the class) are actors playing servants and guests. Group Three will work in pairs with the person sitting next to them.

Worksheet 5: The Capulets and Paris
▶ Pupils in Group One, the Capulets and Paris, decide who will be which character and read aloud to each other the information about their characters on the worksheet. They discuss the questions at the bottom of the sheet. Pupils decide what age their character is, choose an adjective to describe their character and decide what their character's attitude to the party is.

Worksheet 6: The servants and guests
▶ Pupils in Group Three, the servants and guests, are characters at the party. In pairs, they discuss what activity they will be doing at the party and how they will carry it out. Pupils decide what age their character is, choose an adjective to describe their character and decide what their character's attitude to the party is.

▶ Pupils in Group Two, the directors, create the stage space. Decide with them where they think the table and chairs should be and where entrances in the room should be. For example, where do the guests enter from? Where do the Capulets enter from? What about the servants? Move the furniture to establish the layout of the room that they suggest.

'Young women in this society are stared at, policed, controlled, owned. Juliet is a young woman who is under house arrest. One of the first questions in the play is: 'Where is my daughter?'
Neil Bartlett, director of the RSC's 2008 production of Romeo and Juliet.

▶ Main Activity

▶ The directors explain the layout of the room to the rest of the class. Each pair of pupils in Group Three introduces themselves in character as servants or guests and explains what they will be doing during the party. Discuss with the directors the order in which the servants and guests will enter the party. The only rule is that the scene must start with the table being set.

▶ The servants setting the table have the **props** ◧ and the servants and guests enter in the suggested order, interacting in character, remembering their adjective and attitude. They speak to each other in character. When all the servants and guests have entered, pupils in Group One introduce themselves in character as the Capulets and Paris, then enter the scene in the order they have decided. Stop the scene. Explain that the actors will repeat the sequence; the directors must watch carefully and pick out one thing that they like and want to keep in the scene, and one thing they would like to change. Pupils repeat the sequence, then ask the directors what they want to keep and what they want to change.

Resource Sheet 5: Act 1 Scene 4

▶ Ask the actors to take out any improvised spoken words next time the scene is played. Allocate Shakespeare's lines to the actors indicated, and explain that they can use them whenever they like during the sequence.

▶ Pupils play the scene again, this time using only Shakespeare's lines.

▶ Explain that Romeo Montague comes to the party and that somehow Romeo and Juliet meet and talk to one another. Choose one member of Group Three to be Romeo – they form a pair with the pupil playing Juliet. Ask everybody else to work in pairs with the person next to them.

Worksheet 7: The meeting of Romeo and Juliet

▶ All pupils will now look at Romeo and Juliet's first meeting during the party scene. Distribute pencils and ask pupils in pairs to stand back-to-back and read the words aloud to each other, listening carefully. They underline any words that are repeated. Their task is to find the 'secret sign language' in the words by choosing a gesture that could go with the repeated words, for example, opening their hands on *'palm'* and kissing the back of their hand on *'kiss'*. They must not touch one another.

▶ Pupils read the scene face-to-face in their pairs, using their secret sign language, then sit down on the chairs. Collect in the worksheets and pencils, except from the pupils being Romeo and Juliet in the second part of the main activity.

▶ Ask pupils to listen whilst Romeo and Juliet read the scene using their secret sign language. Pupils must consider how Romeo and Juliet could talk to each other in this way without Juliet's family interrupting or overhearing.

▶ Explain that every time this scene is staged, the director has to decide what the other characters are doing at the moment when Romeo and Juliet meet, so that the audience can concentrate on what Romeo and Juliet are doing and saying. Tell the class that they will now decide how to stage the private meeting between Romeo and Juliet within the context of the party scene they have been working on. Ask:

■ *How does Romeo come in to the party?*

■ *When, and exactly how, do they notice each other?*

■ *Where are they when they speak to each other?*

■ *How do they manage to hold this secret conversation without Juliet's family interrupting or overhearing?*

■ *What would Juliet's father do if he knew she was being so secretive with the son of his worst enemy?*

■ *What would Paris do if he saw Juliet being so secretive with another man?*

▶ Ask the actors to run through their entrances into the party again, but this time to continue acting as Romeo enters the scene, meets Juliet and starts speaking to her. The directors must watch carefully.

▶ Ask the directors if anything was confusing or unclear and for their ideas to make the scene clearer. Suggest the following ideas that other directors have tried:

■ Everyone except Romeo and Juliet freezes.

■ Everyone except Romeo and Juliet is distracted by an event outside and goes to the window to look out.

■ Time slows down and everybody except Romeo and Juliet moves in slow motion.

▶ Ask the actors to try out one or two of these ideas. Explain that there is no such thing as the 'right' way of staging this or any other scene in a play; as long as pupils can justify their ideas, they can stage the scene however they like. Ask the directors to comment on which of the ideas they think works best in allowing the audience to see, hear and feel involved in Romeo and Juliet's secret meeting, and why?

▶ Plenary

 ▶ Display the following questions on a whiteboard, flipchart or sugar paper on the wall:

■ *Why does Shakespeare choose the party as the place where Romeo and Juliet meet?* (To make the audience feel anxious or excited for them? To make the audience understand how deeply they feel for each other? To make the audience understand how risky it is for them?)

■ *What do you think should be made clear to the audience in the scene?*

■ *How should the scene be staged to make this clear, and why?*

▶ Explain that Shakespeare often writes scenes like this one in which a big, public event includes a secret conversation between two characters.

■ *Why do you think Shakespeare does this?*

▶ Homework

▶ Ask pupils to imagine they have been asked to direct this scene, then to write an account of what they think should be happening at the moment that Romeo and Juliet meet. The account must include:

■ An explanation of why Shakespeare chooses for Romeo and Juliet to meet at the party.

■ An explanation of what they think is the most important thing to make clear in the scene.

■ A description of how the scene should be staged, explaining their choices.

Group One

LORD CAPULET

■ He is head of the Capulet household.
■ He thinks he knows what is best for his daughter Juliet, and has chosen Paris to be her husband.
■ He has arranged the party so that Paris and Juliet can meet.
■ He expects Juliet to obey his orders.
■ He has been in a long standing dispute with the Montagues.

LADY CAPULET

■ She married Lord Capulet when she was a teenager.
■ She obeys her husband.
■ Juliet is her only child.

TYBALT

■ He is a nephew of the Capulets.
■ He is Juliet's cousin.
■ He has a bad temper.
■ He hates the Montagues.

JULIET

■ She is nearly 14 years old and has never been in love.
■ She is Capulet's only daughter.

NURSE

■ She has looked after Juliet since she was a baby.
■ She loves Juliet and they are very good friends.
■ Lord Capulet pays her wages and she lives with the Capulets.

PARIS

■ He is a rich nobleman, related to the Prince of Verona.
■ He wants to marry Juliet and has arranged this with her father.

▶ Decide:

■ How old is your character?
■ What adjective might best describe your character (for example bossy, shy, fussy, lazy)?
■ What is your character's attitude to the party? Are they pleased to be there or only there because they have to be?
■ How will the characters behave towards one another at the party?
■ Who will enter the room first, and why?
■ Will any of these characters come in together?
■ Who will stick close to whom, and why?

Group Three

TABLE SERVANTS
- Your job is to set the table and provide clean glasses and cutlery when required.

GUARDS
- Your job is security.

CLOAKROOM ATTENDANTS
- Your job is to take people's coats and keep them safe during the party.

RICH FRIENDS OF LORD CAPULET
- You want to see who Lord Capulet has arranged for his only daughter to marry.

OLDER RELATIVES OF THE PRINCE
- You want to find out about the family that Paris intends to marry into.

TEENAGERS
- This is the first big party that you have been to.

FOOD SERVERS
- Your job is to make sure that the guests get their food on time and on demand.

DRINK SERVERS
- Your job is to make sure that anyone who wants a drink has one.

MUSICIANS
- Your job is to entertain the guests.

CLEANERS
- Your job is to make sure that everything stays tidy and organised

▶ **Decide:**

- How old is your character?
- What adjective might best describe your character (for example bossy, shy, fussy, lazy)?
- What is your character's attitude to the party? Are they pleased to be there or only there because they have to be?
- What activity are you doing at the party? What is your relationship with your partner?

Act 1 Scene 5 (edited)

DRINKS SERVER: You are looked for and called for, asked for and sought for.

TABLE SERVANT: We cannot be here and there too.

GUARD: Cheerly, boys, be brisk awhile.

RICH FRIEND OF LORD CAPULET: More light, you knaves.

TEENAGER: Come, musicians, play.

CLEANER: Away with the joint-stools.

FOOD SERVER: Look to the plate.

All character names have been created for the purpose of this exercise.

Act I, Scene 5 (edited)

ROMEO: If I profane with my unworthiest hand
This holy shrine, the gentle sin is this:
My lips, two blushing pilgrims, ready stand
To smooth that rough touch with a tender kiss.

JULIET: Good pilgrim, you do wrong your hand too much,
Which mannerly devotion shows in this,
For saints have hands that pilgrims' hands do touch,
And palm to palm is holy palmers' kiss.

ROMEO: Have not saints lips, and holy palmers too?

JULIET: Ay, pilgrim, lips that they must use in prayer.

ROMEO: O, then, dear saint, let lips do what hands do.

JULIET: You kiss by th' book.

ROMEO AND JULIET
LESSON 6: THE BAND OF BROTHERS (PART ONE)

Key Objective

To introduce Romeo, Benvolio and Mercutio and explore their relationship.

KS3	KS2
4.1 Using different dramatic approaches to explore ideas, texts and issues	Understanding and Interpreting Texts, Engaging and Responding to Text and Drama
5.2 Understanding and responding to ideas, viewpoints, themes and purposes in texts	

LESSON DESCRIPTION

Pupils explore the relationship between Romeo, Mercutio and Benvolio.

Preparation and Resources

You will need:

▶ A hall or drama studio, or classroom with tables pushed back

▶ **Worksheet 8/8a:** one between two pupils

 This is the first of two lessons exploring the relationships between Romeo, Mercutio and Benvolio. The lessons should make the characters come alive for the pupils, evoking their different reactions and opinions: sympathy, empathy, admiration, dislike, etc.

It is easy to imagine that the three young men have been friends for a long time – they share jokes, finish each other's sentences and are relaxed in each other's company. We know that Romeo and Benvolio are cousins and we imagine that perhaps all three were at school together or at least spent time together as children. It is crucial to understand the strength of kinship and loyalty in order to fully appreciate the tragedy of Mercutio's death and its effect on the course of the play. Mercutio is the only one of Romeo's immediate friends who wants to fight, and it is Mercutio who is the first to pay with his life: a strong message in itself. It is Mercutio's desire to fight that sets off the catalogue of disasters that carries us through to the end of the play. This lesson allows pupils the opportunity to explore the depth of the relationship between the three characters and the importance and complexity of kinship and loyalty in the play.

 Worksheet 8a provides an alternative edit of Act 1 Scene 4 for younger or less able pupils.

LESSON STRUCTURE

► Starter Activity

► Ask pupils, in groups of three, to label themselves 'Friend 1', 'Friend 2' and 'Friend 3'. Tell them: *You are going to make **freeze frame** ◘ using just your bodies. You should do this without talking, using body language to communicate.*

► Call out the following titles and ask them to make a freeze frame to match each one. Give them a five-second countdown for each.

■ *Friend 1 and Friend 2 teasing Friend 3*

■ *Friend 1 upset and the other two comforting him/her*

■ *Friend 1 arguing with Friend 2, with Friend 3 being the peacemaker*

■ *Friends 1, 2 and 3 celebrating*

■ *Friends 1 and 2 searching for Friend 3, who is hiding*

■ *Friend 1 giving Friend 2 advice about love, with Friend 3 looking on in amusement*

► As pupils create their freezes and if they are familiar with the story, link them to Romeo, Benvolio and Mercutio, speculating with the class about how the images connect to the three friends. If the class are unfamiliar with the play, use the images to illustrate the relationship between three characters you are going to be exploring in more detail in the lesson.

► Main Activity

Sculpting: Explain that pupils will now work in pairs to explore the characters of Romeo, Benvolio and Mercutio. Ask pupils to label themselves A and B. A is a sculptor and B is the clay. The exercise must take place in silence so that the only communication is physical. B's eyes should remain closed.

► B first of all stands in neutral pose. The sculptor sculpts him/her into a young man trying to stop a fight (allow up to 30 seconds). The sculptor is to imagine the sculpture saying:
'Part, fools!
Put up your swords; you know not what you do.'

► The sculpture then becomes animated by moving between the neutral position and the sculpted position, thinking about how it makes him/her feel. The sculpture should add in the line that the sculptor used for inspiration. Ask the pupils:
Do any other lines, or sounds, come to mind as you change position? If so, you should voice them. (Pupils could be asked to note these down after they have voiced them.)

► Ask the pairs to swap so that B is now the sculptor and A is the clay. A stands in a neutral pose and then B sculpts him/her into a

RSC Shakespeare Toolkit for Teachers   234   **ROMEO AND JULIET**

young man trying to cheer up his friend and get everyone in a party mood. The sculptor is to imagine the sculpture saying:
'Nay, gentle Romeo, we must have you dance'.

▶ The sculpture should become animated and move between the neutral and sculpted positions, thinking about how it makes him/her feel. Again, the sculpture should try saying the inspiration line. Ask them if any other lines or sounds come to mind as they change position. If so, they should voice them.

▶ Finally, ask the pairs to swap again, so that A is the sculptor again and B is the clay. They repeat the exercise, this time making the image of a young man in love. The sculptor imagines the sculpture saying:
'Is the day so young?
Ay me! Sad hours seem long'.

▶ Pupils to come back and sit in a circle. Ask:
Can you guess who you have just created sculptures of?

▶ If pupils are less familiar with the story, tell them that they have created sculptures of Romeo, his cousin Benvolio and his friend Mercutio, and they have used the first line that each of the characters speak in the play to do this. Shakespeare knew he had to seize the audience's imagination right from the very first line; therefore, the first line a character speaks is often crucial in giving clues to the audience about the sort of character they are going to see develop through the play. First lines often arouse instant curiosity.

▶ Ask the pupils to discuss the characters they have just sculpted:

■ *What do the lines suggest about the character who speaks them?*

■ *What do you think they are like?*

■ *Do they remind you of any people you know?*

▶ Tell them they are going to decide on a **backstory** ◻ for how the three young men met.

Worksheet 8/8a: Character stories
▶ Working in groups of three, ask pupils to read through the character stories on the worksheet and invent three **freeze frames** ◻ depicting:

■ *a moment from Benvolio, Mercutio and Romeo's mutual past which encapsulates their friendship*

■ *a happy, shared significant moment*

■ *a sad, shared, significant moment.*

▶ The groups should then **showback** ◻ their work and the freeze frames can be interrogated by the rest of the group, for example:

■ *What is happening in the picture?*

■ *Where is the scene taking place?*

▶ What has just happened in frames can also be *thought tracked* ⟨⟩.

▶ Ask each group to bring one of their freeze frames to life for five seconds. *What does this add to your understanding of what is happening and what the characters are feeling?*

▶ Tell pupils that this kind of improvisation work is commonly used by actors and directors in rehearsals to help create the backstory to different sets of character relationships. Ask:

■ *How does this work add to our understanding of the characters? Who do we empathise with and who do we want to know more about?*

▶ Plenary

▶ Ask pupils what they have learned about the three main characters – Romeo, Mercutio, and Benvolio – and about the friendship between them, for example:

■ *What kind of a person is Mercutio?*

■ *What words would you use to describe him?*

■ *Does he remind you of any other characters from books, films or plays you have seen?*

■ *How would you describe the relationship between the three characters?*

■ *How have the activities helped you develop an understanding of the characters?*

Character stories

MERCUTIO: Relative of the Prince, friend of Romeo and Benvolio

1. Although he is one of Romeo's best friends, there are signs that Mercutio's constant teasing tries Romeo's patience.
2. When Romeo is lovestruck and unable to join in the festive party mood, before gatecrashing the Capulet party, Mercutio tries to tease him out of his sadness.
3. When Romeo is threatened by Tybalt, following Tybalt's discovery that Romeo has gatecrashed the party, Mercutio expects Romeo to fight. However, Romeo refuses because Tybalt is Juliet's cousin and therefore his kinsman.
4. Mercutio is enraged and fights Tybalt himself. Romeo tries to intervene and Mercutio is stabbed under Romeo's arm.
5. As Mercutio dies, he cries out, *'a plague on both your houses'*, meaning a plague on Tybalt's and Romeo's houses: the Montagues and the Capulets.
6. A joker to the end, he makes one final pun: *'ask for me tomorrow and you shall find me a grave man'*.

ROMEO: Son of Lord and Lady Montague, Benvolio's cousin, Mercutio's friend

1. Romeo wants no part in the ongoing feud between his family and the Capulets. When Benvolio tells him of the latest fight in the street, he says, *'Why then, O brawling love, O loving hate, O anything of nothing first create! ... This love feel I, that feel no love in this.'*
2. At the beginning of the play, Romeo is pining with love for Rosaline.
3. He and Benvolio accidentally discover Rosaline is invited to a party at the Capulets' house. They know that, as Montagues, they will not be welcome; however, they decide to gatecrash, along with Mercutio. They wear masks so that no-one will recognise them.
4. At the party, Romeo meets and falls instantly love with the Capulets' only daughter, Juliet.
5. Later that night, Romeo and Juliet meet secretly and agree to marry, despite their families' hatred and long-standing feud.
6. They marry the following day, but their marriage is thrown into chaos when Juliet's cousin Tybalt duels with and kills Romeo's friend Mercutio. Romeo is so enraged about the death of his friend that he kills Tybalt, and the Prince of Verona then banishes him from the city.
7. Meanwhile, Juliet's father plans to marry her off to Paris, a local Count.
8. Desperate, Juliet begs Romeo's friend, Friar Laurence, to help her escape the marriage.
9. He gives her a potion that puts her into a death-like sleep.
10. The plan works, but before Romeo learns the truth of it, he receives word that Juliet is dead and so plans to kill himself.
11. Romeo returns to Juliet's grave, drinks poison and dies.
12. Shortly afterwards, Juliet wakes up; finding her beloved Romeo dead, she kills herself.

BENVOLIO: Nephew of Lord and Lady Montague, friend of Romeo and Mercutio

1. The name Benvolio means good-will or peacemaker.
2. Right from the start he tries to prevent the fighting between the Montagues and the Capulets.
3. Benvolio spends most of Act 1 attempting to distract his cousin Romeo from his infatuation with Rosaline.
4. In the scene where Tybalt kills Mercutio, Benvolio carries the fatally wounded Mercutio offstage, and returns to tell Romeo of Mercutio's death.
5. He then reports the story of Mercutio and Tybalt's deaths truthfully to the Prince. Benvolio does not return to the play after this scene. However, crucially, he is the only one of the young generation from either family to survive the play (as Romeo, Juliet, Paris, Mercutio, and Tybalt are all dead by the end of the play).

Character stories

MERCUTIO: Relative of the Prince, friend of Romeo and Benvolio

1. When Romeo is too lovestruck to join in the festive party mood, before gatecrashing the Capulet party, Mercutio tries to tease him out of his sadness.

2. When Romeo is challenged to a fight by Tybalt, Mercutio expects Romeo to fight. When Romeo refuses, Mercutio is angry and fights Tybalt himself. Romeo tries to stop the fight and Mercutio is stabbed under Romeo's arm.

3. As Mercutio dies, he cries out, *'a plague on both your houses'*, meaning a plague on Tybalt's and Romeo's houses: the Montagues and the Capulets.

ROMEO: Son of Lord and Lady Montague, Benvolio's cousin, Mercutio's friend

1. At the beginning of the play, Romeo is in love with Rosaline. He and Benvolio discover Rosaline is invited to a party at the Capulets' house. They know that, as Montagues, they will not be welcome; however, they decide to gatecrash, along with Mercutio. They wear masks so that no-one will recognise them.

2. At the party, Romeo meets and falls instantly love with the Capulets' only daughter, Juliet. Later that night, Romeo and Juliet meet secretly and agree to marry, despite their families' hatred and long-standing feud.

3. Their marriage is thrown into chaos when Juliet's cousin Tybalt fights with and kills Romeo's friend Mercutio. Romeo, in revenge, kills Tybalt, and the Prince of Verona then banishes him from the city.

4. Meanwhile, Juliet's father plans to marry her off to Paris, a local Count. Juliet is desperate, so Friar Laurence, (Romeo's teacher and friend) gives her a potion that puts her into a death-like sleep.

5. Romeo thinks Juliet is really dead, goes to her grave and kills himself.

6. Shortly afterwards, Juliet wakes up; finds her beloved Romeo dead and kills herself.

BENVOLIO: Nephew of Lord and Lady Montague, friend of Romeo and Mercutio

1. The name Benvolio means good-will or peacemaker. Right from the start he tries to prevent the fighting between the Montagues and the Capulets.

2. In the scene where Tybalt kills Mercutio, Benvolio carries the fatally wounded Mercutio offstage, and returns to tell Romeo of Mercutio's death.

3. He then truthfully reports the story of Mercutio and Tybalt's deaths to the Prince.

4. He is the only one of the young generation from either family to survive the play (Romeo, Juliet, Paris, Mercutio, and Tybalt are all dead by the end of the play).

ROMEO AND JULIET
LESSON 7: THE BAND OF BROTHERS (PART TWO)

Key Objective

To consider the relationship between Romeo, Mercutio and Benvolio through staging Act 1 Scene 4.

KS3

4.1 Using different dramatic approaches to explore ideas, texts and issues

5.2 Understanding and responding to ideas, viewpoints, themes and purposes in texts

KS2

Understanding and Interpreting Texts and Engaging and Responding to Texts

LESSON DESCRIPTION

Pupils continue exploring the relationship between Romeo, Mercutio and Benvolio.

Preparation and Resources

You will need:

▶ A hall or drama studio, or classroom with tables pushed back

▶ Worksheet 9/9a: one per pupil

 This is the second of a two-part lesson. Having made some decisions about the history of the relationship between Romeo, Mercutio and Benvolio, pupils now undertake a close reading of Act I Scene 4 in which Mercutio and Benvolio persuade Romeo to gatecrash the Capulet's party. At this point in the play, Romeo is in love with Rosaline and pining for her. Exploring this early scene gives us the opportunity to look at the dynamics of the relationship between the three men.

 Worksheet 9a provides an alternative edit of Act 1 Scene 4 for younger or less able pupils.

► Starter Activity

► Pupils form a circle. Ask them to listen for a signal from you. When you say *'go'*, they must:

■ Visit all four corners of the room, in any order, as fast as they can, *then*:

■ Return to the centre, make the weirdest most exaggerated shape possible and freeze, *then*:

■ Copy the shape of any person they can see.

► Repeat the copying exercise several times. Each time, pupils should exaggerate the shape they make.

► Explain that during the lesson, pupils will be putting themselves in the shoes of three boys who are gate-crashing a party: Romeo, Mercutio and Benvolio. They will need boldness and bravery to do this. Exaggerating shapes is a way of getting in touch with the kind of energy they'll need to perform the scene the class is about to explore.

► Main Activity

Worksheet 9/9a: Act 1 Scene 4

► Start by getting the pupils into a circle. Explain that the three friends, Romeo, Benvolio and Mercutio are about to gatecrash a party at the Capulet's – the party is a masked ball. Ask for volunteers to play each character. (The parts of Mercutio and Romeo could be divided between two or more pupils.)

► Ask the volunteers to sit in the middle of the circle and read the scene aloud twice in quick succession. Tell them not to worry if they don't understand some of the words. When they have finished the second read through, ask: *Does it make sense? Is it always clear who is talking to whom? Which lines are confusing?*

► Ask the pupils to think about who the characters are: *What is your first impression of each of them? How do the characters enter the space? Remember it is a masked ball. What are they wearing? What are they carrying?*

► Explain the meaning of character status. Ask: *Who has the highest status in the scene? How might this be shown? Does it stay the same throughout the scene, or does it change? If so, where?* Also ask: *How do the others in the scene respond to Mercutio's humour?*

► Ask pupils to form into groups of four or five. Using Worksheet 9/9a, groups should allocate parts to each other being aware that the roles of Romeo and Mercutio can be divided between two or more pupils. Explain that you will be asking groups to work through Act 1 Scene 4 in a variety of ways.

► Ask each group to play the scene in the following ways:

■ First read through the scene as if Romeo is trying to *convince* Mercutio that he is in love and wants Mercutio to take it seriously.

■ Now read the scene as if Mercutio is *fed up* with Romeo's love sickness and determined to make him look stupid.

■ Now as if Mercutio's teasing has been going on for some time and Romeo is *sick and tired* of hearing it.

■ Finally, read the scene as if Benvolio *recognises and understands* that Romeo is fed up and attempts to get them into the house before Romeo changes his mind about going to the party.

▶Plenary

 ▶ Ask:

■ *Which way of playing the scene did you feel worked best? Why?*

■ *What sort of relationship do you think these young men have? Is it like any of the relationships you have with your friends?*

Act 1 Scene 4 (edited)

A street.
Enter ROMEO, MERCUTIO, BENVOLIO, with five or six
Maskers, Torch-bearers, and others

ROMEO: Give me a torch, I am not for this ambling.
Being but heavy, I will bear the light.

MERCUTIO: Nay, gentle Romeo, we must have you dance.

ROMEO: Not I, believe me. You have dancing shoes
With nimble soles, I have a soul of lead
So stakes me to the ground I cannot move.

MERCUTIO: You are a lover, borrow Cupid's wings,
And soar with them above a common bound.

ROMEO: I am too sore enpiercèd with his shaft
To soar with his light feathers and so bound,
I cannot bound a pitch above dull woe:
Under love's heavy burden do I sink.

MERCUTIO: And to sink in it should you burden love,
Too great oppression for a tender thing.

ROMEO: Is love a tender thing? It is too rough,
Too rude, too boist'rous, and it pricks like thorn.

MERCUTIO: If love be rough with you, be rough with love:
Prick love for pricking, and you beat love down.
Give me a case to put my visage in,
A visor for a visor!

BENVOLIO: Come, knock and enter, and no sooner in,
But every man betake him to his legs.

ROMEO: A torch for me:
I'll be a candle-holder, and look on.
The game was ne'er so fair, and I am done.

MERCUTIO: We waste our lights in vain, light lights by day.

ROMEO: And we mean well in going to this masque,
But 'tis no wit to go.

MERCUTIO: Why, may one ask?

ROMEO: I dreamt a dream tonight.

MERCUTIO: And so did I.

ROMEO: Well, what was yours?

MERCUTIO: That dreamers often lie.

ROMEO: In bed asleep, while they do dream things true.

MERCUTIO: O, then I see Queen Mab hath been with you:
She is the fairies' midwife, and she comes
In shape no bigger than an agate-stone
On the forefinger of an alderman,
Drawn with a team of little atomies
Over men's noses as they lie asleep.

ROMEO: Peace, peace, Mercutio, peace!
Thou talk'st of nothing.

MERCUTIO: True, I talk of dreams,
Which are the children of an idle brain,
Begot of nothing but vain fantasy,
Which is as thin of substance as the air.

BENVOLIO: Supper is done, and we shall come too late.

ROMEO: I fear too early, for my mind misgives
Some consequence yet hanging in the stars
Shall bitterly begin his fearful date
With this night's revels and expire the term
Of a despisèd life closed in my breast
By some vile forfeit of untimely death.
But he that hath the steerage of my course,
Direct my suit. On, lusty gentlemen!

Exeunt

Act 1 Scene 4 (edited)

Enter ROMEO, MERCUTIO, BENVOLIO, with five or six Maskers, Torch-bearers, and others

ROMEO: Give me a torch, I will bear the light.

MERCUTIO: Nay, gentle Romeo, we must have you dance.

ROMEO: Not I, believe me.

BENVOLIO: Come, knock and enter.

ROMEO: I'll be a candle-holder, and look on.

MERCUTIO: We waste our lights in vain, light lights by day.

ROMEO: I dreamt a dream tonight.

MERCUTIO: And so did I.

ROMEO: Well, what was yours?

MERCUTIO: That dreamers often lie.

ROMEO: In bed asleep, while they do dream things true.

MERCUTIO: O, then I see Queen Mab hath been with you:
She is the fairies' midwife.

ROMEO: Peace, peace, Mercutio, peace!

BENVOLIO: Supper is done, and we shall come too late.

ROMEO: I fear too early, for my mind misgives
Some consequence yet hanging in the stars
Shall bitterly begin his fearful date
With this night's revels.

Exeunt

Key Objective

To help pupils enjoy Shakespeare's language and understand how poetic technique creates meaning.

KS3	KS2
6.2 Analysing how writers' use of linguistic and literary features shapes and influences meaning	Speaking, Group Discussion and Interaction, Drama, Understanding and Interpreting Texts and Engaging and Responding to Text
10.2 Commenting on language use	

LESSON DESCRIPTION

Pupils explore Shakespeare's verse technique as he applies it to Mercutio's Queen Mab speech, and create a choral piece reflecting their understanding.

Preparation and Resources

You will need:

▶ A hall or drama studio, or classroom with tables pushed back

▶ **Worksheet 10/10a:** one per pupil

▶ Four objects to inspire stories: for example, a rain stick, a brass pot, a chiffon scarf, a small box – anything that might be imagined to have magic properties would be effective

▶ Groups of chairs in four areas of the room. Each group of chairs should face another group of chairs

 Choral speaking ◘ has an ancient and honourable heritage, dating from the ancient Greek plays of Aeschylus, Sophocles, Euripides and Aristophanes. In the first half of the 20th century choral speaking was a part of most childrens' education, until its popularity waned, possibly because it was often taught as a kind of rote learning exercise without pupils fully understanding what they were saying or why they were saying it. In fact, it is an excellent way of giving insight into literary technique and building enthusiasm for speaking aloud image-rich texts. Mercutio's famous Queen Mab speech is certainly one of these. Romeo, Mercutio and Benvolio are going to gate-crash the Capulets' party, but Mercutio is already in party mode: with his colourful imagination, love of word-play and talent for improvisation, he creates a one-man stage performance with his famous description of Queen Mab and her activities, woven from nothing but the feverish workings of his acrobatic mind. Pupils are invited to catch his enthusiasm for words in this choral speaking sequence that incorporates a movement element.

 Worksheet 10a provides an alternative edit of Mercutio's speech for younger or less able pupils.

LESSON STRUCTURE

▶ Starter Activity

▶ Divide the class into four groups. Each group is labelled as either Group A, B, C or D. Group A is paired with Group B and Group C with Group D. The groups sit facing each other.

▶ Give one person from each group a starter sentence and one of the inspirational objects (rainstick, box, etc). Explain that each group is going to create a dream using a starter sentence and every member of the group is going to contribute at least two sentences (i.e. the dream is going to go round the group twice). The object is passed from one storyteller to the next when the responsibility for continuing the story is passed on.

▶ One group listens while the other group weaves its dream; they then swap over. Contextualise the activity by explaining that Mercutio creates a story from his imagination when he and Romeo are going to the Capulets' party and they are now going to have a similar experience – making up a story on the spur of the moment. Examples of starter sentences are:

■ *It was midnight and I was lost in an enormous mansion in the middle of nowhere.*

■ *Where was this place, with tables piled high with food, masked dancers whirling by, drumbeats and the calls of exotic caged birds?*

■ *It started as a vague shape, filling the horizon and getting closer every minute.*

■ *I could hear it before I could see it.*

▶ Main Activity

Worksheet 10/10a: Mercutio's Queen Mab speech

▶ Give each pupil a worksheet and ask them to stand in a circle. Explain they will work on a speech that Mercutio gives just before he, Romeo and Benvolio go to the Capulet's party.

▶ Starting the activity by modelling it, ask pupils to pass around the words of the first part of the speech one word at a time. Each person speaks a word, in sequence, until the end of the speech is reached. Pupils should make the most of the sound of each word (model this with '*O,*' to set a standard).

▶ Now try saying the lines using different speeds. Lead the pupils in speaking the first few lines as quickly as you can. Then speak them as if in slow motion. *Which words and phrases are especially suited to speed or slow motion?* (The first line might be spoken very slowly to accentuate amazement then, '*no bigger than an agate stone*' spoken quickly highlights Mab's smallness. Further on, '*long spinners' legs*' is effective spoken slowly to draw out the long vowels and the long legs; '*wings of grasshoppers*' is quicker with its many, closely-packed consonants.)

► Try out different pitches. Ask pupils to speak the first line in the lowest register possible and to go up their vocal scale on the second, third and fourth lines. Ask them why such choices might suit the content of those lines.

► Investigate Shakespeare's use of vowels and consonants for special effect. Review the use of long vowels for '*long spinner's legs*' and hard consonants for '*wings of grasshoppers.*' Where else can they find a similar contrast ('*moonshine's watery beams*' for long vowels and '*Her whip, of cricket's bone; the lash of film*' for quick consonants)? Speak these aloud so that everyone has an experience of the way the sounds of the words support Shakespeare's meanings.

► Ask pupils to work in groups of five or six and to spread out through the space so that they can move freely. Give them a series of lines from the text and ask them as a group to create **freeze frames** ◊ for these in five seconds. They should work quickly, intuitively and completely in silence (talking and planning can interfere with intuitive choices). Some images to make are:

■ '*She is the fairies' midwife*'

■ '*Her chariot is an empty hazelnut*'

■ '*Sometime she driveth o'er a courtier's nose*'

■ '*Tickling a parson's nose as 'a lies asleep*'

► If time allows, when they have created three or four images, ask the groups to choose their favourite and then take it in turns to present these to the rest of the class, asking pupils which image they think they are looking at.

► Now allocate a section of the speech to each of the small groups (more than one group can have the same section of text). Ask them to use speech and movement to create a short choral piece that illustrates their section of text and captures its spirit. Give them about ten minutes to prepare and then perform these in sequence.

► Plenary

► Ask:

■ *Which freeze frames particularly stood out either from ones you made or ones you saw other groups create? Why?*

■ *Can you create a list of words to describe Mercutio, based on your investigation of his speech.*

■ *What have you discovered from this work about the way Shakespeare writes?*

Act 1 Scene 4

MERCUTIO: O, then I see Queen Mab hath been with you:
She is the fairies' midwife, and she comes
In shape no bigger than an agate-stone
On the forefinger of an alderman,
Drawn with a team of little atomies
Over men's noses as they lie asleep:

Her wagon-spokes made of long spinners' legs,
The cover of the wings of grasshoppers,
Her traces of the smallest spider's web,
Her collars of the moonshine's wat'ry beams,
Her whip of cricket's bone, the lash of film,
Her wagoner a small grey-coated gnat,
Not half so big as a round little worm
Pricked from the lazy finger of a maid.

Her chariot is an empty hazel-nut,
Made by the joiner squirrel or old grub,
Time out o'mind the fairies' coachmakers.
And in this state she gallops night by night
Through lovers' brains, and then they dream of love,

On courtiers' knees, that dream on curtsies straight,
O'er lawyers' fingers, who straight dream on fees,
O'er ladies' lips, who straight on kisses dream,
Which oft the angry Mab with blisters plagues,
Because their breath with sweetmeats tainted are:

Sometime she gallops o'er a courtier's nose,
And then dreams he of smelling out a suit:
And sometime comes she with a tithe-pig's tail
Tickling a parson's nose as a lies asleep,
Then he dreams of another benefice.

Sometime she driveth o'er a soldier's neck,
And then dreams he of cutting foreign throats,
Of breaches, ambuscadoes, Spanish blades,
Of healths five-fathom deep, and then anon
Drums in his ear, at which he starts and wakes,
And being thus frighted swears a prayer or two
And sleeps again.

▶ Notes

'fairies' midwife': she gives birth to people's dreams

'agate-stone': a stone often used in signet rings

'alderman': important member of a local council

'atomies': little atoms or tiny creatures

'spinners': spiders

'traces': reins that link the animals to the chariot

'film': fine thread

'joiner squirrel': because the squirrel chews nuts and therefore carves out the chariot

'old grub': insect larva or worm that bores holes

'state': manner

'sweetmeats': candied fruit

'smelling out a suit': finding someone whom he can charge a fee for his services

'tithe-pig': annually people paid their priests in goods. One kind of payment was the tenth pig of a litter.

'another benefice': a church position

'breaches': gaps in a fortress which artillery has made

'ambuscadoes': ambushes

'healths five-fathom deep': toasts drunk from very deep glasses

'anon': soon

Act 1 Scene 4

MERCUTIO: O, then I see Queen Mab hath been with you:
She is the fairies' midwife, and she comes
In shape no bigger than an agate-stone
On the forefinger of an alderman,
Drawn with a team of little atomies
Over men's noses as they lie asleep:

Her wagon-spokes made of long spinners' legs,
The cover of the wings of grasshoppers,
Her traces of the smallest spider's web,
Her collars of the moonshine's wat'ry beams,
Her whip of cricket's bone, the lash of film,
Her wagoner a small grey-coated gnat,
Not half so big as a round little worm
Pricked from the lazy finger of a maid.

Her chariot is an empty hazel-nut,
Made by the joiner squirrel or old grub,
Time out o'mind the fairies' coachmakers.
And in this state she gallops night by night
Through lovers' brains, and then they dream of love.

▶ Notes

'fairies' midwife': she gives birth to people's dreams

'agate-stone': a stone often used in signet rings

'alderman': important member of a local council

'atomies': little atoms or tiny creatures

'spinners': spiders

'traces': reins that link the animals to the chariot

'film': fine thread

'joiner squirrel': because the squirrel chews nuts and therefore carves out the chariot

'old grub': insect larva or worm that bores holes

Key Objective

To understand why and how Romeo speaks to the audience at the opening of Act 2 Scene 2.

KS3	KS2
1.1 Developing active listening skills and strategies	Speaking, Listening and Responding, Group Discussion and Interaction, Drama, Understanding and Interpreting Texts, Engaging and Responding to Texts.
2.2 Using and adapting the conventions and forms of spoken texts	

LESSON DESCRIPTION

Pupils explore Romeo's speech from Act 2 Scene 2 and develop their awareness of the circumstances in which he speaks.

Preparation and Resources

The lesson is complex and requires thorough preparation for effective classroom management. You will need:

▶ A hall or drama studio, or classroom with chairs pushed back

▶ Chairs: enough for everyone in the biggest circle you can make in the available space. Younger pupils may be more comfortable sitting on the floor

▶ **Worksheet 11/11a:** one per pupil

▶ **Resource Sheet 6:** prepare *interpolated questions* ⟡ for the speech

▶ **Resource Sheet 7**

 There are many sections of text like this one in Shakespeare's plays: long speeches in which a character shares with the audience their intimate perspective on the action. This sequence is a transferable approach, which involves the whole class, and enables pupils to:

■ Break down the speech into individual thoughts.

■ Analyse exactly what the words mean by physically expressing them.

■ Kinaesthetically experience the key words and images in the speech.

■ Understand Romeo's motivations by speaking the words aloud.

 Worksheet 11a provides an alternative edit of Romeo's speech for younger or less able pupils. The edited worksheet cuts the section from '*Arise, fair sun, and kill the envious moon*' down to '*And none but fools do wear it. Cast it off.*' This removes some complex imagery and language. However, we have been surprised by how well younger or less able pupils respond to this exercise so would recommend working with the full speech wherever possible.

▶ Starter Activity

Worksheet 11/11a: Act 2 Scene 2

▶ Pupils sit on the chairs, ready for **Ensemble reading** ⟨⟩. Explain the circumstances in which Romeo speaks (*it is after the party and Romeo has sneaked into the Capulets' orchard in the hope of seeing Juliet again*).

▶ Pupils read the speech aloud, with each pupil reading only up to the next punctuation mark. This may mean that individuals read only one word, or a couple of lines. The punctuation is strictly observed.

▶ Ask:

■ *Which words stand out when we share the reading in this way?*

■ *Was there a place in the speech when we were swapping readers often?*

■ *Did any individual have a more sustained period of speaking?*

■ *Do you notice anything about the pattern of the speech?*

▶ Explain that actors use punctuation as an indicator of the thought patterns of the character. Many contemporary directors and actors make sense of Shakespeare's words by reading to the punctuation rather than to the verse line endings, precisely because the punctuation reveals the pattern of the character's thoughts.

▶ Ask pupils to repeat the **ensemble reading** ⟨⟩, but this time ask them to imagine that Romeo is sharing a secret that he doesn't want anyone else to overhear. Pupils will whisper the words to the next reader, passing on what is said with energy. There should be no pauses between one reader and the next; it should be as if there is only one person speaking. Ask:

■ *What is the effect of this?*

■ *What is Romeo's state of mind?* (Excited? Confused?) Ask pupils to explain their comments and support them with evidence from the text.

▶ Main Activity

Resource Sheet 6: Interpolated questions

▶ **Interpolated questions** ⟨⟩ Pupils speak the whole speech in unison, but you interrupt them with comments or questions in modern English as if you are Romeo's friend. They must listen to what you say, then respond with Romeo's lines. The speech will therefore be a dialogue between the pupils as Romeo and you as his 'friend'.

▶ Open the dialogue with a comment or question; pupils respond in unison using Romeo's words. At the end of the sequence ask:

■ *Did you understand what you were saying?*

■ *How do you think Romeo is feeling when he speaks these words?*

■ *Do you have sympathy for Romeo?*

▶ Explain that everything that is said in a play is said by a character, to someone else, for a good reason. Even though Romeo is not speaking directly to someone else in the play, he is speaking to the audience. Ask:

■ *Why does Shakespeare have Romeo speaking directly to the audience at this point in the play?*

■ *How does it make you feel about him?*

▶ Ask pupils to stand and evenly space themselves around the room. Play **Punctuation Shift** ⟲. After pupils have 'walked' the speech ask:

■ *How does Romeo feel during this speech?*

■ *Where in the speech do Romeo's thoughts change direction rapidly?* (for example, in the middle of the speech, when he is deciding whether or not to speak to Juliet)

■ *What is Romeo talking about when his thoughts are more sustained?* (later in the speech, 'Her eye in heaven/Would through the airy region stream so bright/That birds would sing and think it were not night.')

■ *Why are his thoughts clearer at this point?* (Because he is so involved in thinking about Juliet's beautiful eyes? Because he is so wrapped up in his own imaginary world?)

Resource Sheet 7: Imaging the text
▶ Follow the instructions on the resource sheet and model the first line of the speech with the whole group working in a circle.

▶ Now ask pupils to work with the person next to them. Assign each pair a short section of the speech, no more than a couple of lines. The lines should be allocated in sequence round the circle, until the whole speech is assigned.

▶ Ask pupils to speak their lines aloud, simultaneously, then to speak their lines aloud in a variety of ways:

■ *As if they are market traders.*

■ *As if they are telling a young child a bedtime story.*

■ *As if they are a teacher telling someone off.*

■ *As if they are at a football match.*

▶ Finally, ask pupils to speak their lines without looking at the words on the page. Most will now know their lines.

▶ Ask pupils to find key words in their lines and agree on strong gestures to go with each key word. Give a few minutes to rehearse, so that they are confident to speak their lines and make their gestures.

▶ Re-form the circle. Explain that the whole group will say and do the first lines together, then each pair will deliver their lines and gestures in sequence round the circle. Ask pupils to watch each other carefully and notice which words and images stand out. After pupils have completed the speech ask:

■ *Which words/images stand out?*

■ *Why are there so many images of light in the speech?* (Because Romeo is full of joy? Because Juliet lights up his life? In contrast to the dark despair Romeo has felt earlier in the play?)
Explain that images of light and dark occur throughout the play.

▶ Keeping in their pairs, pupils sit opposite their partner, face to face. They label themselves as A or B. Ask As to speak Romeo's lines to Bs, who are Romeo's friend. Bs must listen very carefully and attentively but they are not allowed to speak.

▶ Ask Bs what they were thinking whilst they were listening to Romeo. (For example *Poor thing, he's so confused. Why doesn't he just get on with it and speak to Juliet? He's a coward. I know what he means. He must be really in love.*)

▶ Repeat the activity, but this time give Bs permission to interrupt As in modern English any time they want to, and explain that As must try not to let Bs get a word in edgeways. Model this by tackling the first couple of lines with one of the As in the group.

▶ Ask As:

■ *As: did you speak the words differently when you were trying to stop B from interrupting? In what way?*

▶ Plenary

▶ Ask:

■ *Why does Romeo speak directly to the audience at this point in the play?* (Because he has to tell someone how he feels? Because he is sharing his secret feelings? Because Shakespeare wants us to feel sympathy for Romeo? Because Shakespeare wants us to connect with Romeo's feelings? Because Shakespeare wants us to feel the suspense that Romeo is feeling before he summons up the courage to speak to Juliet?)

■ *What did you notice about the words and images that Romeo uses in the speech? What does this tell you about him?*

Act 2 Scene 2

ROMEO: But, soft, what light through yonder window breaks?
It is the east, and Juliet is the sun.
Arise, fair sun, and kill the envious moon,
Who is already sick and pale with grief,
That thou her maid art far more fair than she:
Be not her maid, since she is envious:
Her vestal livery is but sick and green
And none but fools do wear it, cast it off.
It is my lady, O, it is my love!
O, that she knew she were!
She speaks yet she says nothing: what of that?
Her eye discourses: I will answer it.
I am too bold, 'tis not to me she speaks:
Two of the fairest stars in all the heaven,
Having some business, do entreat her eyes
To twinkle in their spheres till they return.
What if her eyes were there, they in her head?
The brightness of her cheek would shame those stars
As daylight doth a lamp, her eye in heaven
Would through the airy region stream so bright
That birds would sing and think it were not night.
See how she leans her cheek upon her hand!
O that I were a glove upon that hand,
That I might touch that cheek!

Act 2 Scene 2 (edited)

ROMEO: But, soft, what light through yonder window breaks?

It is the east, and Juliet is the sun.

It is my lady, O, it is my love!

O, that she knew she were!

She speaks yet she says nothing: what of that?

Her eye discourses: I will answer it.

I am too bold, 'tis not to me she speaks:

Two of the fairest stars in all the heaven,

Having some business, do entreat her eyes

To twinkle in their spheres till they return.

What if her eyes were there, they in her head?

The brightness of her cheek would shame those stars

As daylight doth a lamp, her eye in heaven

Would through the airy region stream so bright

That birds would sing and think it were not night.

See how she leans her cheek upon her hand!

O, that I were a glove upon that hand,

That I might touch that cheek!

Interpolated questions

Example, where the questions clarify meaning:

Teacher: *Careful, someone will hear you!*
Pupils: But, soft,

Teacher: *Is that light coming from the window?*
Pupils: What light through yonder window breaks?

Teacher: *It looks like the sunrise!*
Pupils: It is the east, and Juliet is the sun!

Example, where the questions provoke an emotional response:

Teacher: *Is she the one for you?*
Pupils: It is my lady.

Teacher: *And do you love her?*
Pupils: O, it is my love!

Teacher: *But does she know that?*
Pupils: O, that she knew she were!

Teacher: *She's going to be saying something!*
Pupils: She speaks!

Teacher: *No, she's not.*
Pupils: Yet she says nothing.

Teacher: *Maybe she doesn't want to talk to you.*
Pupils: What of that?

Teacher: *She has got a twinkle in her eye.*
Pupils: Her eye discourses.

Teacher: *Go on, speak to her.*
Pupils: I will answer it.

Teacher: *You don't dare!*
Pupils: I am too bold.

Imaging

To model how to do the imaging exercise, try the first line of the speech as a whole group.

'But soft! What light from yonder window breaks?'

First ask pupils to identify the key words in the line: **soft, light, yonder, window, breaks.**

Ask for suggestions from the group for gestures that could go with the key words to make their meaning clear.

soft!	A stroking gesture? A shushing gesture?
light	A sudden opening of the hands like a light coming on? Covering the eyes against a sudden glare?
yonder	Pointing up and out in the direction of the window? With one hand? With both hands?
window	Drawing the shape of the window in the air? Opening the window?
breaks?	A sharp motion like the breaking of sticks? A slow rise of the hands like sunrise?

There are many possibilities for each key word. Agree on the one that most pupils in the group like.

Now, as a group in unison, speak the whole line out loud, making the agreed gestures on the key words. Repeat this until the group can confidently speak the line and make the gestures almost without thinking.

ROMEO AND JULIET
LESSON 10: MENTORS: THE NURSE AND FRIAR LAURENCE

Key Objective

To explore different ways of interpreting Romeo's relationship with the Nurse and the Friar.

KS3

1.2 Understanding and responding to what speakers say in formal and informal contexts

4.1 Using different dramatic approaches to explore ideas, texts and issues

5.2 Understanding and responding to ideas, viewpoints, themes and purposes in texts

KS2

Speaking, Listening and Responding, Group Discussion and Interaction, Drama, Understanding and Interpreting Texts, Engaging and Responding to Texts

LESSON DESCRIPTION

Pupils use physical gestures to explore the dynamic of the relationship between Romeo, the Nurse and Friar in Act 3 Scene 3.

Preparation and Resources

You will need:

▶ A hall or drama studio, or classroom with tables pushed back

▶ **Worksheet 12/12a:** one per pupil

 Act 3 Scene 3 takes place in Friar Laurence's cell. Romeo has fled there following a brawl in which his friend Mercutio has been killed and he has murdered Juliet's cousin, Tybalt. The audience have witnessed the fight and so know to expect Romeo in a desperate state. In the opening lines of the scene we see Romeo become even more frantic as the Friar tells him the Prince has banished him from Verona. However, he then draws some comfort from the Friar and the Nurse as they advise him to go to Juliet. The actor playing Romeo has to go on quite an emotional journey through the scene. He has the text, his imagination and his physical and vocal responses to the words of the Nurse and the Friar, to help him do this. A technique sometimes used in rehearsals to pinpoint and accentuate the swift-changing emotional state of a character is to make large external physical gestures that sum up what the character is feeling internally. It often helps if these are larger than life, or melodramatic, especially to start with. It can help the actor and the company to visualise where the small twists and turns of feeling are, and what words, phrases or actions prompt a direct response in the character.

 Worksheet 12a provides an alternative edit of Act 3 Scene 3 for younger or less able pupils. However, you may want to use this simpler edit in all cases and build up to the fuller version on Worksheet 12 (or the full scene from the play).

LESSON STRUCTURE

▶ Starter Activity

▶ Ask the group to walk freely around an open space until you call out a number. When you do this, pupils should make groups of this number. Once everyone is in a group, tell them to relax and walk as individuals around the space until you call out the next number, and so on. If any pupils are left out, they should be invited to join another group; the rule of inclusion is the most important one to employ and no-one should be left out.

▶ Tell pupils that when you call out the next number you're going to ask them, in that number formation, to create an image.

■ Now call out 'two' and ask the pairs to make a picture of *cruelty*. Choose one pair and ask everyone else to copy their picture.

■ Next time call out 'three' and ask them to make a picture of *mercy*. Choose one and ask everyone else to copy it.

■ Next time call out 'four' and ask them to make you a picture of *banishment*. Choose one and ask everyone to copy it.

You now have a two person, three person and four person picture. Quickly call out the numbers again to recap on all three pictures that you have chosen. Explain that these three words are closely linked to Romeo's journey through the play. Invite pupils to speculate with you on how each word connects to his story.

▶ Main Activity

Worksheet 12/12a: Act 3 Scene 3

▶ In groups of three, allocate pupils a character to read and ask them to sit on the floor back to back and read the scene all the way through. (If there are more than three pupils in any group, ask the additional pupil to take on the role of observer, reflecting back to the group the effect of the choices they are making.) Now ask pupils to try whispering the scene as if they are afraid of being overheard.

▶ Ask: *Which words stood?*

▶ Ask pupils to try playing the scene in a number of different ways. Try the first part of the scene before the Nurse enters, with Friar Laurence whispering, urging Romeo to keep his voice down. Then ask them to try it with the Friar sitting down and Romeo moving freely – then to change when the Nurse enters so that Romeo is sitting down and Friar Laurence and the Nurse are moving freely.

▶ Discuss as a group what this felt like. Ask:

■ *Which was the most effective way to read the scene? Why?*

Worksheet 12/12a

▶ In the same groups of three, and still focusing on the section of text before the Nurse enters, ask pupils to read the scene as if:

■ Romeo has *given up hope* and Friar Laurence is trying to *persuade* him out of his hopelessness

■ Romeo is *desperate* for comfort and the Friar is *cautious,* not wanting to give him false hope

■ Romeo is *seeking comfort* and the Friar is trying to *reassure* him.

▶ Ask the pupils to try the second part of the scene after the nurse enters as if:

■ the Nurse *blames* Romeo for what has happened and he is *desperate* for news

■ the Nurse is deeply *concerned* for Romeo, who is *impatient* with the Nurse.

Worksheet 12/12a

▶ Ask pupils to look at the list of expressions on the bottom of the worksheet. Tell them:
You are going to invent a gesture for each of the expressions on the list, such as both hands clasped to your heart for 'I love her' or pretending to stab yourself and falling to the ground, for 'I want to die'.

▶ Each gesture must be large, slightly over-the-top, or melodramatic. Tell pupils:
Don't censor or give yourselves too much time to think; just make the first gesture that comes to mind.

▶ A good way to begin is to call out each of the expressions and ask pupils to make an instant image or gesture that corresponds to each expression. Look at the examples around the groups and, with the pupils, collectively decide which is the strongest and easiest to copy. Then ask each group to copy the chosen gestures, and to practise performing them together.

Worksheet 12/12a

▶ Now ask each group to choose four of the gestures, which they can repeat as often as they like. They practise these, making them as clear and clean as possible. They should try to remember them.

▶ Next ask them to read through the scene again and discuss the fast-changing emotional states of each of the characters.

▶ Using only the gestures they have chosen and no words they ought to be able to display the emotional state of each of the characters to an audience. Ask them first to do this individually, focusing on one of the characters and creating a kind of monologue without words. Then ask them to work together in their groups to create a sequence, or conversation, with all three characters which follows the arc of Act 3 Scene 3. Remind them:
This is your own performance and there is no right way of playing the scene. It will differ from pupil to pupil as it would differ from actor to actor.

▶ They can then **showback** ▣ to the rest of the group.

▶ Plenary

As a group, discuss what this exercise tells us about Romeo's
relationship with the Friar and Nurse. Ask:

■ *What effect do the Nurse and Friar Laurence have on Romeo in the
scene?*

■ *What techniques or phrases do they use in order to comfort Romeo?*

■ *What is Romeo's state of mind at the beginning of the scene?*

■ *In what ways does it change through the scene?*

■ *Why do you think Shakespeare provided Romeo and Juliet with these
mentors?*

Act 3 Scene 3 (edited): Friar Laurence's cell

FRIAR LAURENCE: Romeo, come forth, come forth, thou fearful man.

ROMEO: Father, what news?

FRIAR LAURENCE: I bring thee tidings of the prince's doom.
Here from Verona art thou banishèd:

ROMEO: There is no world without Verona walls,
But purgatory, torture, hell itself.

FRIAR LAURENCE: O deadly sin! O rude unthankfulness!
Thy fault our law calls death, but the kind prince,
Taking thy part, hath rushed aside the law,
And turned that black word 'death' to 'banishment'.
This is dear mercy, and thou see'st it not.

ROMEO: 'Tis torture and not mercy. Heaven is here,
Where Juliet lives, and every cat and dog
And little mouse, every unworthy thing,
Live here in heaven and may look on her,

FRIAR LAURENCE: Then, fond mad man, hear me a little speak.

Knocking within

FRIAR LAURENCE: Arise, one knocks. Good Romeo, hide thyself.
Hark, how they knock!- Who's there?- Romeo, arise,
Thou wilt be taken.- Stay awhile!- Stand up.

NURSE: [*Within*] Let me come in, and you shall know my errand:
I come from Lady Juliet. [*Enter NURSE*]
O holy friar, O, tell me, holy friar,
Where's my lady's lord? Where's Romeo?

FRIAR LAURENCE: There on the ground, with his own tears made drunk.

NURSE: O, he is even in my mistress' case,
For Juliet's sake, for her sake, rise and stand.
Why should you fall into so deep an O?

ROMEO: Speak'st thou of Juliet? How is it with her?

NURSE: O, she says nothing, sir, but weeps and weeps,
And now falls on her bed, and then starts up,
And Tybalt calls, and then on Romeo cries,
And then down falls again.

ROMEO: [*drawing his sword*] O, tell me, friar, tell me,
In what vile part of this anatomy
Doth my name lodge? Tell me, that I may sack
The hateful mansion.

FRIAR LAURENCE: Hold thy desperate hand.
Art thou a man? Thy form cries out thou art:
Thy tears are womanish: thy Juliet is alive.
Go, get thee to thy love as was decreed,
Ascend her chamber, hence and comfort her:
But look thou stay not till the watch be set,
For then thou canst not pass to Mantua,
Where thou shalt live till we can find a time
To blaze your marriage, reconcile your friends,
Beg pardon of thy prince, and call thee back
With twenty hundred thousand times more joy
Than thou went'st forth in lamentation.

NURSE: My lord, I'll tell my lady you will come. [*Exit NURSE*]

ROMEO: How well my comfort is revived by this!

FRIAR LAURENCE: Give me thy hand, 'tis late. Farewell; goodnight.

Exeunt

▶ **Expressions to be applied to scene:**

I love her	Go and never come back!	Stand up for yourself
I want to die	What shall I do?	Thank you
I'm so sad	Please help me	
I'm so angry	You are a coward	

Act 3 Scene 3 (edited): Friar Laurence's cell

ROMEO: Father, what news?

FRIAR LAURENCE: I bring thee tidings of the prince's doom.
Here from Verona art thou banishèd:

ROMEO: There is no world without Verona walls,
Heaven is here, where Juliet lives.

FRIAR LAURENCE: Then, fond mad man, hear me a little
speak.

Knocking within

FRIAR LAURENCE: Arise, one knocks. Good Romeo, hide
thyself.

NURSE: [*Within*] I come from Lady Juliet. [*Enter NURSE*]
Where's my lady's lord? Where's Romeo?

FRIAR LAURENCE: There on the ground, with his own tears
made drunk.

NURSE: O, he is even in my mistress' case,
For Juliet's sake, for her sake, rise and stand.

ROMEO: Speak'st thou of Juliet? How is it with her?

NURSE: O, she says nothing, sir, but weeps and weeps.

ROMEO: [*draws his sword*]

FRIAR LAURENCE: Hold thy desperate hand.
Art thou a man? Thy tears are womanish,
Thy Juliet is alive.
Go, get thee to thy love as was decreed,
Then pass to Mantua,
Where thou shalt live till we can find a time
To blaze your marriage, reconcile your friends,
Beg pardon of thy prince, and call thee back.

NURSE: My lord, I'll tell my lady you will come. [*Exit NURSE*]

ROMEO: How well my comfort is revived by this!

▶ **Expressions to be applied to scene:**

I love her	I'm so angry	Stand up for yourself
I want to die	Please help me	
I'm so sad	You are a coward	

ROMEO AND JULIET
LESSON 11: THE CAPULETS' FAMILY ARGUMENT

Key Objective

To deepen understanding of a central theme in the play – the conflict between parents and children – and explore the different motivations for Juliet, Lady Capulet and Capulet in Act 3 Scene 5.

KS3	KS2
5.2 Understanding and responding to ideas, viewpoints, themes and purposes in texts	Speaking, Listening and Responding, Group Discussion and Interaction, Drama, Understanding and Interpreting Texts and Engaging and Responding to Text
6.1 Relating texts to the social, historical and cultural context in which they were written	

LESSON DESCRIPTION

Pupils explore the conflict between Juliet and her parents in Act 3 Scene 5.

Preparation and Resources

You will need:

▶ A hall or drama studio, or classroom with tables pushed back

▶ Chairs for all pupils in three groups – or pupils can sit on the floor

▶ A whiteboard or flipchart

▶ **Worksheet 13/13a:** one per pupil

 By this point in the play Romeo and Juliet have secretly married, Romeo has killed Tybalt, the lovers have spent their wedding night together and Romeo has fled to Mantua. Meanwhile, Lord and Lady Capulet have agreed with Paris that he will marry their daughter.

This scene reveals one of the features of Shakespeare's plays that make them so accessible. When Juliet refuses to do her duty and marry Paris, her father's honour is offended and a violent family argument is triggered. Through Capulet's reaction, we see evidence of the social and historical context in which Shakespeare was working; the Elizabethans expected children to obey their parents. But the language of the scene is so vivid that pupils can quickly recognise and engage with the powerful feelings involved. When they tackle the scene actively, they can experience with their whole selves the age old struggle between parent's will and children's wishes, which is as powerful today as it was in Shakespeare's time.

 Worksheet 13a provides an alternative edit of Act 3 Scene 5 for younger or less able pupils.

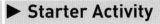

LESSON STRUCTURE

▶ Starter Activity

▶ Write these questions on a whiteboard or flipchart and ask pupils to discuss them with a partner:

■ What are the top three subjects parents and young people have arguments about?

■ What form do these disagreements take (for example, a full-scale row, silent withdrawal, various payback strategies)?

▶ Pairs feed back their responses to the whole group.

▶ Main Activity

Worksheet 13/13a: Act 3 Scene 5

▶ Give each pupil a worksheet and allocate them to one of three groups. Group one will be Juliet, group two Lady Capulet; and group three Lord Capulet. Explain that the whole class will now read the scene with each group reading their character's lines, for example, all the Juliet's speaking together etc. Alternatively, appoint strong readers for each of the three roles and have the others in the group echo all the words which they think are important.

Worksheet 13/13a

▶ Model this activity first by asking for two volunteers. One sits with their eyes closed while you whisper Lord Capulet's attack on Juliet into their ear. (Use the text beginning *'God's bread, it makes me mad!'* and ending *'I'll not be forsworn.'* For younger or less able pupils use Lord Capulet's final two speeches beginning, *'How, will she none?'* and ending *'Do not answer me'*. Exclude Juliet's response.) The other pupil echoes all the important words from the speech into the other ear of the seated pupil as you read the text. Ask the volunteer how it felt to hear these words echoing in his/her head.

▶ Now ask all pupils to work in groups of three and repeat the activity you've just modelled. One person listens with eyes closed while another pupil reads the text and a third echoes and improvises on the key words. When all pupils have had experience of all three roles, ask:

■ *How did it feel to be Juliet on the receiving end of her father's anger?*

■ *What would you do in her position?*

■ *Can you explain her parents' behaviour? Why are they so upset with their daughter?*

Worksheet 13/13a

▶ *Circle Blocking* : Ask pupils to make a circle of fifteen chairs and invite volunteers to play Juliet, Capulet and Lady Capulet. All other pupils stand behind the chairs. The three volunteers decide where in the circle of chairs they want to sit at the start of the scene. These choices should reflect their feelings toward one another at the start. Juliet chooses her seat first, her mother second and father third. As they play the scene they must constantly decide whether they want to stay in the chair they are sitting on or move to a different one. Any character may move to any chair at any point in the scene (the only exception being Lord Capulet before his entrance). All choices about where to sit should reflect the characters' feelings toward one another and should reflect the changes in those feelings.

▶ For younger or less able pupils an alternative approach would be to divide the class into three character groups and for each group to collectively speak their characters lines. Three pupil volunteers would play the three characters in the circle blocking exercise and would move in response to the text as their classmates read it.

▶ Ask the pupils standing behind the chairs:

■ *What did you notice about the movement patterns of the three characters?*

■ *How does this staging of the scene reveal the characters' feelings, in particular Juliet's position at this point?*

▶ Invite three more volunteers to play the roles and do the activity again. Ask:

■ *What differences did you see between the two stagings of the scene?*

■ *Do you think both are acceptable interpretations of the scene?* (You could explain that we may see many productions of a famous play in our lifetime and each one is unique.)

▶ **Stop! Think!** Finally, ask the second group to play the scene once again. This time, any of the pupils standing behind the chairs may interrupt the scene by saying, '*Stop! Juliet* (or one of the other characters), *think!*' The named character must then speak aloud what he/she is thinking privately at that moment.

▶ Plenary

▶ Ask:

■ *What makes Lord and Lady Capulet so angry about their daughter's behaviour?*

■ *Why are they eager for Juliet to marry the County Paris?*

■ *Does this kind of situation apply to our own society?*

■ *How does the action of the scene relate to the Prologue?*

■ *What do you think will happen next?*

▶ Homework

▶ Ask pupils to write diary entries for one or more of the three characters. These could be written as if a few minutes or a few hours after the events of the scene.

Act 3 Scene 5 (edited)

LADY CAPULET: Marry, my child, early next Thursday morn,
The gallant, young and noble gentleman,
The County Paris, at St Peter's Church,
Shall happily make thee there a joyful bride.

JULIET: Now, by St Peter's Church and Peter too,
He shall not make me there a joyful bride.
I will not marry yet, and, when I do, I swear
It shall be Romeo, whom you know I hate,
Rather than Paris. These are news indeed!

LADY CAPULET: Here comes your father: tell him so yourself,
And see how he will take it at your hands.

Enter Capulet

CAPULET: How now, wife?
Have you delivered to her our decree?

LADY CAPULET: Ay, sir, but she will none, she gives you thanks.
I would the fool were married to her grave.

CAPULET: Soft, take me with you, take me with you, wife.
How, will she none? Doth she not give us thanks?
Is she not proud? Doth she not count her blest,
Unworthy as she is, that we have wrought
So worthy a gentleman to be her bridegroom?

JULIET: Not proud you have, but thankful that you have:
Proud can I never be of what I hate,
But thankful even for hate, that is meant love.

CAPULET: How now? How now? Chopped-logic? What is this?
'Proud' and 'I thank you' and 'I thank you not',
And yet 'not proud', mistress minion you?
Thank me no thankings nor proud me no prouds,
But fettle your fine joints gainst Thursday next,
To go with Paris to St Peter's Church,
Or I will drag thee on a hurdle thither.
Out, you green-sickness carrion, out, you baggage,
You tallow-face!

LADY CAPULET: Fie, fie, what, are you mad?

JULIET: Good father, I beseech you on my knees,
Hear me with patience but to speak a word.

CAPULET: Hang thee, young baggage, disobedient wretch!
I tell thee what: get thee to church o'Thursday,
Or never after look me in the face.
Speak not, reply not, do not answer me:
My fingers itch.

LADY CAPULET: You are too hot.

CAPULET: God's bread, it makes me mad!
Day, night, hour, tide, time, work, play,
Alone, in company, still my care hath been
To have her matched: and having now provided
A gentleman of noble parentage,
Of fair demesnes, youthful, and nobly allied,
Stuffed, as they say, with honourable parts,
Proportioned as one's thought would wish a man,
And then to have a wretched puling fool,
A whining mammet, in her fortune's tender,
To answer 'I'll not wed, I cannot love,
I am too young, I pray you pardon me.'
But, an you will not wed, I'll pardon you:
Graze where you will you shall not house with me.
Look to't, think on't, I do not use to jest.
Thursday is near, lay hand on heart, advise:
And you be mine, I'll give you to my friend,
And you be not, hang, beg, starve, die in the streets,
For, by my soul, I'll ne'er acknowledge thee,
Nor what is mine shall never do thee good.
Trust to't, bethink you, I'll not be forsworn.

Exit Capulet

JULIET: Is there no pity sitting in the clouds,
That sees into the bottom of my grief?
O, sweet my mother, cast me not away!

LADY CAPULET: Talk not to me, for I'll not speak a word:
Do as thou wilt, for I have done with thee.

Act 3 Scene 5 (edited):

LADY CAPULET: Marry, my child, early next Thursday morn,
The gallant, young and noble gentleman,
The County Paris, at St Peter's Church,
Shall happily make thee there a joyful bride.

JULIET: Now, by St Peter's Church and Peter too,
He shall not make me there a joyful bride.

LADY CAPULET: Here comes your father: tell him so yourself.

CAPULET: How now, wife?
Have you delivered to her our decree?

LADY CAPULET: Ay, sir, but she will none, she gives you thanks.

CAPULET: How, will she none? Doth she not give us thanks?
Is she not proud? Doth she not count her blest,
Unworthy as she is, that we have wrought
So worthy a gentleman to be her bridegroom?

JULIET: Good father, I beseech you on my knees,
Hear me with patience but to speak a word.

CAPULET: Hang thee, young baggage, disobedient wretch!
I tell thee what: get thee to church o'Thursday,
Or never after look me in the face.
Speak not, reply not, do not answer me.

JULIET: O, sweet my mother, cast me not away!

LADY CAPULET: Talk not to me, for I'll not speak a word:
Do as thou wilt, for I have done with thee.

ROMEO AND JULIET
LESSON 12: INVESTIGATING THE CULTURAL CONTEXT

Key Objective

To explore the similarities and differences between Elizabethan society and our own.

KS3

4.1 Using different dramatic approaches to explore ideas, texts and issues

6.1 Relating texts to the social, historical and cultural contexts in which they were written

KS2

Speaking, Listening and Responding, Group Discussion and Interaction and Drama

LESSON DESCRIPTION

Pupils create a gallery of images representing cultural and historical issues associated with *Romeo and Juliet* and compare these with their own lives.

Preparation and Resources

You will need:

▶ A hall or drama studio, or classroom with tables pushed back

▶ Chairs for all pupils, arranged in a semi-circle – or they can sit on the floor

▶ A whiteboard or flipchart

▶ **Worksheet 14/14a:** one per pupil

▶ **Worksheet 15:** one per pupil

 Of all Shakespeare's plays, *Romeo and Juliet* seems to be the one whose stories and themes are closest to young people's experiences and concerns, as the various updated versions, including *West Side Story* and Baz Luhrmann's film, testify. Even those aspects of the story which at first seem very removed from our own world have strong links with contemporary life. We may question whether young people today can understand the Elizabethan concept of honour, but if we explore the insults Tybalt hurls at Romeo after the death of Mercutio we quickly understand how intolerable those insults would have felt to a young man of that time and might still feel today. This lesson sequence invites pupils to see the events in the play through Elizabethan eyes and then to explore their links to the pupils' own lives and experiences.

 Worksheet 14a provides an edited list of historical facts for younger or less able pupils.

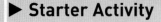

LESSON STRUCTURE

▶ Starter Activity

▶ Explain to pupils that they are going to explore what life was like in Romeo and Juliet's time and compare it with our own contemporary world. Elizabethan England was, of course, different from Verona in Italy, but Shakespeare borrowed many features of sixteenth century England and applied them to the world of his play. Write on a whiteboard or flipchart, 'What do you hope for in the next fifteen years in these areas?'

- Relationships

- Education

- Work or occupation

- Leisure time

- Money

▶ Ask pupils to share with a partner their hopes and plans for the future. Each partner has two minutes to talk about their plans. Encourage them to ask questions, both for clarification and to deepen the speaker's thinking.

▶ Main Activity

▶ Use this warm-up activity. Pupils spread out through the room, equidistant from one another. When you say, *Go*, they walk briskly into the empty spaces, always moving and always trying to stay equidistant from one another. Explain as they walk that you will be giving them a series of situations and will ask them to respond as if they are either SEEING a situation or BEING someone in a particular situation. Pupils will use their bodies and facial expressions to momentarily convey their responses to each situation before continuing with a brisk walk around the space awaiting your next instruction. Possible situations include:

- SEE a doctor tending to someone with the plague.

- BE that person who is infected with an illness very few recover from.

- SEE a group of women, young and old, around a fire doing embroidery and other needlework.

- BE one of those women.

- SEE a group of servants in a grand house setting the enormous table for a banquet.

- BE one of those servants preparing that table.

- SEE a brawl among two gangs of young men.

- BE one of those young men spoiling for a fight.

- SEE a high government official breaking up a street fight involving two dozen people.

- BE that official.

- Ask: *how do these situations relate to the time that Romeo and Juliet was written in? Do any of them also relate to our lives today?*

Worksheet 14/14a: What was it like to live in Romeo and Juliet's time?

▶ Ask for volunteers to read the descriptions of life in Elizabethan England. Pupils listening should close their eyes to help them imagine what is being described. Ask the group for their overall impressions of this world.

Worksheet 14/14a

▶ Divide the class into groups of five or six pupils each and assign one of the descriptions of what it was like to live in Romeo and Juliet's time to each of them. Ask them to create a ***freeze frame*** ◖◗ for this information. Explain that the freeze frame needs to come to life and act out the idea – pupils can move and speak, making up things that the people involved might say. The action should last no more than ten seconds, then everyone should freeze again. Allow about ten minutes for preparation and then position the groups around the space so that their freeze frames are distributed like statues in an art gallery or displays at Madame Tussaud's. Run these action freeze frames in turn, inviting pupils to visit all those in which they are not involved. Ask them to match the pictures and action with the list of facts they have read about life in Romeo and Juliet's time. Then ask:

- *What do you feel and think about each of these experiences.*

▶ Plenary

Worksheet 14a: What was it like to live in Romeo and Juliet's time?

▶ ***Chair thermometer*** ◖◗: Position two chairs across the space from one another, quite far apart. Tell pupils that Chair A represents ideas that are only true of Shakespeare's society and not of our own, and Chair B represents ideas which are just as true today as they were in Shakespeare's time. The space between the chairs is for ideas which are sometimes true of our society but not always: the more true the ideas of our day and age, the closer pupils should position themselves to Chair B.

▶ Now read the twelve statements from Worksheet 14a or a selection of these and ask pupils to make individual choices about where to place themselves between the chairs. As you go along, ask pupils to explain their decisions, especially when they make ones which are quite different from most of the group.

▶ If there is time, ask pupils to record their decisions on Worksheet 15.

What was it like to live in Romeo and Juliet's time?

- In the late sixteenth century, when Romeo and Juliet was written, the idea of marrying for love in high society, as Juliet does in the play, was fairly new. People married for all kinds of other reasons – for money or for political or social advantage, for example.

- Women could marry very young (legally, they could marry from the age of twelve).

- The majority of women in late sixteenth century England were uneducated. However, women who came from families of high social standing were taught by personal tutors at home. They would have studied reading, writing and arithmetic, and languages such as Greek, Latin and French. They were also taught sewing and music.

- While a woman's place in this world was primarily at home and with her family, some women had jobs as midwives and apothecaries (pharmacists); others were employed in trades as shoemakers, milliners (hat makers) and embroiderers. Women were also washerwomen and servants.

- This was a male-dominated society: women in Elizabethan England were of lower status than men. Women were brought up to obey the men in their lives – their fathers, brothers and husbands. They were not allowed to own property once they were married.

- Married women had children on average every two years. About half of the babies born died not long afterward. Many women also died in childbirth.

- Honour, especially male honour, was very important. The slightest insult to male honour was a very serious business and had to be answered. The result of this code was that public fights were common and often ended in bloodshed and death.

- Because of the fights and bloodshed, governments tried very hard to keep public order and rid society of this impulse to row and riot. Punishments for public fights were very severe.

- This was a very Christian society and strict obedience to the laws of the Christian faith was expected.

- There were many life-threatening dangers in Elizabethan times. Fewer than 50% of children reached the age of five and a high percentage of women died during their first childbirth. Many men were killed in wars and great epidemics of smallpox and the plague killed thousands more. If you were ill, there was little the doctors could do. *'Eat, drink, and be merry, for tomorrow you may die'* was a good saying for this period in history.

- In Shakespeare's time the class system was very powerful. You knew your place in society and that was dictated by how much money you had, what you did for a living and who your ancestors were. It was very difficult to move from one class to another – marriage was one opportunity to do this. At the very least, people made every effort not to move down the social rankings.

- In Shakespeare's time there were only about fifty-five noble families in England. These families were very rich and powerful and supported large households of relatives, servants and other associates. You became a nobleman by ancestry or by a grant from the king or queen.

What was it like to live in Romeo and Juliet's time?

1 Marrying for love is uncommon. People marry for money or social advantage.

2 Most women in high society marry young. The legal age for marriage is twelve.

3 This is a male-dominated society, where women are of lower status than men. They are told what to do by their fathers, husbands and brothers.

4 Most women are uneducated. Only women from wealthy families receive any education.

5 If women can afford it, they stay at home as wives and mothers. Poorer women work in a limited range of jobs which don't pay very well.

6 Married women give birth frequently. Babies often die and young mothers often die in childbirth.

7 Honour is a very important concept, especially to men. To insult someone's honour can result in revenge. Sometimes this is fatal.

8 The government is very concerned with law and order and the punishments for breaking the law are severe.

9 This is a very Christian society and strict obedience to the laws of the Christian faith is expected.

10 There are many life-threatening dangers, including wars and epidemics of diseases for which there are very few medicines.

11 The class system is very powerful. Money and your ancestors decide where you fit into this system and it is difficult to improve your social standing.

12 A few very wealthy families run the country.

How times have changed!

Use the chart to record your thoughts on how life has changed since Elizabethan times over 400 years ago. Put the statement numbers from Worksheet 14a (1–12) into the column you think best describes that statement. Give brief reasons for your choices.

True of Elizabethan society but not our own	True of Elizabethan society and also of our own, at least at times or in some places

ROMEO AND JULIET
LESSON 13: THE APOTHECARY'S SHOP

Key Objective

To stage Act 4 Scene 4, the exchange between Romeo and the apothecary, in order to explore Romeo's state of mind.

KS3

4.1 Using different dramatic approaches to explore ideas, texts and issues

4.2 Developing, adapting and responding to dramatic techniques, conventions and styles

KS2

Understanding and Interpreting Texts, Drama, Engaging and Responding to Texts and Speaking, Listening and Responding

LESSON DESCRIPTION

Pupils use physical activities to bring the apothecary's shop to life. They develop an understanding of the dark and foreboding language that Romeo uses when describing the apothecary's shop and begin to speculate on his state of mind.

Preparation and Resources

You will need:

▶ A hall or drama studio, or classroom with tables pushed back

▶ **Resource Sheet 8**

▶ **Worksheet 16:** one per pupil

 Mantua law forbids the sale of lethal poison under penalty of death. However, believing as he does that his wife Juliet is dead, a distraught and desperate Romeo persuades a poverty-stricken apothecary to sell him a dram of poison to aid his suicide.

This lesson encourages pupils to bring the apothecary and his shop to life through close reading of Romeo's speech in Act 5 Scene 1 in which he describes the apothecary and his shop. It also encourages close reading of the subsequent exchange between the two characters to uncover clues in the text about Romeo's state of mind.

LESSON STRUCTURE

► Starter Activity

Resource Sheet 8: Act 5 Scene 1

► Ask pupils to sit on the floor and listen as you read aloud Romeo's description of the apothecary's shop. As they listen, pupils should try to picture what the man and his shop look like.

► Ask the pupils to list some of the things they pictured in their imaginations. Encourage them to make their descriptions as detailed as possible. It's okay if they imagine things that were not listed in Romeo's speech.

► Ask the pupils to stand up and make **freeze frames** ◨ of the following (pupils should do this individually):

■ *A man with tattered weeds, whose sharp misery had worn him to the bones.*

■ *Any other object you remember seeing in the shop.*

► Highlight particular objects that pupils have created and ask them to explain their choices. Pay particular attention to objects that were not mentioned by Romeo but which pupils have imagined will form part of the apothecary's shop.

► Main Activity

Worksheet 16: Act 5 Scene 1

► Divide pupils into three groups; group one should be larger than groups two and three. Distribute the worksheet. Start by working with one group at a time to help them get started. The other two groups can sit on the floor and offer suggestions about how the group you are working with could approach the task you are setting them.

► **Group One** physically make the apothecary's shop, using their bodies to make the walls, the front and back door, the counter and all the objects found inside. Then send them away to brainstorm what the shop might sound like – communally they should create a **soundscape** ◨ of the shop which they will perform at the same time as creating the physical structure for the shop.

► **Group Two** look at the worksheet and read the apothecary's lines out loud, which have the numbers 1 to 4 in front of them. As there will be more than four people in the group, ask them to find a way of dividing the lines equally, using the punctuation as a guide. The pupils in this group are collectively responsible for bringing the apothecary to life; speaking the text with high energy and finding a way of physically representing him. They should think about how he moves and how he speaks his lines. Encourage pupils to be as imaginative as possible. For example:

■ One pupil plays the head and the mouth and each pupil then whispers their lines into the ears of the pupil playing the head, so that he can repeat the lines back to Romeo.

■ Pupils collectively make the apothecary's mouth with their

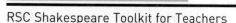

hands and so each speaks their line whilst moving their hands to represent the mouth.

■ Pupils create an 'apothecary puppet' with many controllers.

▶ **Group Three** nominate one pupil to play Romeo who will read all of Romeo's lines which *do not* have a letter in front of them. The rest of the pupils divide up the Romeo lines which have the letter A, B or C in front of them. The A, B and C lines represent either Romeo's darkest thoughts and fears, or his urging himself on to buy the poison. All pupils in the group should practise saying their lines in the order they are written, trying to clearly convey Romeo's state of mind as they do.

▶ All the groups practise their task, then bring them back together and make it clear where the playing space is. When they are ready group one stands in the centre of the space and makes the shop, remembering to make it clear where the doors and the counter are. They also play their soundscape at a low level.

▶ Romeo from Group Three, accompanied by his backing group, enters the space next. They should find a way of entering the shop and looking around it. (Group One may decide to have triggers for the soundscape so that they get louder or quieter depending on where the Romeo group is standing or looking). After looking around, Romeo calls out to the apothecary with his first line.

▶ Group Two enters the space and goes into the shop through the back door. They should do this on Romeo's cue line, '*What ho, apothecary!*' They wait behind the counter watching Romeo. Romeo has to find a way of convincing the apothecary to sell him some of the poison; his support team help him to do this, using the lines they have been allocated and other appropriate gestures.

▶ Plenary

▶ Romeo, '*the star crossed lover*', is destined to die; we are told this in the Prologue at the beginning. However, ironically, he believes the poison from the apothecary was the only thing that would '*shake the yoke of inauspicious stars*' from his '*world-wearied flesh*'. Ask:

■ *What have you discovered from this scene about Romeo's state of mind at this point in the play? Support your ideas with evidence from the text.*

■ *How does the apothecary feel about selling him the poison?*

■ *How does Romeo persuade the apothecary to sell it to him?*

■ *Is the apothecary to blame for Romeo's death?*

Act 5 Scene 1

ROMEO: I do remember an apothecary.
And hereabouts a dwells, which late I noted
In tattered weeds, with overwhelming brows,
Culling of simples: meagre were his looks,
Sharp misery had worn him to the bones,
And in his needy shop a tortoise hung,
An alligator stuffed, and other skins
Of ill-shaped fishes, and about his shelves
A beggarly account of empty boxes,
Green earthen pots, bladders and musty seeds,
Remnants of packthread and old cakes of roses,
Were thinly scattered, to make up a show.
Noting this penury, to myself I said
'An if a man did need a poison now,
Whose sale is present death in Mantua,
Here lives a caitiff wretch would sell it him.'
O, this same thought did but forerun my need,
And this same needy man must sell it me.
As I remember, this should be the house.

Act 5 Scene 1: The Apothecary's Shop

Romeo enters the shop, he looks around and calls out to the apothecary.

ROMEO: What ho, apothecary!

Apothecary enters

1 **APOTHECARY:** Who calls so loud?

ROMEO: Come hither, man. I see that thou art poor.
Hold, there is forty ducats: let me have
A dram of poison, such soon-speeding gear
As will disperse itself through all the veins

B That the life-weary taker may fall dead.

2 **APOTHECARY:** Such mortal drugs I have, but Mantua's law
Is death to any he that utters them.

ROMEO: Art thou so bare and full of wretchedness?

C The world is not thy friend, nor the world's law:

A The world affords no law to make thee rich,
Then be not poor, but break it and take this.

3 **APOTHECARY:** My poverty, but not my will, consents.

ROMEO: I pay thy poverty, and not thy will.

4 **APOTHECARY:** Put this in any liquid thing you will
And drink it off, and if you had the strength
Of twenty men, it would dispatch you straight.

ROMEO: Farewell, buy food, and get thyself in flesh.

B Come, cordial and not poison, go with me

A To Juliet's grave, for there must I use thee.

Key Objective

To draw together the skills utilised in this chapter so far.

To reflect on the tragic events of the play and how they may have been avoided.

KS3	KS2
3.1 Developing and adapting discussion skills and strategies in formal and informal contexts	Speaking, Listening and Responding, Understanding and Interpreting Texts, Engaging and Responding to Text and Drama, Group Discussion and Interaction
4.2 Developing, adapting and responding to dramatic techniques, conventions and styles	

LESSON DESCRIPTION

Pupils use the frame of a *Living Newspaper* to consolidate their knowledge and understanding of events in the play.

Preparation and Resources

You will need:

▶ A hall or drama studio, or classroom with tables pushed back

▶ **Resource Sheet 9**

▶ **Worksheet 17:** one per pupil

▶ A whiteboard or flipchart

TN During this lesson pupils develop and build on the skills they have learnt during their work on *Romeo and Juliet*. They will use a theatrical technique called **Living Newspaper** ◻; originally invented in America in the 1930s, it is a theatrical form which presents factual information and comment on current events to a general audience through live performance. In this lesson the class will use the technique to explore the tragic events of *Romeo and Juliet* from multiple points of view. Through this process they will also start to make links between the dilemmas faced and decisions taken by some of the characters in the play, and consider how they are similar to real-life figures in similar circumstances.

LESSON STRUCTURE

▶ Starter Activity

▶ Pupils stand in a circle. Hold your hands out and tell them: *I am holding an imaginary red ball.* You then make eye contact with someone on the other side of the circle, call *'[Their name], red ball'*, and 'throw' it to them. The person who 'catches' it must hold eye contact and say *'red ball, thank you'* before turning and passing it to someone else. For example:

- *Teacher*:   John, red ball

- *John*:   Red ball, thank you

- *John*:   Aisha, red ball

- *Aisha*:   Red ball, thank you

- *Aisha*:   Jade, red ball

▶ Once the rhythm of throwing, catching and speaking is running smoothly you can add in other objects, such as a blood-soaked dagger, a party invitation, bottle of poison, etc.

▶ More than one object can be thrown at once. Encourage pupils to stay calm and maintain the rhythm. Tell them:
Keeping up the rhythm and staying focused is extremely useful for all drama work, but especially when improvising, which you will doing in this next exercise.

▶ Main activity

Resource Sheet 9: The Prince's speech
▶ Read the Prince's last speech out loud to the pupils. As a group, discuss what the Prince is saying. Ask, for example:

■ *What does the Prince mean specifically by 'a glooming peace this morning with it brings'?*

■ *Why might the Prince be asking those gathered at the Capulet tomb to 'go hence and have more talk of these sad things'?*

■ *What do you think he is hoping to achieve by getting people to talk about it?*
Write pupils' ideas and suggestions up on a whiteboard or flipchart.

▶ In pairs, pupils discuss and list all the people who have died in the play. Ask one pair to feed back to the rest of the class and note their responses onto a flipchart or whiteboard. If they miss anyone out, invite another pair to contribute until you have a complete list.

▶ We are told at the beginning of the play that the ancient quarrel between the Capulets and the Montagues has a vague origin: it is *'bred of an airy word'.* It seems no one can quite remember how it started. Ask pupils to discuss in pairs what they think the quarrel might have been about. Hear back some of the ideas and note them.

▶ Ask the class to imagine that they are newspaper reporters who have been called to the Capulet tomb to hear the Prince's speech. Using **teaching in-role** ⟨⟩ read the speech aloud again with pupils in-role as reporters. Let them know you'll be asking for their personal reactions to the deaths and to your speech. For example, they might think about who is to blame for the tragedy or about which elements of the story they want to publicise to ensure the same mistakes aren't repeated.

▶ When you have finished the speech, nominate individual pupils and ask them for an immediate response to the speech they have just heard.

Worksheet 17: Living Newspaper ideas

▶ Divide the class into eight groups (or less, depending on the size of your class). Tell the pupils: *You are going to create a 'living newspaper' aimed at young people of your age. A 'living newspaper' is one which dramatises news stories, social comment, personal stories, interviews and other traditional aspects of the newspaper. This means that, instead of reading about news stories, the audience can see the stories acted out in front of them. Your edition of the 'living newspaper' is to be devoted entirely to the events surrounding the tragic death of star-crossed lovers, Romeo and Juliet.*

▶ Assign each group a section of the paper as listed on Worksheet 17. This is not an exhaustive list – encourage pupils to think of more sections, such as Sports, which could report on the annual football match between the Capulets and the Montagues.

▶ Ask pupils to revisit the information gathered from the discussion exercise, which is written on a flipchart or whiteboard. They are going to use this as the starting point for devising their section of the newspaper.

▶ Pupils have 20 minutes to devise and rehearse their section and will then be asked to present back to the rest of the class.

▶ When pupils **showback** ⟨⟩ their work to the class, all of the groups together should result in a whole newspaper. Start with the front page and work all the way through to the back page.

▶ Homework

▶ Continuing with the newspaper theme, ask pupils to write a newspaper report on the tragic events using the Prologue and the Prince's speech as source material.

Act 5 Scene 3

PRINCE: A glooming peace this morning with it brings,
The sun, for sorrow, will not show his head.
Go hence to have more talk of these sad things:
Some shall be pardoned, and some punishèd.
For never was a story of more woe
Than this of Juliet and her Romeo.

Living newspaper

Group One: The front page

This group should cover the most important facts of the main story – the double suicide of Romeo and Juliet. What is the headline? What are the exact circumstances surrounding the two deaths? Reporters for the Living Newspaper should establish the facts first of all, then decide how they will present them. Where will the headline come or will this be performed? Is there a photograph? How will you make it?

Group Two: Features

This group should concentrate on the 'human interest stories'. Which news, taken from the play, would most appeal to your audience (other pupils of your age)? It could include interviews with witnesses to the main events, such as Benvolio, Friar Laurence, the Nurse, and Romeo and Juliet's parents, or with the servants from the households who may have the 'inside story'! It should contain opinions and different viewpoints. Facts and fictions may emerge as a result of placing different accounts next to one another.

Group Three: Editorials

In this section, the editor chooses one of the stories in the paper that he or she would like to write about. It is their personal opinion and therefore this article should be strictly from one person's viewpoint. Reporters for the Living Newspaper could take on an Editor 'collective role' and so together they should decide which story they would like to concentrate on, what their opinion is, and how they are going to present it. For example, they may look at the front page story of the double murder, weigh up the facts and then express their opinion on how the whole thing may have been prevented.

Group Four: Opinion polls

This group will ask the citizens of Verona their opinion about issues based on the events in the play. Reporters should choose carefully which opinion poll questions they are going to ask. Some possible questions could be:

- How many people think that, as a result of the recent tragedy, there should be a curfew imposed on the city of Verona?

- Following the recent tragic events, how many people think that the Prince should step down?

Group Five: Comic strip

This group should think about the messages in the play. What do you learn from it? Is there some brilliant piece of advice, warning, or political joke that can be summed up simply in a comic strip or cartoon? What is it, and how will you present it?

Group Six: Agony Uncle/Aunt

For this section, readers write letters or ask questions related to the action of the play. These are anonymous. They are sent in to the newspaper and they call upon the agony aunt or uncle to respond and provide advice. Both the questions and the responses should be written and dramatised by the pupils.

Group Seven: Who is in the limelight?

This section highlights one character from the play. It should give basic information about them, such as their name, age, place of study, likes and dislikes, hobbies, etc. They could then address more specific questions to do with the recent events in Verona. There should be a quote from the person in the limelight to end.

Group Eight: The story in photos

The newspaper could finish with a section which tells the story of the recent tragic events using pictures. You should think of the most important or significant moments in the play, and what photographs would best show these moments.

COMMON BANK OF
ACTIVITIES AND TERMS

Backstory

The events that have happened before a play begins.

Often the backstory is discovered during the course of the play through characters reporting past events. Sometimes there are only hints as to what might have happened in the past, and director and actors must decide what they think the backstory of the characters might have been.

In the classroom, our approach enables pupils to:

■ Use reported action to experience the back story.

■ Make interpretive choices based on the hints that are found in a close reading of the script.

Blocking

The process of negotiating and setting the action of a scene. Director and actors negotiate the thought processes, moves, gestures, interactions, eye contact, facial expressions that most aptly express what they feel is going on in the scene. This is a fundamental skill of working actively with a script.

In the classroom, our approach enables pupils to:

■ Take concrete steps towards making their own active blocking choices.

Chair Thermometer

A strategy often used for active reflection. Essentially it asks pupils to place themselves somewhere on a continuum of opinion about a particular topic. For example, would they be prepared to sacrifice their good name for power, as Macbeth does? In inviting a response to this question, the teacher might position two chairs at opposite sides of the room, one representing power and the other representing Macbeth's good name. Pupils place themselves along an imaginary line nearer to one chair or the other as they individually respond to the question posed. Chair Thermometer is usually preceded by other exercises which elicit thoughts and feelings from the pupils about the topic in focus.

Choral Characters

This is useful for bringing great energy to a scene and for including pupils who are not yet confident speakers of Shakespeare's words. One pupil is chosen as the 'Choral Leader' for each role in the scene. The remainder of the pupils support the choral leaders in equal numbers, gathering behind them. The chorus echoes all the words spoken by their leader which they want to emphasise. These choices may be made spontaneously or through prior negotiation among the group. If this exercise follows on from *One-word Dialogues* ◪, the chorus echoes each of the words and copies the accompanying gesture immediately after their choral leader speaks and before another character speaks the next word.

Choral Speaking

When speaking chorally, pupils are highlighting meanings in a text by emphasising the features of its language. Choral work uses such strategies as:

■ Different numbers of voices speaking at different times.

■ Echoing key words and sounds.

- Emphasising the rhythm of the words.

- Emphasising long vowels and hard consonants.

- Creating non-verbal sounds to complement and comment on the text.

- Making the most of onomatopoeic words.

- Using a variety of vocal qualities to create characters, represent action and convey a variety of other meanings in the text.

Choral speaking is a particularly powerful approach to use for verse because poetry relies so heavily on verbal and non-verbal effects for its impact. This approach can help pupils become very sensitive to ways in which authors use sounds to create meaning and it is a powerful tool for giving young people a sense of ownership of Shakespeare and other authors. It is also a highly effective way of engaging less confident speakers; they are able to explore the sounds, rhythms and patterns of speech through this accessible and supported activity. Choral speaking is often accompanied by movement.

Circle Blocking

Circle blocking offers an approach to staging a scene without requiring pupils to make complex movement choices. It reflects very clearly character relationships and motivations at different moments in the scene. The usual approach is to create a circle of chairs between three and five times as great as the number of characters in the scene. Those playing the characters then choose the chairs they want to sit on at the start of the scene. As the scene is played, characters must constantly decide where in the circle they want to sit. Any character may move at any point in the scene. This exercise is effectively paired with 'Stop. Think!'

Conscience Threes

An active strategy for exploring a character dilemma. The dilemma is first of all discussed objectively - what are the arguments for or against a decision that the character must make. Pupils work in groups of three. The pupil in the middle is the character who must listen to the arguments that the other two pupils make. One pupil argues for the decision, the other argues against. These pupils are competing to make the pupil in the middle follow their advice. The pupil in the middle takes a step towards the decision if the 'for' arguments are strongest, and a step away if the 'against' arguments are strongest. So the dilemma is argued live and the pupil in the middle moves backwards and forwards. The imperative to make the strongest argument to win the competition means that pupils adopt all sorts of persuasive strategies and the dilemma becomes much harder to solve - exactly as it would be in life.

Editing

The process of cutting the text until it suits your purposes. There are several different versions of every Shakespeare play and directors will often work with all the available versions to edit together the one that makes most sense in rehearsals.

In the classroom, reasons for editing include:

- Reducing the amount of text to one that is suitable for the reading age of the learners in your class.

- Focusing on the linguistic devices that Shakespeare has used.

- Focusing on the key ideas in a speech or a scene.

- Highlighting the action in a speech or a scene.

- Highlighting the vocabulary that the characters are using.

- Highlighting a particular character, relationship or theme.

Ensemble

The Cambridge dictionary definition of ensemble is "*a group of people acting together as a whole.*" Mikhail Stronin (Dramaturg at St Petersburg's Maly Drama Theatre) describes ensemble work as "*...one body with many heads – but many heads who work in the same direction.*"

Ensemble theatre was the principle way of working for the actor companies of Shakespeare's day. At the Royal Shakespeare Company we define ourselves as an ensemble: a group of people engaged in a collaborative act of enquiry around the work we create.

In the classroom, an ensemble approach encourages pupils to:

- Work as a mutually supportive group.

- Build a cumulative, collaborative understanding of the play.

- Listen to and respect each other's ideas and opinions.

- Allow for difference.

- Be inclusive.

Ensemble Reading

Pupils stand in a circle. The speech is read aloud, with each pupil reading only up to the next punctuation mark. Each time there is a punctuation mark, the next pupil reads. This may mean that individuals read only one word or a couple of lines. The punctuation is strictly observed. Afterwards, discuss the speech with the pupils and work out with them what they think any unfamiliar words mean. Actors use the punctuation as an indicator of the thought patterns of the speech. Most contemporary directors and actors make sense of these words by reading to the punctuation precisely because it reveals the pattern of the character's thoughts.

Follow Chase

The Follow Chase, like **Circle Blocking** ⬦, is an approach to staging which avoids asking participants to 'act' a scene and instead gives them tight movement guidelines through which to explore the text.

It is useful for two-character scenes where one character is in control and trying to dominate the other character who at some point rebels or for some reason refuses to be further influenced. The example used in this book is Lady Macbeth trying to influence Macbeth about the murder of Duncan. The character in control sets off at a brisk pace moving through the space and the other character follows. At some point in the scene the following character refuses to go any further and stops. The leading character then decides how to regain influence. Tell pupils to 'let their feet do the talking', and work instinctively: their feet will know when they no longer want to follow. The debrief will often reveal that there are various options in the text for when the 'following' character stops as well as a range of strategies for the leading character to use to regain their influence.

Five Point Chase

An active reading strategy for exploring a scene. Useful for scenes with two or more characters and can be used in combination with **scene studies** ◖. Pupils stand facing each other about ten paces apart. As they read the scene aloud to each other they are restricted to five movement choices:

- To stand still.

- To take a step towards another character.

- To take a step away from another character.

- To turn their back on another character.

- To turn towards another character.

These choices are rigidly observed during the scene. Actors use this exercise to pinpoint exactly how their character is behaving towards the other character/s, and the restricted choice makes their behaviour very deliberate. The choices are made instinctively, in the moment and on your feet. The point of the exercise is to make the actor consciously aware of their movement choices in order for them to develop an intimate understanding of the relationship dynamics in the scene. So, it is important to discuss with pupils the choices they have made and why they made them.

Freeze Frames

The creation by a group of people of a physical image. This could represent a paused moment in time, a photograph, a sculpture, an illustration.

Reasons for using freeze frames include:

- Giving the group an opportunity to negotiate their readings of the play.

- Developing interpretive choice.

- Capturing ideas around a theme or an idea.

- Developing presentation skills.

You can enable pupils to share their freeze frames in a variety of ways. There may be interesting shapes to comment on. Ask the rest of the pupils why a group has chosen to use those shapes to illustrate the story - often this will reveal major themes in the play. There may be significant characters represented. You could ask the rest of the pupils what a character may be about to say, or **thought track** ◖ the characters. There may be a freeze frame that is a frozen moment of action. You could ask this freeze frame to come to life for a moment and re-freeze it, then ask the rest of the pupils which moment they think it is from the story and why.

Guided Imaginary Journey	One pupil leads their partner, who has their eyes closed, around the room. They must be careful to look after their blinded partner and ensure that they come to no harm. As the pupil guides their partner around the room they describe the world that they want them to see in their imaginations. Painting pictures with words, they illustrate the landscape, or the interior of a building, they portray the atmosphere, the temperature, the flora and fauna, the colours, everything that will help their partner visualise the world in full technicolor in their own imagination.
Iambic Pentameter	The verse rhythm most frequently used in Shakespeare's plays, it consists of five iambic feet. Each iambic foot is made up of an unstressed syllable followed by a stressed syllable. The rhythm of an iambic pentameter line would therefore go: De DUM de DUM de DUM de DUM de DUM. This is a very easy, conversational rhythm and resembles the beating of our hearts. It's the kind of rhythm that we regularly use in everyday speech, for example. I REAlly WANT to HAVE a CUP of TEA is a perfect iambic line. An example of a line of iambic pentameter from *Romeo and Juliet* would be '*But, soft, what light through yonder window breaks?*' Shakespeare regularly breaks the rhythm of iambic pentameter and when he does it is usually a clue; it gives us additional information about the emotional state of the character who is speaking the line or the situation at the time. Being a very skilled poet, Shakespeare uses many other metrical rhythms but iambic pentameter is the one he employs most often.
Imaging	Pupils work in pairs or threes, using their bodies to find a physical expression for the words. Reasons for imaging: ■ To explore the meaning of the words with peers. ■ To connect the words to a physical memory, aiding recall. ■ To highlight the ideas and images in the text. ■ To highlight the repetition of strong ideas and images.
Improvising	The act of inventing performance and spoken text, in the moment, often in response to stimuli or a set of instructions. It is really useful for inventing new ideas or clarifying thoughts and for bringing out what a pupil may instinctively feel about a situation or character, without censoring. In the classroom, our approach enables pupils to improvise as individuals, pairs, small groups and as a whole group.
In-Role Meeting	Pupils and teacher adopt roles with different points of view on the events in the play. They hold a meeting to debate a dilemma as if they are characters in the play. Pupils can research the social and historical context of the play in advance, and use their research to prepare their role. Every group of actors which tackles a Shakespeare play for performance

will discuss the relevance of the text for a contemporary audience. Some productions place the action very firmly in the time and place that Shakespeare chose for the play, and rely on the audience to make the connections between the action of the play and their own life experiences. Others may choose to place the action in a very specific contemporary context to emphasise the relevance of the themes and ideas in the play.

An in-role meeting similarly brings the action of the play directly into the lives and experiences of the teachers and pupils working together. . Reasons for holding an in-role meeting include:

■ To deepen understanding of the society in which the play is set.

■ To personalise the dilemma faced by that society.

■ To draw out parallels between the world of the play and pupils' own life experiences.

In every classroom there is a diverse group of learners. The individuals will bring both their own life experience and their understanding of the fictional context to the debate. The fictional context is very useful to the teacher in extending the thinking of the group. For example, using this activity in *Romeo and Juliet* (Lesson 3), individuals might express a controversial point of view: for example *"I think we should hang anyone who causes trouble."* Someone in role as a weapons' maker might say, *" Why shouldn't everyone have the freedom to defend themselves?"* or someone in role as a Montague teenager might say, *"I hate these Capulets, they shouldn't be allowed to live here, send them away somewhere else till they can behave themselves."* Hence, some of the big questions for citizenship will arise but they can be safely dealt with, not as the personal views of the speaker but as the views of the character. If an in-role discussion does become heated, the teacher always has the option to stop the action and ask the pupils why. Indeed, reflecting out of role should always follow an in-role exercise.

Interpolated Questions	Pupils speak a whole speech in unison. The teacher adopts a pertinent point of view and interrupts the pupils with comments or questions in modern English, voicing the chosen point of view. Pupils must listen to what the teacher says and then say aloud the next part of the speech in reply to what they have heard. The speech will therefore be a dialogue.
Living Newspaper	A form of theatre which originated in America in the 1930s. A 'living newspaper' dramatises news stories, social comment, personal stories, interviews and other traditional aspects of the newspaper. This means that, instead of reading about news stories, the audience can see the stories acted out in front of them. The technique allows students to collectively explore events from multiple points of view.
One-Word Dialogues	This exercise reduces the number of words in a scene to a fraction of the original, usually one word for each speech. Thus a two-page scene may be limited to ten words. Choosing the words is the first activity; pupils are asked to decide with their playing partners which words best tell the story of the scene. Then they rehearse this mini-scene finding at least one gesture for every word. Encouraging pupils to make their movements as large as possible helps to sharpen the interpretative choices. This

exercise is helpful for:

■ Involving pupils who are not confident in speaking large sections of Shakespeare's text.

■ Finding the 'spine' or heart of the scene.

■ Appreciating patterns in Shakespeare's language.

This exercise can be paired with *Choral Characters* ⟨⟩.

Props

Physical artefacts that are part of the action, usually carried by an actor. Props often have a symbolic meaning as well as a literal one. For example, a sword is literally a weapon used for fighting but may be used in the action to symbolise authority or brutality or bravery. Props are carefully chosen by the designer to give the audience clues about the *World of the Play* ⟨⟩.

Punctuation Shift

Pupils are asked to walk with pace and energy around the room and to read a speech aloud as they walk. Whenever they come to a full stop or equivalent strong punctuation mark they will stop and turn 180 degrees and walk in a new direction. If they reach a comma, they will stop and turn 90 degrees. Pupils do this simultaneously but not in unison. They should take the speech at their own pace.

Afterwards, the teacher discusses with the pupils what the physical pattern of the character's thoughts are, and whether 'walking' the speech gave them any insight into how the character feels or what their state of mind is. If there's lots of punctuation, pupils will often say, for example, *"He feels confused, his thoughts are all over the place, he is dizzy."* The teacher can deepen this response by asking pupils to identify if there were any parts of the speech where they found themselves walking for a long time in one direction. What is the character talking about when this happens? The most sustained thoughts, the ones most clear in the character's mind, stand out.

Reasons for using punctuation shift:

■ To experience the pattern of the character's thoughts.

■ To find a physical connection with the language.

Role on the Wall

A character is depicted in a visual way. For example, a simple outline of a human figure is drawn and displayed on a large sheet of paper. As pupils explore what they know about a character and develop their ideas about what that character is like, they add these to the drawing. For example, inside the drawing could be words describing the feelings of the character, or things they say about themselves, and outside the drawing could be words describing or reporting things that other characters say or feel about the person.

Scene Studies

Active reading strategies for scenes between two characters.

1. Back to back reading
Pupils work in pairs and choose characters. They read the scene aloud with their partner, standing back to back, so that they cannot see each other. They are asked to listen closely to what their partner says. This device allows pupils to read the scene without 'acting' it and develops active listening skills. You can pair the pupils for peer reading support, pairing an able reader with a less able one. The whole class does the exercise simultaneously, which allows a moment for you or support staff to work one to one with any pupils who need extra support. It is important to stress that there are no right or wrong answers and that the scene can be interpreted in many different ways.

2. Whispered reading
Pupils work in pairs and read the scene as if they do not want to be overheard, keeping their voices at a whisper, but still making sure that their partner can hear all the sounds in the words. The teacher encourages pupils to talk about any moments in the scene where speaking the words in this way felt right and to speculate about why that might be. (For example, the character is saying something particularly dangerous or sensitive.) It is important to stress that there are no right or wrong answers and that the scene can be interpreted in many different ways.

3. Sharing the words across space
Pupils work in pairs and stand about ten paces apart. They read the scene at full volume, as if they do not care who hears them, sending their voice across the space between them. The teacher encourages pupils to talk about any moments in the scene where speaking the words in this way felt right and to speculate about why that might be. (For example, the character is so full of emotion that they are out of control.) It is important to stress that there are no right or wrong answers and that the scene can be interpreted in many different ways.

4. Experimenting with movement
Pupils work in pairs. One of the characters has to stand rooted to the spot whilst the other character can move wherever they like in relation to their partner. They can circle them, or stand too close for comfort, or walk away from them, or whisper in their ear, or go behind them. They can kneel down, stand up, turn their back on their partner. They should move wherever feels instinctively right to them as they read the scene with their partner. Then the scene can be tried with the positions reversed and the other character rooted to the spot. The teacher encourages pupils to talk about any moments in this exercise where they found out something new about the relationship between the two characters (for example, *character A feels powerless*). It is important to stress that there are no right or wrong answers and that the scene can be interpreted in many different ways.

Sculpting

Pupils work in pairs: person A is the sculptor and person B is the clay that the sculpture is made from. A moves B into the position they feel best reflects the character, emotion or dilemma they are trying to portray. The exercise must take place in silence so that the only communication is physical and the eyes of the person being sculpted must remain closed. A time limit of thirty seconds is always helpful in setting up the exercise with a five second countdown given at the end for final adjustments.

You can then ask sculptures to stay in their positions as sculptors move around the space which has now become an art gallery peopled with representations of whatever the class is working on.

Shared Line

Refers to occasions when a single line of iambic pentameter is shared by two or more characters. Editors often indicate that a line is shared by spacing it out on the page so that it looks like a sequence of steps. Usually shared lines indicate a high degree of intimacy between the two characters at that moment, almost as if they are breathing in unison. Sometimes a line will be shared when one character interrupts another or is trying to influence another.

Showback

This is an opportunity for the pupils to show the rest of the group what they have been working on. It is important when showing back that they do so in a supportive environment. Encourage pupils to quickly arrange themselves into an audience, to watch quietly and afterwards to say what they liked about the presentation and what they thought could be improved on for next time.

Spider Diagrams

Spider diagrams give structure to the idea of diagramming the components of a concept or idea in order to aid its exploration. The ones proposed in this book are quite simple but could make very attractive displays. Traditionally, spider diagrams begin with the expression of a central idea either in words or as a drawing. Connected by lines to this central idea, rather like the drawing of a family tree, are lists of various aspects or sub-divisions of the idea. Connections among the sub-divisions are again made evident through connecting lines. The teacher or leader usually proposes the sub-divisions for the diagram. Anything can be the subject of a spider diagram – characters, places, themes, even text extracts.

Spotlighting

A technique for quickly and efficiently sharing small group or pairs work. The teacher holds up a hand to represent a spotlight and moves around the room, shining the 'spotlight' on a pair or small group at work. All the other pupils in the room stop what they are doing and watch the work in the spotlight. When the teacher moves on, pupils return to their work. No one knows where the spotlight will shine next so there is a playful raising of anticipation and expectation. It's also a useful technique for ensuring pupils stay focused.

Staging

The process of deciding exactly how a scene should be constructed so that the audience know what it is they should focus on.

Soundscapes

Soundscapes are auditory experiences created from sounds or words or both. Soundscapes are used for:

- Understanding mood and atmosphere.

- Deepening appreciation of a character's emotional state.

- Creating a sense of place and time.

■ Drawing special attention to words and resonance.

Soundscapes can be quite elaborate, with pupils creating a whole world from non-verbal and verbal sound and then sharing this invention with visitors to the soundscape experience. A soundscape for the Athenian wood in *A Midsummer Night's Dream* is an example of a more elaborate soundscape opportunity. On the other hand, soundscapes can be quite simple exercises, with just the words of the text whispered and perhaps echoed into the ears of a listener whose eyes are shut in order to focus more intently on the words and sounds.

'Stop. Think!'

This activity is similar to **Thought Tracking** ◪ because it asks pupils to speak aloud the thoughts of the characters they are playing. It is different only in that it is used during rather than after a piece of acting. Any member of the audience may call out 'Stop. Think!' during the course of a scene, and must then name a character. That character must say in as much detail as possible what they are thinking at that moment. The aim is obviously to deepen pupils' understanding of character motivation.

Teaching In-Role

The means by which a teacher can address their educational objectives for the lesson by using an appropriate role that will allow them to enter and influence the active work accordingly.

Reasons for using teacher in role include:

■ Building and deepening belief in the given circumstances of the play.

■ Building tension.

■ Challenging an attitude or introducing another point of view.

■ Provoking confrontation.

■ Introducing a complex dilemma from the play.

The teacher can adopt a high or a low status role as appropriate. Many teachers are concerned about dealing with disruptive behaviour during an in-role exercise. However, a high status role modelled with confidence gives the teacher a further dimension in the teaching and learning relationship. Most pupils relish the opportunity to play a role, and respect an adult who shares that relish. Within a high status role, you can use the authority of the character to bolster your own authority. Adopting a role also means that the teacher is liberated from pupils' expectations that they will have all the answers. In-role, the teacher can say, "*I don't know, what do you think? I would appreciate your advice,*" and, because it is the character that needs help, most pupils will respond by offering that help.

The teacher can use a role:

■ As a way of progressing the pupils exploration of a play.

■ As a way of questioning what is happening in the play.

■ As a way of gauging pupils understanding of a character or a dilemma.

■ As a way of exploring unanswered questions about the events and

	relationships in the play.
Thought Tracking	Pupils are asked to speculate about what a character might be thinking. The pupil representing that character speaks their thoughts out loud, using first person narrative. Alternatively, other pupils speak the thoughts of the character out loud, by placing a hand on the character's shoulders and speaking as if they are the character.

Reasons for using thought tracking include:

■ To deepen empathy with the character.

■ To explore what is going on in a character's head; sometimes this is different from what they say.

■ To personalise understanding of the character. |
| **Voices in the Head** | A group of pupils speak aloud what a character is thinking. Teacher in-role can be one side of a conversation in which a small group improvise the other character. One of them is the "mouth" of the character, and speaks aloud the things that the rest of the group whisper to them. This activity is described in detail in *A Midsummer Night's Dream* Lesson 2. |
| **Wants and Tactics** | This approach is based on one of the most important and fundamental of all acting principles - that a character is always trying to achieve something and whatever the character does or says is geared towards achieving their goal. For example, Lady Macbeth <u>wants</u> Macbeth to murder Duncan. There are various tactics she can use to achieve this and the actor's interpretation will ultimately depend upon which tactics she chooses. Does she coax him? Does she reason with him? Does she insult or bully him into the decision? Very different Lady Macbeths would emerge from each of these choices.

This approach is readily accessible to young people. Simply agree with them on the ambition of the character – the <u>want</u> - and then ask them to suggest ways in which this could be achieved. It is important to use transitive verbs. For example, I flatter you; I beg you; I reject you; I charm you. Avoid 'to be' verbs because these don't build a relationship with the other characters and create self-consciousness as the actor tries to look or be a particular way – frightened or happy or angry. The verbs chosen should attempt to change the character to whom the line is directed.

It is interesting that this approach exactly mirrors our behaviour in life. At every waking moment we are trying to achieve something (to please our mum, to get to sleep, to lose weight, to attract someone) and we have varying tactics we use to get what we want. For example, when trying to get something from a parent we might flatter them, beg them or tease them. |
| **Whoosh!** | A quick, physical participatory telling of a story that uses text and action to establish consensual understanding and invite participants to play. There are two Whooshes in the toolkit (one in *Romeo and Juliet* and the other in *A Midsummer Night's Dream*). However, it is easy to write your own which can be specific to the part of the play you want to look at. |

Whooshes can tell the whole story of the play (as we've done in *Romeo and Juliet*), or can be broken down into smaller chunks and interspersed with discussions or other practical exercises (as we've done in *A Midsummer Night's Dream*). It is described in detail in *Romeo and Juliet* Lesson 4. The activity necessitates certain interpretative choices being made about character attitudes and motivations through the telling of the story and this can be discussed with pupils. For example, *in what other ways might Juliet have responded to the idea of marrying Paris?*

World of the Play

The three-dimensional, multi-sensory, fictional place in which the play happens.

Shakespeare created a whole world in each of his plays, and each world is created and discovered in the very sounds of the words he chooses. As an audience, we experience that world along with the actors, and a successful production will make use of every little clue that the playwright offers to bring that world to us. An ensemble like the Royal Shakespeare Company uses all the tools of the theatre to do this: design, costume, lighting, sound and music, special effects, but the key to any interpretation is always found in the language. In the rehearsal room, the director, actors and designers refine their interpretation of the world that Shakespeare offers in his script, and then carefully, cumulatively, they build their version of that world together with the production team. Each play has a very different world to explore and interpret. Shakespeare's extraordinary skill as a playwright does far more than just evoke a particular place and time. In each play he brings us a whole experience of a whole world, in all its complexity, with all its fascinating human dimensions - an intriguing world that we want to find out more about.

In the classroom, our approach enables pupils to:

■ Make instinctive discoveries about the world of the play through speaking the words aloud.

■ Find links between the world of the play and their own lives.

■ Use multi-sensory stimuli to inhabit the world of the play in their imaginations.

■ Physically create the actions of the characters in the world of the play.

■ Interpret the world of the play by making active choices.

ACKNOWLEDGEMENTS

We are deeply indebted to the following people for their inspiration and guidance in the creation of this book and for the development of the pedagogy at its heart:

Cicely Berry
Director of Voice, RSC

Mick Connell
School Improvement Advisor, English and the Arts, Rotherham

Sarah Downing Stanton
Freelance theatre arts practitioner

Maria Evans
Coach and consultant to the cultural and education sectors

Juliet Forster
Director

Fiona Lindsay
Arts programmer, producer and presenter

Jonothan Neelands
Professor of Drama and Theatre Education, University of Warwick

Miles Tandy
Advisor to the Educational Development Services, Warwickshire

Joe Winston
Associate Professor of Drama and Theatre Education, University of Warwick.

Our thanks go to Georghia Ellinas, Senior Adviser – English, The National Strategies, Secondary for her careful reading of draft chapters and subsequent invaluable advice. Final thanks go to the many thousands of teachers and young people that we have worked with over the years and learnt so much from. We are particularly indebted to schools in the RSC Learning and Performance Network for their support in developing many of the ideas in the toolkit.

All text extracts based on Jonathan Bate and Eric Rasmussen, *The RSC Shakespeare: The Complete Works*, published by Macmillan, 2007, reproduced with permission of Palgrave Macmillan.

The Whoosh activity in *Romeo and Juliet* and *A Midsummer Night's Dream* is based on an original idea by Joe Winston, Associate Professor of Drama and Theatre Education, University of Warwick.

Punctuation shift in the Common Bank of Activities is based on an exercise from *The Actor And His Text* by Cicely Berry, published by Virgin Books. Reprinted by permission of The Random House Group Ltd

We are grateful to the following for their support of the RSC's education programme:

Arts Council England, The Ernest Cooke Trust, Creative Partnerships, The Equitable Charitable Trust, Paul Hamlyn Foundation, The Alan Edward Higgs Charity, John Lyons Charity, Ohio State University, The Polonsky Foundation, RSC Friends and Stratford-upon-Avon Town Trust as well as the many individual donors who annually support our work.

WRITER ACKNOWLEDGEMENTS:

Written by: Rachel Gartside, Rebecca Gould and Mary Johnson with additional material by Tracy Irish, Jacqui O'Hanlon and Kate Wolstenholme. Edited for the RSC by Jacqui O'Hanlon.

STAND UP FOR SHAKESPEARE

A MANIFESTO FOR SHAKESPEARE IN SCHOOLS

We want young people to feel that Shakespeare belongs to them. Having worked with thousands of teachers, students, policy-makers and theatre companies exploring what makes Shakespeare vivid, accessible and enjoyable for students of all abilities and backgrounds, we know that children and young people get the most out of Shakespeare when they:

■ Do it on their feet

■ See it live

■ Start it earlier

DO IT ON THEIR FEET - Explore the plays as actors do.

The best classroom experience we can offer is one which allows young people to approach Shakespeare's plays as actors do – as an ensemble, using active, problem-solving methods to develop a greater understanding and enjoyment of the plays.

SEE IT LIVE - Participate as members of a live audience.

A play script is like a musical score, telling only half the story. The physical dynamic of the actors and the sensory act of hearing, seeing and feeling the sounds, rhythms and words brings the world of the play to life in a way that reading a text cannot. There is no substitute for the shared experience of seeing Shakespeare live.

START SHAKESPEARE EARLIER - Experience Shakespeare from a younger age.

Shakespeare holds no fear for younger children as they find delight in using new and unusual language. They can confidently engage with the stories and dilemmas long before formally studying the plays. Starting Shakespeare early generates an excitement in children about his work that can last into secondary school and beyond.

"My dad said Shakespeare was boring, but he's got it wrong! I'm gonna tell him about Hamlet. It's got murders and ghosts and castles and stuff and that's not boring. What are we doing next?"

Ben, age 8, Stokeinteignhead Primary School, Devon after doing a unit of work with his teacher on *Hamlet*

For further information about the work of the RSC Education Department please visit **www.rsc.org.uk/education** or email **education@rsc.org.uk**.

Find out about *Teaching Shakespeare*, our new online Professional Development programme: **www.teachingshakespeare.ac.uk. Experience this groundbreaking approach to professional development and transform classroom experiences of Shakespeare in your school.**

To keep up to date with the latest RSC news and enjoy a range of other benefits, your school could become an Education Member for just £18 per year. Visit **www.rsc.org.uk/membership** or phone **01789 403 440** for further details.

Alternatively you can sign up for free email updates by visiting **www.rsc.org.uk**, join us at **facebook.com/RSCTeachers** or follow us on **twitter.com/theRSC**